Beginning Reading Intervention Activities

Five-Day Units on Short-Vowel Words to Strengthen Phonemic Awareness, Letter-Sound Correspondence, and Word Recognition

by Debra Olson Pressnall

Key Education
An imprint of Carson-Dellosa Publishing, LLC
Greensboro, North Carolina

keyeducationpublishing.com

CONGRATULATIONS ON YOUR PURCHASE OF A KEY EDUCATION PRODUCT!

The editors at Key Education are former teachers who bring experience, enthusiasm, and quality to each and every product. Thousands of teachers have looked to the staff at Key Education for new and innovative resources to make their work more enjoyable and rewarding. We are committed to developing educational materials that will assist teachers in building a strong and developmentally appropriate curriculum for young children.

PLAN FOR GREAT TEACHING EXPERIENCES WHEN YOU USE EDUCATIONAL MATERIALS FROM KEY EDUCATION

About the Author

Debra Olson Pressnall has been an editor, writer, and product developer in the educational publishing field for over 20 years. She earned her bachelor of science degree in elementary education from Concordia College (Minnesota) and then spent 12 years as a teacher in elementary classrooms before entering the supplemental education publishing field. She has authored dozens of classroom teaching aids as well as 14 teacher resource books. Debra has been the recipient of two Directors' Choice Awards, three *Creative Child* Magazine Awards, and a Parents' Choice Approved award.

Acknowledgments

Thanks to Linda Kimble and Janice Hass for their excellent contributions. Their fine work as elementary classroom reading teachers inspires me! ~ D. P.

Credits
Author: Debra Olson Pressnall
Copy Editor: Karen Seberg
Illustrations: Vanessa Countryman
Cover Design: Creative Department
Cover Photograph: © Shutterstock

Key Education
An imprint of Carson-Dellosa Publishing, LLC
PO Box 35665
Greensboro, NC 27425 USA
keyeducationpublishing.com

Food Activities

Caution: Before beginning any food activity, ask families' permission and inquire about students' food allergies and religious or other food restrictions.

ISBN 978-1-620573-67-9
01-002138091

TABLE OF CONTENTS

INTRODUCTION

For children who are beginning readers, it is imperative that they acquire the following foundation skills:

- **Phonological awareness** (ability to hear and manipulate phonemes in spoken words)
- **Letter recognition skills** (orthographic knowledge)
- **Letter-sound correspondence skills** (*alphabetic principle*—ability to map sounds onto letters in predictable ways)
- **Rapid automatic naming (RAN) letters skills** (influences word-reading ability)

How to Use This Book

Teachers can use the multisensory five-day lessons, phonemic awareness activities, read-at-home activities, word cards, templates for writing words and sentences, and RAN boards for letter- and word-naming activities to boost the fundamental skills identified above. Select lessons that target your students' underdeveloped decoding and phonological processing skills as identified by formal assessments. You may also create your own units (pages 126–127) by using the materials provided in this resource.

According to the research study *Developing Early Literacy: Report of the National Early Literacy Panel—A Scientific Synthesis of Early Literacy Development and Implications for Intervention* (2008), these are key literacy skills, along with the ability to write alphabet letters in isolation, that children must acquire. Children who lack these skills have difficulty sounding out words.

ISOLATING PHONEMES IN PICTURE NAMES AND IMPROVING LETTER NAMING

Before starting any phonological-processing lessons, it is important to assess how well your students can isolate, identify, and manipulate speech sounds in words. This is known as *phonemic awareness*. If the student has difficulty with identifying beginning and final sounds in spoken words or needs pictures to hold the words in short-term memory, start with the picture-word activities (pages 5 and 6). When the child demonstrates an understanding of these concepts, provide more challenging exercises. Let students follow oral directions—without relying on picture prompts—to manipulate speech sounds in spoken words.

In reviewing the research on word-reading ability, one can conclude that the ability to **read letter names quickly** and accurately is also a fundamental literacy skill that students must develop. First, assess your students to find out which letters they can identify correctly (page 7). Then, determine how rapidly your students can read random letters by completing the Rapid Automatic Naming (RAN) Letters Assessment (page 14). Suggestions for creating your own RAN boards are provided on page 6 along with reproducible boards on page 129. These boards can be used for letters and words to strengthen fluency skills.

Isolating and Saying Beginning Sounds in Words

Activity 1: Matching Beginning Sounds

Things You'll Need: For each pair of students, copy the picture cards (pages 8 and 9) onto card stock. Cut out the pictures and store them in a zippered plastic bag.

Follow These Steps
Introduce the picture cards to the students. Then, scatter the cards *faceup* in the playing area and let the children take turns finding two pictures whose names begin with the same sound. Continue until all matches have been made.

Activity 2: Sound the Letters!

Things You'll Need: For each student in the group, copy the work mat (page 11) onto card stock. Make one copy of the picture cards (page 10) on card stock for the group. Cut out the pictures and store the materials in a zippered plastic bag. Include 20 chips for each work mat.

Follow These Steps
Give each student a work mat and 20 chips. Show one of the picture cards. Have students identify that picture and then say the beginning phoneme in that word, like *pie* = /p/. Finish the exercise for that word by letting the child cover the letter *p* in the first row with a chip. Repeat this step with

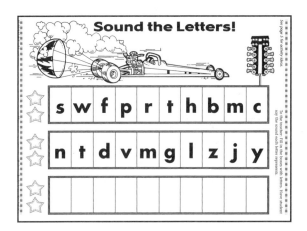

other picture cards. When the pictures for *top* and *money* are shown, make sure students cover the corresponding letters in both rows. Continue the activity until all of the boxes in the first or second row have been covered. Clear the boards and do the activity again if time allows. Wrap up the lesson by having students say the sound for each letter in the first or second row of boxes to "speed" across the work mat.

Variation: Fill in the third row of boxes with single consonants. Call out CVC words. Have students identify the beginning phonemes in those words and cover the corresponding letters in the boxes.

Isolating and Saying Final Sounds in Words

Activity 1: Matching Final Sounds

Things You'll Need: For each pair of students, copy the picture cards (page 12) onto card stock. Cut out the pictures and store them in a zippered plastic bag.

Follow These Steps
Introduce the picture cards to the students. Then, scatter them on the playing area and let the children take turns finding two pictures whose names end with the same sound to make a match. Continue the activity until all matching pairs of cards have been found.

Pictures Cards:
Set A—gum, duck, leaf, bib, sled, tent, pen, bus, pop, leg
Set B—chain, coat, cab, bug, stick, drum, sheep, kiss, cloud, knife

Matching pairs: gum—drum, duck—stick, leaf—knife, bib—cab, sled—cloud, tent—coat, pen—chain, bus—kiss, pop—sheep, leg—bug

Activity 2: Sound at the End!

Things You'll Need: For each student in the group, copy the picture cards (page 12) and work mat (page 13) onto card stock. Cut out the pictures and store the materials in a zippered plastic bag along with 10 chips or buttons.

Follow These Steps

Select picture cards whose names have three phonemes, like *bug*. Show one of the cards. Have students identify that picture and then touch each box on the train illustration while saying the individual phonemes in that word. Finish the exercise for that word by letting the child cover the letter *g* on the grid. Repeat this step with other picture cards.

Reinforce the lesson by letting students do this activity with partners. Give each child a work mat and six to eight chips or buttons. Mix up the picture cards and place them *facedown* in a stack. Have students take turns drawing a card, naming the picture, and covering the corresponding

ending consonant letter with a chip. When all of the boxes have been covered, clear the board and complete the activity again if time allows.

Variation: Fill in the second row of boxes with single consonants. Call out CVC and CCVC words. Have students identify the final phonemes in those words and cover the corresponding letters in the boxes.

Assessing and Improving Rapid Automatic Naming (RAN) Ability

Students who show evidence of slow-processing speed and automaticity issues relating to letter names would benefit in doing RAN activities. First, assess the student's knowledge by using the form on page 7. Document which letter names are troublesome for the student. Have the child work on learning those letter names and practice reading select letters rapidly. To support these educational goals, provide the student with RAN letters activities. First, make several copies of page 129. Choose six letters for one of the boards and fill in the boxes, repeating each letter four times. (Make sure to incorporate letters that the child can identify easily with letters that look similar to boost visual discrimination skills.) Repeat this step to complete additional boards. *Note: Even though the student may be able to name each letter in isolation, the length of time taken to read a RAN letters board may indicate that the student lacks proficiency in naming letters. In the Neuhaus and Swank (2002) study, the researchers*

recommended that students continue improving their letter-naming ability even after they start reading words. You may also use page 14 to assess how well the student can name a set of 12 letters on each board.

Note: The letters *q* and *x* are not included on this assessment (page 14). It is essential for beginning readers to learn that *q* is usually paired with *u* in written words. The letter *x* usually stands for the sounds /ks/ in words, like *box* and *fox*.)

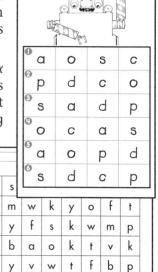

Reference: Neuhaus, Graham F., and Swank, Paul R. (2002). "Understanding the Relations Between RAN Letter Subtest Components and Word Reading in First-Grade Students." *Journal of Learning Disabilities*, 35 (2), 158–174.

LETTER IDENTIFICATION AND SOUNDS ASSESSMENT

Student's name: _____

Teacher's name: _____

First assessment date: _____

Second assessment date: _____

1. **Say the Letter Names:** Have the student read the letters in Box 1.

e y f p c x r b z a o d u j v l w i q k g m h s t n

2. **Say the Sounds:** Have the student say the corresponding sound for each consonant in Box 2. (Use *c* = /k/ and *g* = /g/ sounds. The letters *x* and *q* are not included to focus on common speech sounds in words.)

m b f p c r z d j v g k l n h t w s y

✂ -

Box 1

Say the Letter Names

e	y	f	p	c	x	r
b	z	a	o	d	u	j
v	l	w	i	q	k	g
m	h	s	t	n		

Box 2

Say the Sounds

m	b	f	p	c	r	z
d	j	v	g	k	l	n
h	t	w	s	y		

MATCHING BEGINNING SOUNDS

See page 5 for activity directions.

Pictures: bear, bat, cat, can, dog, dock, fish, fan, goat, gum,
horse, hair, jellyfish, jacket, lion, leaves, mouse, mittens

Pictures: narwhal, nut, porcupine, puppet, raccoon, ring, seal, submarine, turtle/tortoise, tent, vulture, vase, walrus, window, yak, yard, zebra, zero

ISOLATING AND SAYING BEGINNING SOUNDS CARDS

See page 5 for activity directions.

Pictures: Column 1—socks, wagon, feet, pie, rake, hat; Column 2—bib, car, top, money, nose, dot; Column 3—vest, game, lip, zipper, jug, yo-yo

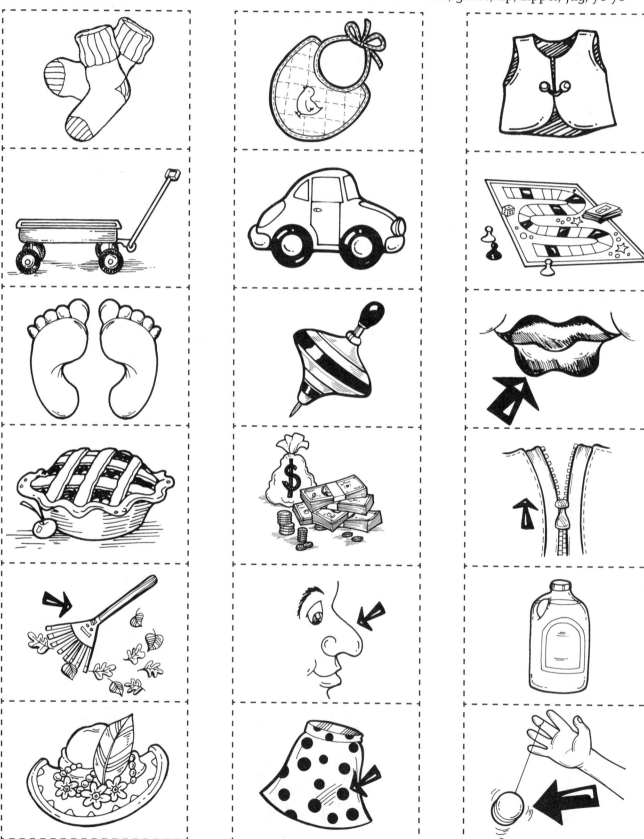

See page 5 for activity ideas.

To the teacher: Fill in the boxes with letters. Have student say the sound each letter represents.

Sound the Letters!

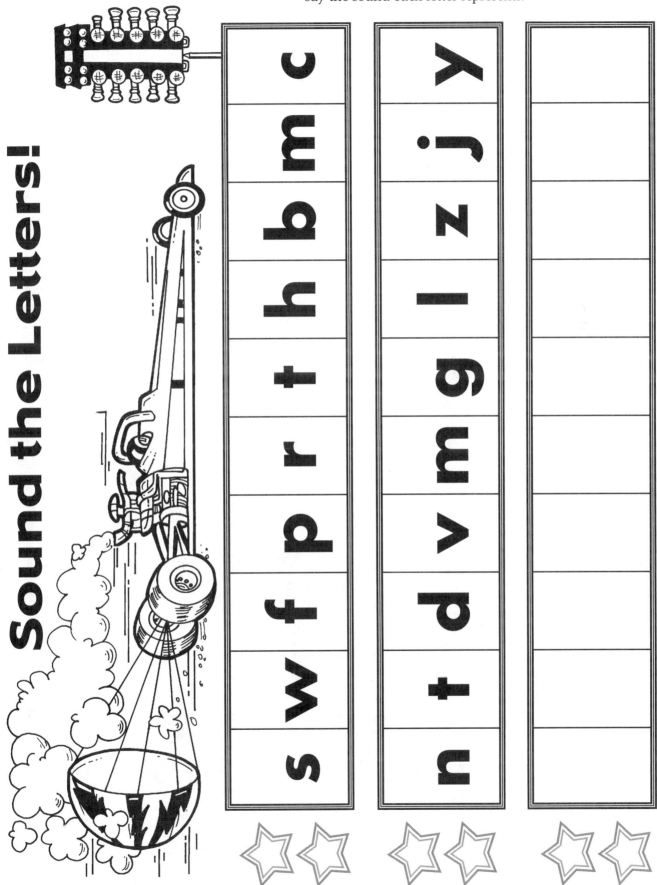

c m b h t p r f w s	y j z l g m v d t n	

☆ ☆   ☆ ☆   ☆ ☆

ISOLATING AND SAYING FINAL SOUNDS CARDS

Set A

See pages 5 and 6 for activity directions.

Set B

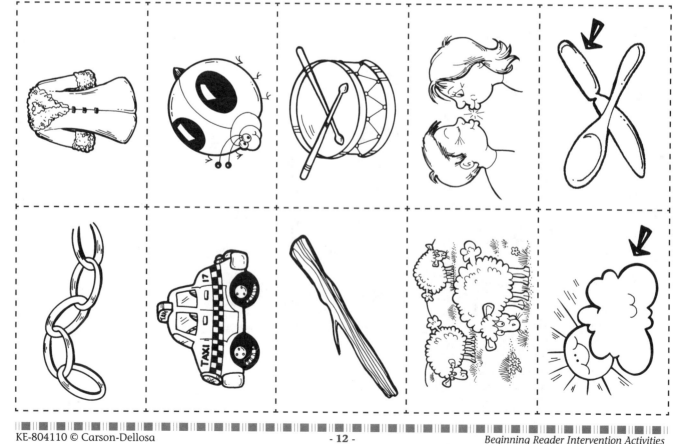

- 12 - *Beginning Reader Intervention Activities*

To the teacher: Fill in the boxes with letters for the final sounds in words that the student needs to practice identifying.

Sound at the End!

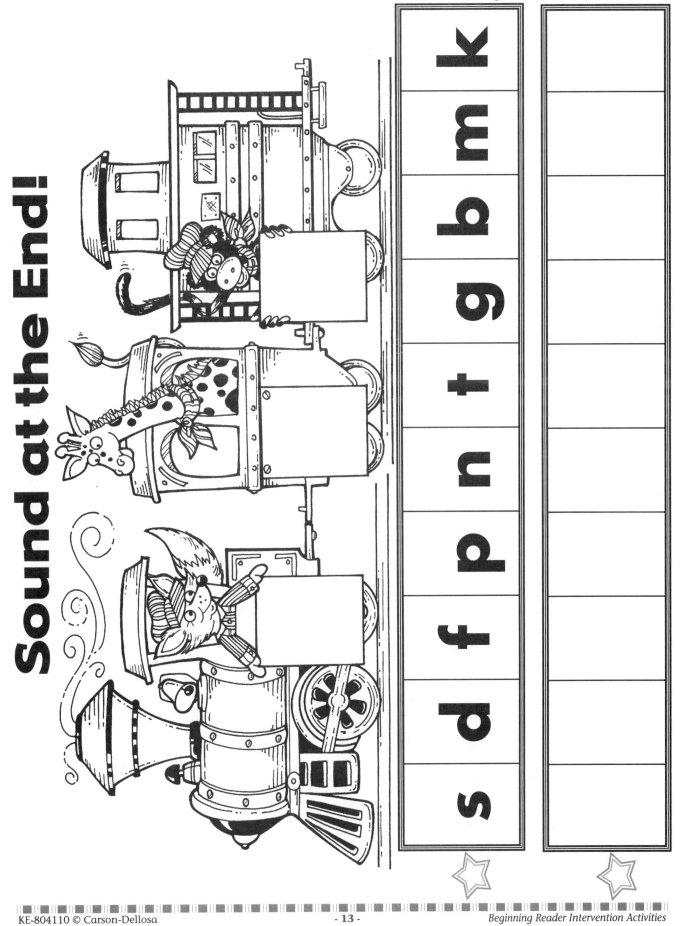

s   d   f   p   n   t   g   b   m   k

See page 6 for additional information.

RAPID AUTOMATIC NAMING (RAN) LETTERS ASSESSMENT

Student's name: _____

Assessment date: _____

 Board A

w	m	s	p	b	o	a	y	v
b	a	m	w	k	y	o	f	t
t	v	y	f	s	k	w	m	p
f	p	b	a	o	k	t	v	k
s	o	y	v	w	t	f	b	p

Total Named Correctly: _____   Duration of Time Used: _____ seconds

Board B

n	c	h	z	r	d	j	e	g
z	g	r	l	e	h	n	u	c
d	j	n	u	g	c	i	h	l
z	r	e	i	u	n	l	d	j
e	i	d	h	l	r	g	u	z

Total Named Correctly: _____   Duration of Time Used: _____ seconds

BUILDING SOUND-TO-LETTER KNOWLEDGE WITH TACTILE EXPERIENCES

Easy No-Flour Play Clay Recipe

Things You'll Need
1 cup (237 mL) cornstarch
2 cups (473 mL) baking soda
1 1/4 cups (300 mL) water
1 tbsp. (15 mL) vegetable oil
food coloring or fruit and vegetable juices
saucepan and stirring utensil

Follow These Steps
Mix the cornstarch and baking soda together in the saucepan. Slowly add the water, oil, and food coloring (or juice) for desired color. Cook on the stove over a low heat for approximately 15 minutes while stirring constantly. When the clay has reached the consistency of mashed potatoes, turn off the heat. Remove it from the saucepan. Allow the clay to cool on a hard surface that has been coated with a light dusting of cornstarch. Then, knead the clay until it has a smooth consistency. Store in an air-tight container in a cool location up to two weeks. This play clay will harden if air dried, and it may be painted.

Molding Words

Things You'll Need
Use the Easy No-Flour Play Clay recipe or your own favorite recipe to prepare play clay for the children. Make two batches, each a different color—

one color for vowel letters and the other for consonants. Cut cardboard into small pieces for displaying the clay letters.

Follow These Steps
Give students a small amount of clay in two different colors. Have them form the letters for the designated word family on a piece of cardboard (e.g., the letters *op* to spell words *hop*, *top*, *mop*, and *bop*). Talk about the selected words and then let children form the initial consonants on smaller pieces of cardboard.

More Ideas for Creating Multisensory Words
- Bend chenille stems into letters and lay out the letters to spell words.
- Finger paint letters. Add salt to the paint to create an additional texture.
- Provide glitter glue for students to use to print the words. When the glue is dry, let children "feel" the words.

Puffy Words

Things You'll Need: Make large tactile cards by forming the individual letters (see page 140) with puff paint or craft glue on pieces of poster board. Make one set for each student in the small group.

Follow These Steps
Give each student a set of puffy letters. Call out a word. Have children lay out the cards to spell the word and then trace over each letter with a pointer finger while saying its corresponding sound (phoneme).

Pinching Letters

Things You'll Need: Collect 27 milk jug caps for each basic set. Cover their tops with self-adhesive circles. Then, label the caps individually with the single consonants and vowels shown on page 140. (Add digraphs and silent-letter pairs caps to the set as needed.) Make one set for each pair of students in the group. Also, supply a large plastic tweezers for each child.

Follow These Steps
Display the letter caps in the center of the playing area. Give plastic tweezers to each child. Call out a word for each pair of students. Have them take turns picking up and arranging the corresponding caps to spell the word and then return the caps to the playing area.

MATCHING SOUNDS TO LETTERS ACTIVITIES

Children who struggle to learn how to read usually have not fully mastered "sound-to-letter relationships." Activities 1–4 help students focus on isolated phonemes (single speech sounds) and connect them with the corresponding graphemes (letters which stand for phonemes). Activities 5–8 target words having three or four phonemes. For these activities, the student is asked to move chips or buttons when articulating each phoneme in a spoken word—a strategy commonly known as using Elkonin boxes, named after D. B. Elkonin who developed this method of instruction. These activities help students who have limited phonological processing skills "see" and "hear" the sounds.

Activity 1: What's the Word?

Things You'll Need: For each student in the group, photocopy the letter cards (page 140) onto card stock and cut them out. Copy the picture for the chosen word family.

Basic: Select four to six words from a targeted word family (e.g., the –at family on page 24 and picture for *cat* or *hat* on page 26).

More challenging: Choose words from two or more word families for comparing vowels or different rimes.

Follow These Steps

1) Point to the word-family picture (cat) and let the child identify the vowel card for the word *cat*. Place the vowel (letter "a") in the center of the work area and say the short vowel sound represented by that letter (/a/).

2) Lay a consonant card (letter "m") in front of the vowel card and say the sounds by blending the two phonemes (/m/ and /a/) together while moving your pointer finger under each card. Say the phonemes again by stretching the vowel sound (/mmmmmmaaaaaa/). (This method works well to keep the consonant phoneme pure.) Ask the student: *What word can you make with these sounds that rhymes with* cat*?* (Answer: *mat*) Place the consonant card (letter "t") after the vowel and once again pronounce the phonemes by blending the sounds while simultaneously pointing to the letters. Repeat these steps using other chosen words.

Extend the lesson: Give each student an initial consonant and a vowel to sound out and use to build a word that rhymes with the picture.

Activity 2: Letters on Stones

Things You'll Need: For each student in the group, photocopy the letter cards (page 140) and the stone wall mats (page 130) onto card stock. Cut out the letters and store them in a zippered plastic bag.

Basic: Select four to six words from a targeted word family and copy the word-family picture.

More challenging: Choose words from two or more targeted word families for comparing vowel sounds or different rimes.

Follow These Steps

Have students "chisel" letters on the stone wall. Place the work mat in front of the child and scatter the letter cards in the work area. Follow the same steps used for the activity "What's the Word?"

Extend the lesson: Call out a word and let the child use the letters to build the word on the stone wall by first placing the vowel card on the work mat followed by the consonants. When the word is spelled correctly, have the child practice blending the phonemes while pointing to the corresponding letters.

Activity 3: Rev Up for Words

Things You'll Need: For each student in the group, photocopy the letter cards (page 140) and the racetrack billboard work mats (page 131) onto card stock. Cut out the letters and store them in a zippered plastic bag. Copy the word-family picture for the chosen word family.

Follow These Steps
Have students "display" words on the racetrack billboard. Place the selected mat in front of the child and scatter the letter cards in the work area. Follow the same steps used for the activity "What's the Word?" to spell words on the mat.

Activity 4: Blast Off!

Things You'll Need: For each student in the group, photocopy the letter cards (page 140) and the launch pad work mats (page 132) onto card stock. Cut out the letters and store them in a zippered plastic bag. Copy the word-family picture for the chosen word family.

Follow These Steps
Students will have a blast building words on the launch pad! Place the selected mat in front of the child and scatter the letter cards in the work area. Follow the same steps used for the activity "What's the Word?" to spell words on the mat.

Activity 5: Load the Truck

Things You'll Need: For each student in the group, photocopy the letter cards (page 140) and the truck work mats (page 133) onto card stock. Cut out the letters and store them in a zippered plastic bag. Include four playing chips or buttons in the bag.

Basic: Select four to six words from a targeted word family.

More challenging: Choose words from two word families for comparing different rimes.

Follow These Steps
Listening for sounds in words and loading the truck to make words—this is another fun task to help students understand the relationship between phonemes and letters. Place the selected truck mat in front of the student and scatter the letter cards on the work area.

1) Counting the phonemes: Tell the child to listen to the word (e.g., *red*). Say, *Listen to the word* red. *Say each sound separately with me.* (/r/ /e/ /d/) *How many sounds do you hear?* (three) Have the student place a chip on the truck trailer while saying each phoneme. (red = 3) Important: Be sure the child says each phoneme while touching each chip to reinforce what is being heard in the spoken word.

2) Making the word: Say the designated word aloud again. Have the student "load" the truck by finding the correct letters and placing them on the mat.
   • Start with the vowel letter card.
   • Find the beginning consonant and lay it in front of the vowel.
   • Then, add the final consonant.

When the word is spelled correctly, have the child practice saying the corresponding phoneme for each letter while touching the chip under it. Celebrate by "unloading" the truck and gearing up for a new word!

Activity 6: Pack the Words

Things You'll Need: Cut an egg carton in half so that there are two rows of three cavities in each piece. Obtain 32 plastic eggs (2 for each vowel [10 yellow in total] and 22 eggs in other colors for consonants) and two shoe boxes. *Note: To spell certain CCVC, CVCC, and CCVCC words, collect and prepare extra eggs (digraphs and silent-letter pairs) as needed. Also, use an egg carton that has 12 cavities.*

Labeling the eggs: For the vowels, print the letters (two of each—*a, e, i, o,* and *u*) on the yellow eggs. Place them in a small box.

On the other colors of eggs, print these letters: two of each—*b, d,* and *g;* one of each—*c, f, h, j, k, l, m, n, p, r, s, t, v, w, y,* and *z.* Store these eggs in a larger box.

Basic: Select four to six words from a targeted word family and its picture card.

More challenging: Choose words from two word families for comparing vowels or different rimes.

Follow These Steps
Make colorful words with plastic eggs!

1) Place the egg carton section in front of the child along with the two boxes of eggs.

2) Call out a word for the child to build (*big*). Have the student "pack" the egg carton by finding the correct letters. Remember: start with the vowel egg, next find the beginning consonant, and then finish the word by adding the final consonant.

3) When the word is spelled correctly, have the child practice decoding the word by saying the phoneme for each letter while touching the corresponding egg.

Be sure to fill the second row of cavities with another word to finish "packing" the eggs.

Activity 7: Catch High-Flying Sounds

Things You'll Need: For each student in the group, photocopy the letter cards (page 140) and playing catch mats (page 134) onto card stock. Cut out the letters and store them in a zippered plastic bag. Include four playing chips or buttons in the bag.

Follow These Steps
Have students "catch" these sounds in words! Place the selected work mat in front of the child and scatter the letter cards in the work area. Follow the same steps used for the activity "Load the Truck" on page 17. First, have the student place a chip on each mitt while saying each phoneme. Then, let the student build the word on the "billboard." Celebrate and clear the work mat for another round of play.

Activity 8: Unlock the Code

Things You'll Need: For each student in the group, photocopy the letter cards (page 140) and safe mats (page 135) onto card stock. Cut out the letters and store them in a zippered plastic bag. Include four playing chips or buttons in the bag.

Follow These Steps
Have students break the code to sound out these words! Place the selected safe work mat in front of the child and scatter the letter cards in the work area. Follow the same steps used for the activity "Load the Truck" on page 17 by placing a chip on the safe for each phoneme in the word and building the word on the work mat. Celebrate when the safe has been cracked and then "close" its door to play again.

SOUNDING OUT & READING WORDS ACTIVITIES

Activity 1: Where Is . . . ?

Things You'll Need: Select words (pages 143–160) and make photocopies of them on card stock. Cut out the word cards and store them in a zippered plastic bag.

Follow These Steps
Scatter six to eight word cards *faceup* on a flat surface. Without looking at the cards, call out one of the words. Repeat the word and then have a student point to the correct card. Continue in this manner until all of the cards have been matched with a spoken word.

Extend the lesson: Create a "cloze" activity for each word. Without looking at the word cards, tell the student a sentence that is missing one of the featured words. Then, have the child complete the sentence by finding the corresponding card and tell you the finished statement. For example, say, *The dog ____ through the park.* (The student then repeats the sentence and adds the word *ran.*) Alternatively, encourage students to think of sentences for the featured words and have you point to the word that would complete each statement. This switch in roles helps students apply their language skills.

Activity 2: Read 'n' Climb to See the View

Things You'll Need: For each student in the group, select six to eight words (pages 143–160) and make photocopies of them along with the tree house work mat (page 136) on card stock. Cut out the word cards and store them in a zippered plastic bag.

Follow These Steps
Scatter the word cards *faceup* on a flat surface. Let the child read aloud each word and then lay it on the ladder when decoded correctly. Continue in this manner until the child reaches the tree house to see the view. (Extra words that are read can be placed below the mat.)

Activity 3: Mr. Word Muncher

Things You'll Need: For each student in the group, select eight to ten words (pages 143–160) and make photocopies of them along with the monster work mat (page 137) on card stock. Cut out the word cards and store them in a zippered plastic bag.

Follow These Steps
Scatter the word cards *faceup* on a flat surface. Let the child read aloud each word and then lay it on the monster if decoded correctly. Continue the activity until all of the word cards have been read.

Activity 4: "Sticky" Words

Things You'll Need: For each pair of students, obtain two family-size soup cans (empty and clean). Cover them with colorful self-adhesive paper or felt. Select six to eight words (pages 143–160). Make two photocopies of each word on card stock. Cut out the word cards. Mount short magnetic strips or pieces of hook-and-loop tape on the backs of the cards. Store the prepared cards in a zippered plastic bag.

Follow These Steps
Arrange the word cards *faceup* on a flat surface. Taking turns, have students find a matching pair of cards and read the word aloud. If the word is decoded correctly, the student attaches one card to each metal can. When all of the words are sticking to cans, each student gets to "clean up" a can by reading the words aloud before removing them.

Activity 5: Yummy Words

Things You'll Need: For each student in the group, select six words (pages 143–160) and two extra ones to practice reading. Make two photocopies of each word onto card stock. Cut out the words. Also, make a copy of the sandwich pattern (page 138). Print each targeted word on a sandwich as shown in the example. Cut out the sandwiches and store them along with the word cards in a zippered plastic bag. Provide a small colorful paper bag to "pack" the sandwich for each featured word.

Follow These Steps
Scatter the word cards and the sandwiches *faceup* on a flat surface. Have the child select a sandwich, find the two matching word cards, and read aloud the word. Repeat the steps until all of the matches have been found. To "pack" the sandwiches, let the child read aloud each pair of words again and place them along with the sandwich in a paper bag.

SPELLING & WRITING ACTIVITIES

Activity 1: Word Family Mini-Book

Things You'll Need: For each student, cut small index cards in half or obtain eight sheets of self-adhesive note paper. Staple the pieces of index cards or paper to make a small booklet.

Follow These Steps
Let the child write each word on a page in the mini-book. Send the booklet home so that the child can read the words aloud to family members.

Activity 2: Clip, Read, 'n' Write

Things You'll Need: For each student, select one or two word families and glue the word-family ending label for each one in the center of a small sturdy paper plate. Make a copy of the word-family picture for the activity. Determine which word-family words the students needs to practice spelling and then print the initial consonants or letter clusters for those words on clothespins. Also, prepare extra clothespins to make nonsense words. Make a copy of the writing template (page 141) for recording the words.

Follow These Steps
Give the student the prepared paper plate. Talk about the name of the picture and its rime. Have the child print the corresponding word ending on the recording sheet. Set the clothespins and the prepared paper plate on the work surface. Direct the child to think of words that rhyme with the picture, clip the corresponding initial consonants to the plate, and write the words on the paper.

Activity 3: Finish the Sentence

Things You'll Need: Write a variety of simple sentences on sentence strips or card stock. The sentences can be generic or very specific for certain word family words (to make a cloze activity). Indicate with blanks where students should add the words to complete the sentences. Laminate the prepared sentences so that they can be reused. Provide a watercolor marker for the activity.

Examples may include:
Look at the _____.
The _____ is small (big).
The _____ is under the _____.
The _____ is on the _____.
The _____ is by the _____.
See the _____ over there?
I see a _____.
I feel _____.

Follow These Steps

Place a few selected word cards *faceup* on the tabletop. Ask students to read aloud the words before selecting a sentence strip to complete. Let students fill in the blanks on the laminated paper strips by writing the missing word(s) and reading aloud their work. Cleanup is easy! Wipe off the writings with a damp cloth and then have students in the group exchange sentence strips.

Extend the lesson: Write an open-ended story (fantasy or silly) that has blanks for students to fill in with words from a prepared word bank. Print the story on poster board and laminate it. This activity is a fun way to encourage students to practice reading high-frequency words, too!

Activity 4: Write Down—Back to the Ground

Things You'll Need: Use the materials that were prepared for the activity "Read 'n' Climb to See the View." Review the directions (page 19) if needed. Provide a copy of the writing template (page 141).

Follow These Steps

To begin the activity, make sure there are word cards on the ladder and then tell the student it is time to "climb" down from the tree house. To reach the ground, the child reads aloud each word, prints it on the writing paper, and then places that card in a discard pile.

Activity 5: Feed Mr. Word Muncher

Things You'll Need: Use the materials that were prepared for the activity Mr. Word Muncher. Review the directions (page 19) if needed. Provide a copy of the writing template (page 141) with a word-family chunk filled in.

Follow These Steps

After students have placed word cards on the work mat for Mr. Word Muncher, tell them it is time to "feed" the monster with some "crunchy" sounds. To do this, let the child read each word again and print it on the writing paper. When finished, the child can make the card "disappear" by sliding it under Mr. Muncher while saying the sounds in the word and "yum." (e.g., *bat* = /b/ /a/ /t/—"yum")

Activity 6: Robot Writing!

Things You'll Need: Make a copy of the robot form (page 139).

Follow These Steps

Fill in each box on the form with a selected word-family word. Then, let the student think of and write down sentences that incorporate the words.

Activity 7: I Write, You Write Sentences!

Things You'll Need: Make a copy of the writing template (page 142) for each student. Choose four or five words that have been read aloud several times by the student for the student to use.

Follow These Steps

To strengthen word recognition, it is important for students to write word-family words in sentences. Explain to the child how the selected words will be used in sentences that either stand alone or build on each other. Then, start the activity by choosing one of the featured words, using it in an oral sentence and recording that sentence on the paper. Direct the child to follow the same steps with another word. Continue taking turns until all of the targeted words have been incorporated into sentences. Wrap up the activity by letting the child read aloud the writing for extra decoding practice!

What to do with reluctant writers: Scribe their thoughts. Struggling learners might feel more comfortable sharing their ideas verbally, especially those who have weak fine motor skills.

Points to Remember

Letters and Sounds

⭐ A **phoneme** is the smallest unit of sound within a spoken word.

⭐ A **grapheme** is the letter or letter cluster within a written word that represents one sound.

⭐ To indicate the speech sound for a letter, it is written between slashes, or **virgules**, such as m = /m/.

⭐ Consonants which stand for single phonemes are *b, d, f, g, h, j, k, l, m, n, p, r, s, t, v, w, y,* and *z*. On the word-card pattern pages, the letter *c* stands for the /k/ sound. Words with *c* = /s/ are not used in any of the lessons.

⭐ If a student struggles to hear and identify phonemes, demonstrate how consonant sounds are made. Some consonant sounds are **plosive**, like /b/, /d/, /g/, /k/, /p/, and /t/. This means that a burst of air leaves the mouth when the sound is articulated. Let the child place her hand in front of her mouth to feel the rush of air when making these sounds. Make sure to articulate each phoneme without tacking on a vowel sound; for example, when teaching the letter *b*, say /b/ instead of /buh/.

⭐ Some consonant sounds can be held continuously, such as /f/, /h/, /m/, /n/, /r/, /s/, and /z/. Have students look in a child-safe mirror while making these sounds if they have difficulty identifying them. This strategy helps them understand how they position their lips and tongue to prolong the sounds of these phonemes.

⭐ When two adjacent consonants in a written word stand for a unique sound—such as *ch, sh, th, wh,* and *ng,* that phoneme is called a **digraph**. Note how a digraph is different than the phoneme for each individual consonant. For example, within the spoken word *chat,* there are three phonemes, /ch/ /a/ /t/.

⭐ Some pairs of consonants in written words are known as letter clusters because each individual letter stands for a phoneme. Each pair—*bl, cl, gl, pl, br, dr, gr, sc,* and others—represents sounds that are blended together, hence the name **blend**. For example, within the spoken word *flat,* there are four phonemes, which are /f/ /l/ /a/ /t/.

⭐ Words in text may also have silent-letter consonant pairs, like *ck, ff, ll, ss,* and *wr*. (These consonant pairs are also included on the letter-card reproducible on page 140 as a tool to use when spelling certain words.)

⭐ The letter pair *qu* actually stands for the sounds /kw/. To reinforce that the letter *q* is usually followed by the letter *u*, this unique common consonant team is included on the letter-card reproducible.

Phonemic Awareness Activities

⭐ Encourage students to tap two fingers on a hard surface while simultaneously saying each phoneme in a word. This kinesthetic strategy helps students with special needs "hear" and "feel" the sounds they are articulating. For example, make three taps for the word *cat,* (/k/ /a/ /t/).

⭐ Another kinesthetic strategy is to have a student slide or place a chip or button into a box drawn on paper when articulating each phoneme in a spoken word. This strategy, commonly known as "using Elkonin boxes," is named after D. B. Elkonin, who developed this method of instruction. Several work mats in this resource are actually modified Elkonin boxes. The fun, engaging illustrations on the work mats will fuel students' imaginations as they sound out and spell words.

⭐ Hearing and identifying short vowels sounds is very challenging for many young children. When creating lessons, have students compare the vowel sounds of two different word-family words that are not similar. For example, let children practice reading and spelling words from the *-an* and *-in* families. Avoid using *-an* words with *-en* words at first.

Assessing Rapid Automatic Naming (RAN) Ability

⭐ At various times, have students read RAN Letters Boards (page 129) that you have prepared. It is important for children to overlearn the names of the letters so that they can recall them rapidly, which impacts their decoding skills. Include RAN words exercises (page 126) as well.

Helping Your Child Learn How to Sound Out Words

Dear Parent,

Now that your child can recite the alphabet and identify the letters in print, there is more to be done to help your child learn how to sound out words. During small group sessions, your child will be doing activities to . . .

- understand that spoken words are made up of small individual sounds (called *phonemes*) and change single sounds to make new words;
- identify isolated letters and make the sounds they represent; and
- articulate and blend the sounds for letters together in printed words to read them.

In addition to the materials that your child will be bringing home for reading practice, use this page as a resource for more activity ideas and teaching suggestions.

Please continue reading aloud stories to your child and talking about the words your child sees on the pages. The discussion about the story, letters in the text and the sounds they stand for, rhyming words, words that begin with the same letters, and so on should take place after you and your child have enjoyed the book. Also, try to locate stories that include the word-family words your child has been learning to read in school. Take turns with your child reading aloud passages from those books to work on word fluency. Make sure to keep the sessions fun and engaging!

Sincerely,

Hearing Sounds in Spoken Words

Choose small words when playing oral word games.

Examples: word = # of sounds
bat = 3 (/b/ /a/ /t/)*
chat = 3 (/ch/ /a/ /t/)
flat = 4 (/f/ /l/ /a/ /t/)
*The speech sounds are indicated with slash marks.

How Many Sounds? Say a word and have your child tap on a surface while pronouncing each individual sound in the word. Ask how many taps were made.

What's the New Word? Say a word. Have your child change its beginning sound to a new sound. (Example: Change the /s/ in *sat* to a /k/ sound. What is the new word? Answer: *cat*)

Connecting Sounds to Letters

When talking about a letter and its corresponding sound, say, "What sound does this letter stand for?" (Letters do not say sounds.)

Remember when making a consonant sound, be careful not to add an extra vowel sound. Example: b = /b/, not /buh/

I Spy a Letter. Choose a secret letter on a book page, billboard, street sign, cereal box, and so on. Say the sound and then have your child point to and identify the corresponding letter.

What's the Sound? Point to a letter and have your child tell you its corresponding sound.

Sounding Out Words

To begin, choose three-letter words, known as consonant–vowel–consonant (CVC) words. Point out how those words end with a consonant and have a short vowel sound. This knowledge is also used when decoding and spelling longer words because a CVC syllable has a short vowel sound as well.

When sounding out a new CVC word, have your child first look at the vowel and say its sound. Next, focus on the initial consonant. While moving your finger under the first two letters, have your child blend those sounds together out loud. Finally, have your child look at the ending consonant, say its corresponding sound, and then blend the three sounds together.

MEET AND READ THE "-AT" FAMILY

Getting Started! Determine which letter-sound correspondences and letter patterns the student needs to practice.

• **Learning to Read CVC Words**—If the student cannot easily identify the phonemes for the consonants *b, c, f, h, m, p, r,* and *s,* use Day 1–5 activities. Otherwise, begin on Day 2. Select CVC words from the list. Start with about six words for the targeted practice on the first day. Add more words and the letter-sound relationship for *v* when the child is ready for a challenge.

• **Learning to Read CCVC Words**—If the student can read the three-letter words, provide lessons on sounding out and reading CCVC words. Select three days of activities. Introduce the digraphs *th* and *ch* and consonant clusters with a tactile activity. During the lessons, include various CVC words to strengthen decoding skills (*bat* with *brat, hat* with *chat* and *that, cat* with *scat, pat* with *spat*) and word-recognition fluency.

Word List

at	pat*	flat*
bat*	rat*	scat
cat*	sat*	slat
fat*	vat	spat
hat*	brat*	that*
mat*	chat*	

*See page 143 for reproducible word cards. Add to the set by printing other words on card stock.

DAY 1

Materials: Copy the pictures on page 26 (CVC Words). Follow the directions for the Molding Words activity on page 15.

• Show the pictures of the *cat* and the *hat.* Ask the child to tell you the beginning sound of each word (*cat* = /k/ and *hat* = /h/) and make those letters in clay. Continue the lesson by calling out other *-at* words. Have the child identify the beginning sounds and make the letters in clay to spell the words.
• To teach CCVC words, form the letters for digraphs, blends, and rimes in clay.
• Have students write the words.

DAY 2

Materials: Copy of letter cards (page 140) and word cards (page 143); prepared mini-book

Use letters and selected word cards in the following activities:

• Show and talk about the words.
• Phonemic Awareness (See page 25.)
• Puffy Words—if tactile activity is needed (See page 15.)
• What's the Word? (See page 16.)
• Where Is . . . ? (See page 19.)
• Word Family Mini-Book (See page 20.)

DAY 3

Materials: Copy of letter cards (page 140), word cards (page 143), truck mat (page 133), and tree house mat (page 136)

Use letters and selected word cards in the following activities:

• Review and use words in sentences. (See Finish the Sentence, page 21.)
• Phonemic Awareness (See page 25.)
• Load the Truck (See page 17.)
• Read 'n' Climb to See the View (See page 19.)
• Write Down—Back to the Ground (See page 21.)

DAY 4

Materials: Copy of word cards (page 143), monster mat (page 137), and robot form (page 139); labeled plastic eggs and egg carton (page 18)

Select word cards and use them in the following activities:

• Review and use words in sentences. (See Robot Writing!, page 21.)
• Phonemic Awareness (See page 25.)
• Pack the Words (See page 18.)
• Mr. Word Muncher (See page 19.)
• Feed Mr. Word Muncher (See page 21.)

DAY 5

Materials: Copy of word cards (page 143); children's storybook featuring *-at* words; self-adhesive flags (office supply item)

Select word cards and use them in the following activities:

• Read 'n' Spell Words (Take turns reading aloud a word to a partner who spells it.)
• Flag It!—Take turns reading aloud a passage from a classroom book that has *-at* words in the text. Each time a word-family word is used, mark it with a sticky flag. (Draw attention to the rime *-at.*)
• I Write, You Write! (See page 21.)

More Suggestions!

Spend a few minutes each day introducing or reviewing the *-at* word family by reading aloud passages (pointing to the words) from children's storybooks. Let students be word-family detectives and identify those words used in the text.

Read at Home Activity

Copy the take-home direction sheet and the cat picture (page 26) for each student. Include a copy of the word cards on card stock for the student to read. Place all of the materials in a zippered plastic bag.

Working with Sounds in "-at" Words

LESSON 1
BASIC

Isolating Initial Sounds—Model for your students: *Listen carefully. I am going to say a word. The word is bat. What is the first sound you hear in bat? The first sound is /b/.* Words to practice: *Say the first sound you hear in . . . cat, mat, rat, fat, sat, hat.*

Blending Sounds—Model for your students: *Listen carefully. I am going to say the sounds slowly in my secret word. I would like you to blend those sounds together. The sounds are: /m/ /a/ /t/. What is*

the secret word? When I blend the sounds /m/ /a/ /t/ together, I hear the word mat.* Words to practice: *rat, vat, fat, bat, pat*

MORE CHALLENGING

• *Listen to the words: bat, ball, cat. Which words rhyme?* (bat, cat)
• *What word begins with /m/ and rhymes with cat?* (mat)
• *Listen closely because I want to tell you a secret word. It is /h/ /a/ /t/. Say the sounds with me: /h/ /a/ /t/. What is my secret word?* (hat)
• *Listen to the words: pad, mat,*

pat. Which two words rhyme?* (mat, pat)
• *Here is another secret word for you. It is /r/ /a/ /t/. Say the sounds: /r/ /a/ /t/. What is my secret word?* (rat)
• *Say the word fat. How many sounds do you hear in the word fat?* (three) *Now, say the word without the /f/ sound. What is the new word?* (at)
• *Listen to the words: chat, chair, that. Which two words rhyme?* (chat, that)
• *Here is one more secret word for you. It is /s/ /a/ /t/. Say the sounds: /s/ /a/ /t/. What is the secret word?* (sat)

LESSON 2
BASIC

Segmenting Sounds—Model for your students: *Listen carefully. I would like you to tell me each sound you hear in a word. If the word is hat, what are the sounds? I would say /h/ /a/ /t/.* Words to practice: *Tell each sound you hear in . . . fat, mat, cat, sat, rat.*

Adding Sounds—Model for your students: *Listen carefully. I am going to say a word and then add a sound to make a new word. My secret word rhymes with at and*

begins with the /p/ sound. What is the word? (Repeat the sounds: /p/ /at/.) The word is pat.* Words to practice: *bat, vat, that, chat*

MORE CHALLENGING

• *Say each sound you hear in the word sat. What are those sounds?* (/s/ /a/ /t/)
• *Listen closely because I want to tell you a secret word. It is /v/ /a/ /t/. Say the sounds with me: /v/ /a/ /t/. What is the secret word?* (vat)
• *What word rhymes with at and begins with /ch/?* (chat)

• *Here's another word clue: This secret word begins with /p/ and rhymes with the word at. What is the word?* (pat)
• *Now think about the word rat. How many sounds do you hear in the word?* (three) *Stretch the sounds in the word.* (/rrrrrr/ /aaaaaa/ /t/)
• *Listen to the word at. What word rhymes with at and begins with /th/?* (that)
• *What word begins with /b/ and ends with at?* (bat)
• *Say each sound you hear in the word cat. What are those sounds?* (/k/ /a/ /t/)

LESSON 3
BASIC

Blending Sounds—Model for your students: *Listen carefully. I am going to say some sounds slowly. I would like you to blend those sounds together and then tell me the word. The sounds are /ch/ /a/ /t/. (Repeat the sounds.) What is the word? The word is chat.* Words to practice: *that, flat, spat, slat, and CVC words*

Substituting Sounds—Model for your students: *Listen to the word hat. Let's change the /h/ sound to /k/. What is the new word? I can blend the sounds /k/ /at/ together*

to make the word cat.* Words to practice: *sat—change /s/ to /b/ = bat; bat—change /b/ to /m/ = mat; mat—change /m/ to /p/ = pat*

MORE CHALLENGING

• *Listen to the word sat. Change the /s/ sound to /r/. What new word did you make?* (rat)
• *I want to tell you my secret word. It is /f/ /l/ /a/ /t/. (Repeat the sounds.) Blend the sounds together. What word can you make with the sounds?* (flat)
• *Listen to the sounds: /s/ /l/ /a/ /t/. (Repeat the sounds.) Blend the sounds together. What word can*

you make with the sounds?* (slat)
• *Say the word spat. Now, say it without the /s/ sound. What is the new word?* (pat)
• *This time say the word flat. Now, say it without the /f/ sound. What is the new word?* (lat) *Is this a real word?* (no)
• *Say the sounds /s/ /p/ /a/ /t/. (Repeat the sounds.) Blend the sounds together. What word can you make with the sounds?* (spat)
• *Say the word rat. Add the sound /b/ to the beginning of the word. What is the new word?* (brat)
• *Listen to the word pat. Change the /p/ sound to /v/. What new word did you make?* (vat)

See page 140 for initial letter cards to make words. Pictures: cat, hat

_at **_at** **_at**

_at _at

Read at Home—the "_at" Word Family

Where Is the Cat?

To Parent:
Your child has been learning how to read words that end with "at." In the zippered bag are word cards and a picture of a cat. Please provide a hat.

Where Is the Cat?
How to play the game:
- Cut out the phrase cards.
- Set the hat in the center of the playing area.
- Turn the cards facedown.
- Have your child turn over a phrase card and read it aloud.
- Let your child show what the phrase means using the hat and the picture of the cat.

Ready, Set, Read! Have your child read the word cards aloud as a practice run and then a second time at a faster speed!

| cat on a hat |
| cat in a hat |
| cat by a hat |
| cat under a hat |
| cat behind a hat |

MEET AND READ THE "-AN" FAMILY

Getting Started! Determine which letter-sound correspondences and letter patterns the student needs to practice.

• **Learning to Read CVC Words**—If the student cannot easily identify the phonemes for the consonants *b, c, d, f, m, p, r,* and *t,* use Day 1–5 activities. Otherwise, begin on Day 2. Select CVC words from the list. Start with about six words for the targeted practice on the first day. Add more words and the letter-sound relationship for *v* when the child is ready for a challenge.

• **Learning to Read CCVC Words**—If the student can read the three-letter words, provide lessons for sounding out and reading CCVC words. Select three days of activities. Introduce the digraph *th* and consonant clusters with a tactile activity. During the lessons, include CVC words to strengthen decoding skills (*ban* with *bran, can* with *clan* or *scan, pan* with *plan* or *span, tan* with *than*) and word-recognition fluency.

Word List

an	pan*	plan*
ban	ran*	scan*
can*	tan*	span*
Dan*	van*	than*
fan*	bran*	
man*	clan*	

See pages 143 & 144 for reproducible word cards. Add to the set by printing other words on card stock.

DAY 1

Materials: Copy the pictures on page 29 (CVC Words). Follow the directions for the Molding Words activity on page 15.

• Show the pictures of the *fan* and the *van*. Ask the child to tell you the beginning sound of each word (*fan* = /f/ and *van* = /v/) and make those letters in clay. Continue the lesson by calling out other *-an* words. Have the child identify the beginning sounds and make the letters in clay to spell the words.
• To teach CCVC words, form the letters for the digraph, blends, and rimes in clay.
• Have students write the words.

DAY 2

Materials: Copy of letter cards (page 140), word cards (pages 143 and 144), and stone wall mats (page 130); "Sticky" Words materials (page 19); prepared mini-book

Use letters and selected word cards in the following activities:

• Show and talk about the words.
• Phonemic Awareness (See page 28.)
• Puffy Words—if tactile activity is needed (See page 15.)
• Letters on Stones (See page 16.)
• "Sticky" Words (See page 19.)
• Word Family Mini-Book (See page 20.)

DAY 3

Materials: Copy of word cards (pages 143 and 144); labeled plastic eggs and egg carton (page 18); copy of monster mat (page 137)

Select word cards and use them in the following activities:

• Review and use words in sentences. (See Finish the Sentence, page 21.)
• Phonemic Awareness (See page 28.)
• Pack the Words (See page 18.)
• Mr. Word Muncher (See page 19.)
• Feed Mr. Word Muncher (See page 21.)

DAY 4

Materials: Copy of letter cards (page 140), word cards (pages 143 and 144), and playing catch mat (page 134); materials for Yummy Words (page 20) and Clip, Read, 'n' Write materials (page 20)

Use letters and selected word cards in the following activities:

• Review and use words in sentences. (See Robot Writing!, page 21.)
• Phonemic Awareness (See page 28.)
• Catch High-Flying Sounds (See page 18.)
• Yummy Words (See page 20.)
• Clip, Read, 'n' Write (See page 20.)

DAY 5

Materials: Copy of word cards (pages 143 and 144); children's storybook featuring *-an* words; self-adhesive flags (office supply item)

Select word cards and use them in the following activities:

• Read 'n' Spell Words (Take turns reading aloud a word to a partner who spells it.)
• Flag It!—Take turns reading aloud a passage from a classroom book that has *-an* words in the text. Each time a word-family word is used, mark it with a sticky flag. (Draw attention to the rime *-an*.)
• I Write, You Write! (See page 21.)

More Suggestions!

Spend a few minutes each day introducing or reviewing the *-an* word family by reading aloud passages (pointing to the words) from children's storybooks. Let students be word-family detectives and identify those words used in the text.

Read at Home Activity

Copy the take-home direction sheet (page 29) for each student. Include a copy of the word cards on card stock and a die. Place all of the materials in a zippered plastic bag.

Working with Sounds in "-an" Words

LESSON 1
BASIC

Isolating Initial Sounds—Model for your students: *Listen carefully. I am going to say a word. The word is fan. What is the first sound you hear in fan? The first sound is /f/.* Words to practice: *Say the first sound you hear in . . .* man, ban, ran, can.

Blending Sounds—Model for your students: *Listen carefully. I am going to say the sounds slowly in my secret word. I would like you to blend those sounds together. The sounds are: /v/ /a/ /n/. What is the secret word? When I blend the sounds /v/ /a/ /n/ together, I hear the word van.* Words to practice: *tan, Dan, pan, than, fan*

MORE CHALLENGING

- *Listen to the words: ran, ring, man. Which words rhyme? (ran, man)*
- *What word begins with /p/ and rhymes with an? (pan)*
- *Listen closely because I want to tell you a secret word. It is /r/ /a/ /n/. Say the sounds with me: /r/ /a/ /n/. What is my secret word? (ran)*

- *Listen to the words: vase, van, tan. Which words rhyme? (van, tan)*
- *Here is another secret word for you. It is /m/ /a/ /n/. Say the sounds: /m/ /a/ /n/. What is my secret word? (man)*
- *Listen to the words: can, fun, fan. Which words rhyme? (can, fan)*
- *Say the word ban. How many sounds do you hear in ban? Hold up your fingers to show me the number. (three) Now, say the word without the /b/ sound. What is the new word? (an)*
- *What word begins with /t/ and ends with the word an? (tan)*

LESSON 2
BASIC

Segmenting Sounds—Model for your students: *Listen carefully. I would like you to tell me each sound you hear in a word. If the word is ran, what are the sounds? I would say /r/ /a/ /n/.* Words to practice: *Tell each sound you hear in . . .* man, van, fan, ban.

Adding Sounds—Model for your students: *Listen carefully. I am going to say a word and then add a sound to make a new word. My secret word rhymes with an and begins with the /p/ sound. What is the word? (Repeat the sounds: /p/ /an/.) The word is pan.* Words to practice: *ran, Dan, tan, can, than*

MORE CHALLENGING

- *What word rhymes with an and begins with /v/? (van)*
- *Say each sound you hear in the word Dan. What are those sounds? (/D/ /a/ /n/)*
- *Now think about the word can. How many sounds do you hear in the word? (three) Stretch the sounds in the word.* (/c/ /aaaaaa/ /nnnnnn/)
- *What word begins with /f/ and ends with an? (fan)*
- *Listen closely because I want to tell you a secret word. It is /t/ /a/ /n/. Say the sounds with me: /t/ /a/ /n/. What is the secret word? (tan)*
- *Say each sound you hear in the word ban. What are those sounds? (/b/ /a/ /n/)*
- *Listen to the word an. What word rhymes with an and begins with /r/? (ran)*
- *Here's another word clue: This secret word begins with /m/ and rhymes with the word an. What is the word? (man)*

LESSON 3
BASIC

Blending Sounds—Model for your students: *Listen carefully. I am going to say some sounds slowly. I would like you to blend those sounds together and then tell me the word. The sounds are /b/ /r/ /a/ /n/. (Repeat the sounds.) What is the word? The word is bran.* Words to practice: *clan, scan, plan, span, and CVC words*

Substituting Sounds—Model for your students: *Listen to the word pan. Let's change the /p/ sound to /k/. What is the new word? I can blend the sounds /k/ /an/ together to make the word can.* Words to practice: *can—change /k/ to /d/ = Dan; Dan—change /d/ to /r/ = ran; ran—change /r/ to /th/ = than*

MORE CHALLENGING

- *Say each sound you hear in the word span. What are those sounds? (/s/ /p/ /a/ /n/)*
- *I want to tell you my secret word. It is /b/ /r/ /a/ /n/. (Repeat the sounds.) Blend the sounds together. What word can you make with the sounds? (bran)*
- *Listen to the word plan. Change the /p/ sound to /c/. What new word did you make? (clan)*

- *Say the word an. Add the sound /th/ to the beginning of the word. Now, what is the new word? (than)*
- *Listen to the word clan. Change the /k/ sound to /p/. What new word did you make? (plan)*
- *Now listen to the word bran. Say the word bran without the /b/ sound. What is the new word? (ran)*
- *Listen to the sounds: /s/ /c/ /a/ /n/. (Repeat the sounds.) Blend the sounds together. What word can you make with the sounds? (scan)*
- *Say the word span. Now, say it without the /s/ sound. What is the new word? (pan)*

See page 140 for initial letter cards to make words.

Pictures: fan, van

an

an

_an _an _an

an

Read at Home—the "_an" Word Family

Rolling Out a Sentence

To Parent:
Your child has been learning how to read words that end with "an." Please use the word cards and die to play the following game. You will need to provide a sheet of paper and pencil.

Rolling Out a Sentence
How to play the game:
- Cover each face of the die with a small piece of masking tape.
- Choose five "an" words and write them on the die. On the sixth face, write the word *man*.
- Have your child roll the die and record the word on a sheet of paper. Do this again two more times.
- Then, let your child use the three words in a sentence that can be silly or factual. Record the sentence for your child.
- Continue playing the game by taking a turn. When you are finished, invite your child to read the sentences that were generated for additional reading practice.

Ready, Set, Read! Lay the word cards faceup on a table. Have your child read the words aloud as a practice run and then a second time at a faster speed!

Reading for Fun: Take turns with your child reading aloud passages from children's storybooks.

MEET AND READ THE "-AB" FAMILY

Getting Started! Determine which letter-sound correspondences and letter patterns the student needs to practice.

• **Learning to Read CVC Words**—If the student cannot easily identify the phonemes for the consonants *c, d, g, j, l, n,* and *t,* use Day 1–5 activities. Otherwise, begin on Day 2. Select CVC words from the list. Start with about six words for the targeted practice on the first day. Add more words when the child is ready for a challenge.

• **Learning to Read CCVC Words**—If the student can read the three-letter words, provide lessons for sounding out and reading CCVC words. Select three days of lessons. Introduce the consonant clusters with a tactile activity. During the lessons, include CVC words to strengthen decoding skills (*cab* with *crab* or *scab, lab* with *blab, gab* with *grab, tab* with *stab*) and word-recognition fluency.

Word List

cab*	nab*	grab*
dab*	tab*	scab*
gab*	blab*	slab*
jab*	crab*	flab*
lab*	drab*	

See page 144 for reproducible word cards.

DAY 1

Materials: Copy the pictures on page 32. Follow the directions for the Molding Words activity on page 15.

• Show the picture of the *cab.* Ask the child to tell you the beginning sound of the word (*cab* = /k/) and make the letter in clay. Continue the lesson by calling out other *-ab* words. Have the child identify the beginning sounds and make the letters in clay to spell the words.
• To teach CCVC words, show the picture of the crab and form the letters for the blends and rimes in clay.
• Have students write the words.

DAY 2

Materials: Copy of letter cards (page 140) and word cards (page 144); racetrack billboard mat (page 131); prepared mini-book

Use letters and selected word cards in the following activities:

• Show and talk about the words.
• Phonemic Awareness (See page 31.)
• Puffy Words—if tactile activity is needed (See page 15.)
• Rev Up for Words (See page 17.)
• Where Is . . . ? (See page 19.)
• Word Family Mini-Book (See page 20.)

DAY 3

Materials: Copy of letter cards (page 140) and word cards (page 144); materials for Yummy Words (page 20) and Clip, Read, 'n' Write (page 20)

Use letters and selected word cards in the following activities:

• Review and use words in sentences. (See Finish the Sentence, page 21.)
• Phonemic Awareness (See page 31.)
• Catch High-Flying Sounds (See page 18.)
• Yummy Words (See page 20.)
• Clip, Read, 'n' Write (See page 20.)

DAY 4

Materials: Copy of letter cards (page 140), word cards (page 144), robot form (page 139), safe mat (page 135), and tree house mat (page 136)

Use letters and selected word cards in the following activities:

• Review and use words in sentences. (See Robot Writing!, page 21.)
• Phonemic Awareness (See page 31.)
• Unlock the Code (See page 18.)
• Read 'n' Climb to See the View (See page 19.)
• Write Down—Back to the Ground (See page 21.)

DAY 5

Materials: Copy of word cards (page 144); children's storybook featuring *-ab* words; self-adhesive flags (office supply item)

Select word cards and use them in the following activities:

• Read 'n' Spell Words (Take turns reading aloud a word to a partner who spells it.)
• Flag It!—Take turns reading aloud a passage from a classroom book that has *-ab* words in the text. Each time a word-family word is used, mark it with a sticky flag. (Draw attention to the rime *-ab.*)
• I Write, You Write! (See page 21.)

More Suggestions!

Spend a few minutes each day introducing or reviewing the *-ab* word family by reading aloud passages (pointing to the words) from children's storybooks. Let students be word-family detectives and identify those words used in the text.

Read at Home Activity

Copy the take-home direction sheet (page 32) for each student. Include a copy of the word cards on card stock and a small paper bag. Place all of the materials in a zippered plastic bag.

Working with Sounds in "-ab" Words

LESSON 1
BASIC

Isolating Initial Sounds—Model for your students: *Listen carefully. I am going to say a word. The word is tab. What is the first sound you hear in tab? The first sound is /t/.* Words to practice: *Say the first sound you hear in . . . gab, cab, lab, dab.*

Blending Sounds—Model for your students: *Listen carefully. I am going to say the sounds slowly in my secret word. I would like you to blend those sounds together. The sounds are: /n/ /a/ /b/. What is*

the secret word? When I blend the sounds /n/ /a/ /b/ together, I hear the word nab.*
Words to practice: *jab, cab, tab, lab*

MORE CHALLENGING

- *Listen to the words:* cat, cab, dab. *Which words rhyme?* (cab, dab)
- *What word begins with /j/ and rhymes with* tab? (jab)
- *Listen closely because I want to tell you a secret word. It is /c/ /a/ /b/. Say the sounds with me: /c/ /a/ /b/. What is my secret word?* (cab)
- *Listen to the words:* crab, lamp,

lab. *Say the words. Which two words rhyme?* (crab, lab)
- *Say the word* gab. *How many sounds do you hear in the word* gab? (three) *Now, say the word without the /g/ sound. What is the new word?* (ab) *Is this a real word?* (yes)
- *Listen to this secret word. It is /l/ /a/ /b/. Say the sounds: /l/ /a/ /b/. What is the word?* (lab)
- *Listen to the words:* drab, scab, drop. *Which two words rhyme?* (drab, scab)
- *Here is another secret word. It is /n/ /a/ /b/. Say the sounds: /n/ /a/ /b/. What is the secret word?* (nab)

LESSON 2
BASIC

Segmenting Sounds—Model for your students: *Listen carefully. I would like you to tell me each sound you hear in a word. If the word is* cab, *what are the sounds? I would say /k/ /a/ /b/.*
Words to practice: *Tell each sound you hear in . . .* dab, jab, nab, gab.

Adding Sounds—Model for your students: *Listen carefully. I am going to say a word and then add a sound to make a new word. My secret word rhymes with* cab *and begins with the /d/ sound. What*

is the word? (Repeat the sounds: /d/ /ab/.) The word is dab.*
Words to practice: *gab, tab, jab, lab*

MORE CHALLENGING

- *Say each sound you hear in the word* cab. *What are those sounds?* (/c/ /a/ /b/)
- *What word rhymes with* tab *and begins with /g/?* (gab)
- *Listen closely because I want to tell you a secret word. It is /d/ /a/ /b/. Say the sounds with me: /d/ /a/ /b/. What is the secret word?* (dab)
- *Here's another word clue: This*

secret word begins with /j/ and rhymes with the word* cab. *What is the word?* (jab)
- *What word begins with /c/ and ends with /ab/?* (cab)
- *Now think about the word* lab. *How many sounds do you hear in the word?* (three) *Stretch the sounds in the word.* (/lllllll/ /aaaaaa/ /b/)
- *Say each sound you hear in the word* nab. *What are those sounds?* (/n/ /a/ /b/)
- *Listen to the word* dab. *What word rhymes with* dab *and begins with /t/?* (tab)

LESSON 3
BASIC

Blending Sounds—Model for your students: *Listen carefully. I am going to say some sounds slowly. I would like you to blend those sounds together and then tell me the word. The sounds are /l/ /a/ /b/. (Repeat the sounds.) What is the word? The word is lab.*
Words to practice: *slab, crab, drab, scab,* and CVC words

Substituting Sounds—Model for your students: *Listen to the word* crab. *Let's change the /k/ sound to /g/. What is the new word? I can blend the sounds /g/ /rab/ together*

to make the word* grab.
Words to practice: *grab*—change /g/ to /d/ = *drab*; *drab*—change /d/ to /k/ = *crab*; *slab*—change /s/ to /b/ = *blab*

MORE CHALLENGING

- *Say the word* lab. *Add the sound /b/ to the beginning of the word. What is the new word?* (blab)
- *I want to tell you my secret word. It is /c/ /r/ /a/ /b/. (Repeat the sounds.) Blend the sounds together. What word can you make with the sounds?* (crab)
- *Listen to the word* crab. *Change the /k/ sound to /d/. What new word did you make?* (drab)

- *Say the word* scab. *Now, say it without the /s/ sound. What is the new word?* (cab)
- *Say the sounds: /g/ /r/ /a/ /b/. (Repeat the sounds.) Blend the sounds together. What word can you make with the sounds?* (grab)
- *This time say the word* flab. *Now, say it without the /f/ sound. What is the new word?* (lab)
- *Say the sounds /s/ /l/ /a/ /b/. (Repeat the sounds.) Blend the sounds together. What word can you make with the sounds?* (slab)
- *Listen to the word* slab. *Change the /s/ sound to /b/. What new word did you make?* (blab)

See page 140 for initial letter cards to make words.   Pictures: cab, crab

_ab _ab _ab

_ab _ab

Read at Home—the "_ab" Word Family

Ouch!

To Parent:
Your child has been learning how to read words that end with "ab." In the zippered bag are word cards and a small paper bag.

Ouch!
How to play the game (two players):
- Cut out the picture and glue it onto the front of the paper bag.
- Place the word cards in the prepared bag.
- Take turns with your child drawing a card without looking in the bag, reading the word out loud correctly, and placing the card faceup on the table. Drop the card back into the bag if the word is not read correctly. If you draw the word *crab*, say "Ouch!" and return your collected cards to the bag.
- The first player to collect five cards wins the game.

Ready, Set, Read! Lay the word cards faceup on a table. Have your child read the words aloud as a practice run and then a second time at a faster speed!

Ouch!

Watch out for the crab!

MEET AND READ "-AD" AND "-AN" FAMILIES

Getting Started! Determine which letter-sound correspondences and letter patterns the student needs to practice.

- **Learning to Read CVC Words**—If the student cannot easily identify the phonemes for the consonants, use Day 1–5 activities. Otherwise, begin on Day 2. Select CVC words from the list. Start with about eight words for the targeted practice on the first day. Add more words when the child is ready for a challenge.

- **Learning to Read CCVC Words**—If the student can read the three-letter words, provide lessons for sounding out and reading CCVC words. Select three days of lessons. Introduce the digraph *th* and consonant clusters with a tactile activity. During the lessons, include pairings of CVC and CCVC words to strengthen decoding skills (*lad* with *clad* or *glad, fad* with *fan, mad* with *man, pan* with *pad* or *span, can* with *clan* or *clad, tan* with *tad* or *than*) and word-recognition fluency.

Word List

bad*	sad*	Dan*	bran*
dad*	tad*	fan*	clan*
fad*	clad*	man*	plan*
had*	glad*	pan*	scan*
lad*	an	ran*	span*
mad*	ban	tan*	than*
pad*	can*	van*	

See pages 143–145 for reproducible word cards. Add to the set by printing other words on card stock.

DAY 1

Materials: Copy the pictures on pages 29 and 35. Follow the directions for the Molding Words and Pinching Letters activities on page 15.

- Show the pictures for *fan* and the *sad*. Ask the child to tell you the beginning sound of each word (*fan* = /f/, *sad* = /s/) and make the letters in clay. Continue the lesson by calling out other selected words. Let the child identify the beginning sounds and make the letters in clay to spell the words.
- Have students write the words.
- Pinching Letters (See page 15.)

DAY 2

Materials: Copy of letter cards (page 140), word cards (pages 143–145), and launch pad mat (page 132); materials for "Sticky" Words (page 19); prepared mini-book

Use letters and selected word cards in the following activities:

- Show and read the words.
- Phonemic Awareness (See page 34.)
- Puffy Words—if tactile activity is needed (See page 15.)
- Blast Off! (See page 17.)
- "Sticky" Words (See page 19.)
- Word Family Mini-Book (See page 20.)

DAY 3

Materials: Copy of letter cards (page 140), word cards (pages 143–145), safe mat (page 135), and tree house mat (page 136)

Use letters and selected word cards in the following activities:

- Review and use words in sentences. (See Finish the Sentence, page 21.)
- Phonemic Awareness (See page 34.)
- Unlock the Code (See page 18.)
- Read 'n' Climb to See the View (See page 19.)
- Write Down—Back to the Ground (See page 21.)

DAY 4

Materials: Copy of letter cards (page 140), word cards (pages 143–145), robot form (page 139), truck mat (page 133), and monster mat (page 137)

Use letters and selected word cards in the following activities:

- Review and use words in sentences. (See Robot Writing!, page 21.)
- Phonemic Awareness (See page 34.)
- Load the Truck (See page 17.)
- Mr. Word Muncher (See page 19.)
- Feed Mr. Word Muncher (See page 21.)

DAY 5

Materials: Copy of word cards (pages 143–145); children's storybooks featuring *-ad* and *-an* words; self-adhesive flags (office supply item)

Select word cards and use them in the following activities:

- Read 'n' Spell Words (Take turns reading aloud a word to a partner who spells it.)
- Flag It!—Take turns reading aloud a passage from a classroom book that has *-ad* and *-an* words in the text. Each time a word-family word is used, mark it with a sticky flag.
- I Write, You Write! (See page 21.)

More Suggestions!

Spend a few minutes each day introducing or reviewing the *-ad* and *-an* word families by reading aloud passages (pointing to the words) from children's storybooks. Let students be word-family detectives and identify those words used in the text.

Read at Home Activity

Copy the take-home direction sheet on page 35 for each student. Include a copy of the word cards on card stock and a small paper bag. Place all of the materials in a zippered plastic bag.

Working with Sounds in "-ad" and "-an" Words

LESSON 1
BASIC

Isolating Initial Sounds—Model for your students: *Listen carefully. I am going to say a word. The word is sad. What is the first sound you hear in sad? The first sound is /s/.* Words to practice: *Say the first sound you hear in . . .* mad, bad, tad, dad.

Blending Sounds—Model for your students: *Listen carefully. I am going to say the sounds slowly in my secret word. I would like you to blend those sounds together. The* sounds are: /m/ /a/ /n/. *What is the secret word? When I blend the sounds /m/ /a/ /n/ together, I hear the word* man. Words to practice: *fan, ran, can, tan*

MORE CHALLENGING

- *Listen to the words:* bad, ban, sad. *Which words rhyme?* (bad, sad)
- *What word begins with /m/ and rhymes with* dad? (mad)
- *Listen closely because I want to tell you a secret word. It is /l/ /a/ /d/. Say the sounds with me: /l/ /a/ /d/. What is my secret word?* (lad)

- *Listen to the words:* man, fan, fad. *Which words rhyme?* (man, fan)
- *Here is another secret word for you. It is /t/ /a/ /d/. Say the sounds: /t/ /a/ /d/. What is my secret word?* (tad)
- *Listen to the words:* pan, pad, dad. *Which words rhyme?* (pad, dad)
- *Say the word* Dan. *How many sounds do you hear in* Dan? *Hold up your fingers to show me the number.* (three) *Now, say the word without the /d/ sound. What is the new word?* (an)
- *What word begins with /th/ and ends with the word* an? (than)

LESSON 2
BASIC

Segmenting Sounds—Model for your students: *Listen carefully. I would like you to tell me each sound you hear in a word. If the word is* Dan, *what are the sounds? I would say /d/ /a/ /n/.* Words to practice: *Tell each sound you hear in . . .* can, pan, ban, than.

Adding Sounds—Model for your students: *Listen carefully. I am going to say a word and then add a sound to make a new word. My secret word rhymes with* ad *and* begins with the /l/ sound. What is the word? *(Repeat the sounds: /l/ /ad/.) The word is* lad. Words to practice: *bad, pad, fad, had*

MORE CHALLENGING

- *What word rhymes with* mad *and begins with /t/?* (tad)
- *Say each sound you hear in the word* had. *What are those sounds?* (/h/ /a/ /d/)
- *Now think about the word* dad. *How many sounds do you hear in the word?* (three) *Stretch the sounds in the word.* (/d/ /aaaaaa/ /d/)

- *What word begins with /b/ and rhymes with* mad? (bad)
- *Listen closely because I want to tell you a secret word. It is /s/ /a/ /d/. Say the sounds with me: /s/ /a/ /d/. What is the secret word?* (sad)
- *Say each sound you hear in the word* ran. *What are those sounds?* (/r/ /a/ /n/)
- *Listen to the word* ran. *What word rhymes with* ran *and begins with /f/?* (fan)
- *Here's another word clue: This secret word begins with /f/ and rhymes with the word* mad. *What is the word?* (fad)

LESSON 3
BASIC

Blending Sounds—Model for your students: *Listen carefully. I am going to say some sounds slowly. I would like you to blend those sounds together and then tell me the word. The sounds are /g/ /l/ /a/ /d/.* (Repeat the sounds.) *What is the word? The word is* glad. Words to practice: *clad, span, scan, than,* and CVC words

Substituting Sounds—Model for your students: *Listen to the word* tan. *Let's change the /t/ sound to /th/. What is the new word? I can blend the sounds /th/ /an/ together* to make the word than. Words to practice: *than*—change /th/ to /r/ = ran; *ran*—change /r/ to /v/ = van; *plan*—change /p/ to /k/ = clan

MORE CHALLENGING

- *Say each sound you hear in the word* Chad. *What are those sounds?* (/ch/ /a/ /d/)
- *I want to tell you my secret word. It is /b/ /r/ /a/ /d/.* (Repeat the sounds.) *Blend the sounds together. What word can you make with the sounds?* (Brad)
- *Listen to the word* had. *Change the /h/ sound to /f/. What new word did you make?* (fad)

- *Listen to the sounds: /c/ /l/ /a/ /d/.* (Repeat the sounds.) *Blend them together. What word can you make with the sounds?* (clad)
- *Listen to the word* clad. *Change the /k/ sound to /g/. What new word did you make?* (glad)
- *Now listen to the word* bran. *Say the word* bran *without the /b/ sound. What is the new word?* (ran)
- *Listen to the sounds: /c/ /l/ /a/ /d/. Blend the sounds together. What word can you make with the sounds?* (clad)
- *Say the word* span. *Now, say it without the /s/ sound. What is the new word?* (pan)

See page 140 for initial letter cards to make words. The pictures and cards for -an words are on page 29.

Pictures: glad, sad

_ad **_ad** **_ad**

_ad **_ad**

Read at Home—the "_an" and "_ad" Word Families

Pad or Pan?

To Parent:
Your child has been learning how to read words that end with "ad" or "an." Along with the word cards and small paper bag that have been provided, please supply a small frying pan and a notepad for this activity.

In the Pan or on the Pad?
How to play the game (two players):
- Cut out word cards if needed and the Wild Cards on this page. Place all of the cards in the paper bag.
- Ask your child to choose either the pad (for "ad" words) or the pan (for "an" words) for making matches. (You will match the remaining object.)
- Take turns with your child drawing a card without looking in the bag and reading the word out loud. If the word matches, lay the word card faceup near your chosen object. If not, drop the card back into the bag. Also, return the word card to the bag if it is not read correctly.
- The first player to collect five words wins the game. Watch out for the "Game over!" card. Then, the player who has collected the most cards wins!

Ready, Set, Read! Lay the word cards on a table. Have your child read the words aloud as a practice run and then a second time at a faster speed!

Draw and read
2 cards.

Ouch! Hot pan!
Lose a turn.

Pencil broke!
Lose a turn.

Draw and read
2 cards.

Game over!

MEET AND READ "-AM" AND "-AB" FAMILIES

Getting Started! Determine which letter-sound correspondences and letter patterns the student needs to practice.

• **Learning to Read CVC Words**—If the student cannot easily identify the phonemes for the consonants, use Day 1–5 activities. Otherwise, begin on Day 2. Select CVC words from the list. Start with about eight words for the targeted practice on the first day. Add more words when the child is ready for a challenge.

• **Learning to Read CCVC Words**—If the student can read the three-letter words, provide lessons for sounding out and reading CCVC words. Select three days of lessons. Introduce the consonant clusters with a tactile activity. During the lessons, pair CCVC words (*gram* with *grab*, *crab* with *cram*, *slam* with *slab*) and include CVC words to strengthen decoding skills (*ram* with *tram*, *Sam* with *scam* or *slam*, *Tam* with *tab* or *tram*, *cab* with *crab*, *gab* with *grab*) and word-recognition fluency.

Word List

am*	clam*	cab*	blab*
jam*	cram*	dab*	crab*
Pam*	gram*	gab*	drab*
ram*	scam	jab*	flab*
Sam*	slam*	lab*	grab*
Tam*	swam*	nab*	scab*
yam*	tram*	tab*	slab*

See pages 144 & 145 for reproducible word cards. Add to the set by printing scam on card stock.

DAY 1

Materials: Copy the pictures on pages 32 and 38. Follow the directions for the Molding Words and Pinching Letters activities on page 15.

• Show the pictures for *jam* and the *cab*. Ask the child to tell you the beginning sound of each word (*jam* = /j/, *cab* = /k/) and make the letters in clay. Continue the lesson by calling out other selected words. Let the child identify the beginning sounds and make the letters in clay to spell the words.
• Have students write the words.
• Pinching Letters (See page 15.)

DAY 2

Materials: Copy of letter cards (page 140) and word cards (pages 144 and 145); prepared mini-book

Use letters and selected word cards in the following activities:

• Show and use the words in sentences.
• Phonemic Awareness (See page 37.)
• Puffy Words—if tactile activity is needed (See page 15.)
• What's the Word? (See page 16.)
• Where Is . . . ? (See page 19.)
• Word Family Mini-Book (See page 20.)

DAY 3

Materials: Copy of letter cards (page 140), word cards (pages 144 and 145), truck mat (page 133), and monster mat (page 137)

Use letters and selected word cards in the following activities:

• Review and use words in sentences. (See Finish the Sentence, page 21.)
• Phonemic Awareness (See page 37.)
• Load the Truck (See page 17.)
• Mr. Word Muncher (See page 19.)
• Feed Mr. Word Muncher (See page 21.)

DAY 4

Materials: Copy of word cards (pages 144 and 145) and robot form (page 139); labeled plastic eggs and egg carton (page 18); materials for Yummy Words (page 20) and Clip, Read, 'n' Write (page 20)

Select word cards and use them in the following activities:

• Review and use words in sentences. (See Robot Writing!, page 21.)
• Phonemic Awareness (See page 37.)
• Pack the Words (See page 18.)
• Yummy Words (See page 20.)
• Clip, Read 'n' Write (See page 20.)

DAY 5

Materials: Copy of word cards (pages 144 and 145); children's storybook featuring -*am* and -*ab* words; self-adhesive flags (office supply item)

Select word cards and use them in the following activities:

• Read 'n' Spell Words (Take turns reading aloud a word to a partner who spells it.)
• Flag It!—Take turns reading aloud a passage from a classroom book that has -*am* and -*ab* words in the text. Each time a word-family word is used, mark it with a sticky flag.
• I Write, You Write! (See page 21.)

More Suggestions!

Spend a few minutes each day introducing or reviewing the -*am* and -*ab* word families by reading aloud passages (pointing to the words) from children's storybooks. Let students be word-family detectives and identify those words used in the text.

Read at Home Activity

Copy the take-home direction sheet (page 38) for each student. Include a copy of each word card on card stock in two different colors for the student to read. Place all of the materials in a zippered plastic bag.

Working with Sounds in "-am" and "-ab" Words

LESSON 1
BASIC

Isolating Initial Sounds—Model for your students: *Listen carefully. I am going to say a word. The word is ram. What is the first sound you hear in ram? The first sound is /r/.* Words to practice: *Say the first sound you hear in . . . Tam, jam, Sam, Pam, yam.*

Blending Sounds—Model for your students: *Listen carefully. I am going to say the sounds slowly in my secret word. I would like you to blend those sounds together. The sounds are: /l/ /a/ /b/. What is* the secret word? When I blend the sounds /l/ /a/ /b/ together, I hear the word lab.
Words to practice: *cab, tab, gab, jab, dab*

MORE CHALLENGING

- *Listen to the words: tab, tram, yam. Which words rhyme?* (tram, yam)
- *What word begins with /s/ and rhymes with am?* (Sam)
- *Listen closely because I want to tell you a secret word. It is /n/ /a/ /b/. Say the sounds with me: /n/ /a/ /b/. What is my secret word?* (nab)

- *Listen to the words: dab, lab, jam. Which two words rhyme?* (dab, lab)
- *Here is another secret word for you. It is /j/ /a/ /m/. Say the sounds: /j/ /a/ /m/. What is my secret word?* (jam)
- *Say the word yam. How many sounds do you hear in the word yam?* (three) *Now, say the word without the /y/ sound. What is the new word?* (am)
- *Listen to the words: scam, scab, swam. Which two words rhyme?* (scam, swam)
- *What word begins with /p/ and rhymes with Sam?* (Pam)

LESSON 2
BASIC

Segmenting Sounds—Model for your students: *Listen carefully. I would like you to tell me each sound you hear in a word. If the word is nab, what are the sounds? I would say /n/ /a/ /b/.*
Words to practice: *Tell each sound you hear in . . . jab, dab, cab, tab, gab.*

Adding Sounds—Model for your students: *Listen carefully. I am going to say a word and then add a sound to make a new word. My* secret word rhymes with am and begins with the /p/ sound. What is the word? (Repeat the sounds: /p/ /am/.) The word is Pam.
Words to practice: *yam, ram, Sam, Tam*

MORE CHALLENGING

- *Say each sound you hear in the word dab. What are those sounds?* (/d/ /a/ /b/)
- *Listen closely because I want to tell you a secret word. It is /sh/ /a/ /m/. Say the sounds with me: /sh/ /a/ /m/. What is the secret word?* (sham)
- *What word rhymes with yam and* begins with /j/? (jam)
- *Here's another word clue: This secret word begins with /l/ and rhymes with the word cab. What is the word?* (lab)
- *Now think about the word Sam. How many sounds do you hear in the word?* (three) *Stretch the sounds in the word.* (/sssss/ /aaaaa/ /mmmmm/)
- *Listen to the word yam. What word rhymes with yam and begins with /r/?* (ram)
- *What word begins with /g/ and ends with /ab/?* (gab)
- *Say each sound you hear in the word Pam. What are those sounds?* (/p/ /a/ /m/)

LESSON 3
BASIC

Blending Sounds—Model for your students: *Listen carefully. I am going to say some sounds slowly. I would like you to blend those sounds together and then tell me the word. The sounds are /k/ /l/ /a/ /m/.* (Repeat the sounds.) *What is the word?* (clam)
Words to practice: *gram, swam, slam, tram, and CVC words*

Substituting Sounds—Model for your students: *Listen to the word cab. Let's change the /k/ sound to /n/. What is the new word? I can blend the sounds /n/ /ab/ together* to make the word nab.
Words to practice: nab—change /n/ to /t/ = tab; tab—change /t/ to /g/ = gab; crab—change /k/ to /g/ = grab

MORE CHALLENGING

- *Listen to the word ham. Change the /h/ sound to /sh/. What new word did you make?* (sham)
- *I want to tell you my secret word. It is /b/ /l/ /a/ /b/.* (Repeat the sounds.) *Blend the sounds together. What word can you make with the sounds?* (blab)
- *Listen to the sounds: /d/ /r/ /a/ /b/.* (Repeat the sounds.) *Blend the sounds together. What word can*

you make with the sounds? (drab)
- *Say the word gram. Now, say it without the /g/ sound. What is the new word?* (ram)
- *This time say the word stab. Now, say it without the /s/ sound. What is the new word?* (tab)
- *Say the sounds /s/ /l/ /a/ /m/.* (Repeat the sounds.) *Blend the sounds together. What word can you make with the sounds?* (slam)
- *Say the word ram. Add the sound /t/ to the beginning of the word. What is the new word?* (tram)
- *Listen to the word drab. Change the /d/ sound to /c/. What new word did you make?* (crab)

See page 140 for initial letter cards to make words. The pictures and cards for -ab words are on page 32.

Pictures: jam, clam

am

am

_am _am _am

Read at Home—the "_am" and "_ab" Word Families

Match and Read

To Parent:
Your child has been learning how to read words that end with "am" and "ab." In the zippered bag you will find word cards in two different colors.

Match and Read
How to play the game:

• Cut out the word cards if needed. Sort them into two sets by color.
• Scatter the first set of cards faceup in the center of the playing area.
• Place the second set of cards facedown in a pile.
• Have your child work with both sets of cards to find the matching pairs and then read the words.
• Variation: Draw a smiley face in front of two of the words in the second set. Take turns finding the matching pairs. When a smiley-face card is drawn, that player draws one more card to make another match. When all of the matches have been found, the game ends. The player who collects the most matches wins the game.

Ready, Set, Read! Arrange all of the word cards in several rows on a table. Have your child read the words aloud as a practice run and then a second time at a faster speed!

MEET AND READ "-AP" AND "-AT" FAMILIES

Getting Started! Determine which letter-sound correspondences and letter patterns the student needs to practice.

• **Learning to Read CVC Words**—If the student cannot easily identify the phonemes for the consonants, use Day 1–5 activities. Otherwise, begin on Day 2. Select CVC words from the list. Start with about eight words for the targeted practice on the first day. Add more words when the child is ready for a challenge.

• **Learning to Read CCVC Words**—If the student can read the three-letter words, provide lessons for sounding out and reading CCVC words. Select three days of lessons. Introduce the digraphs *ch* and *th* and consonant clusters with a tactile activity. During the lessons, include pairings of CVC and CCVC words to strengthen decoding skills (*cap* with *chap* or *cat* or *chat*, *lap* with *clap* or *flap, slat* with *slap, mat* with *map, nap* with *snap, rap* with *trap* or *rat*) and word-recognition fluency.

Word List

cap*	tap*	snap*	pat*	scat
gap*	yap*	trap*	rat*	slat
lap*	zap*	bat*	sat*	spat
map*	clap*	cat*	vat	that*
nap*	chap*	fat*	brat*	
rap*	flap*	hat*	chat*	
sap*	slap*	mat*	flat*	

See pages 143, 145 & 146 for reproducible word cards. Add to the set by printing other words on card stock.

DAY 1

Materials: Copy the pictures on pages 26 and 41. Follow the directions for the Molding Words and Pinching Letters activities on page 15.

• Show the pictures for *hat* and the *map*. Ask the child to tell you the beginning sound of each word (*hat* = /h/, *map* = /m/) and make the letters in clay. Continue the lesson by calling out other selected words. Let the child identify the beginning sounds and make the letters in clay to spell the words.
• Have students write the words.
• Pinching Letters (See page 15.)

DAY 2

Materials: Copy of letter cards (page 140) and word cards (pages 143, 145, and 146), "Sticky" Words materials (page 19); copy of stone wall mat (page 130); prepared mini-book

Use letters and selected word cards in the following activities:

• Show and read the words.
• Phonemic Awareness (See page 40.)
• Puffy Words—if tactile activity is needed (See page 15.)
• Letters on Stones (See page 16.)
• "Sticky" Words (See page 19.)
• Word Family Mini-Book (See page 20.)

DAY 3

Materials: Copy of word cards (pages 143, 145, and 146); labeled plastic eggs and egg carton (page 18); materials for Yummy Words (page 20) and Clip, Read, 'n' Write (page 20)

Select word cards and use them in the following activities:

• Review and use words in sentences. (See Finish the Sentence, page 21.)
• Phonemic Awareness (See page 40.)
• Pack the Words (See page 18.)
• Yummy Words (See page 20.)
• Clip, Read, 'n' Write (See page 20.)

DAY 4

Materials: Copy of letter cards (page 140), word cards (pages 143, 145, and 146), robot form (page 139), playing catch mat (page 134), and tree house mat (page 136)

Use letters and selected word cards in the following activities:

• Review and use words in sentences. (See Robot Writing!, page 21.)
• Phonemic Awareness (See page 40.)
• Catch High-Flying Sounds (See page 18.)
• Read 'n' Climb to See the View (See page 19.)
• Write Down—Back to the Ground (See page 21.)

DAY 5

Materials: Copy of word cards (page 143, 145, and 146); storybook featuring *-ap* and *-at* words; self-adhesive flags (office supply item)

Select word cards and use them in the following activities:

• Read 'n' Spell Words (Take turns reading aloud a word to a partner who spells it.)
• Flag It!—Take turns reading aloud a passage from a classroom book that has *-ap* and *-at* words in the text. Each time a word-family word is used, mark it with a sticky flag.
• I Write, You Write! (See page 21.)

More Suggestions!

Spend a few minutes each day introducing or reviewing the *-ap* and *-at* word families by reading aloud passages (pointing to the words) from children's storybooks. Let students be word-family detectives and identify those words used in the text.

Read at Home Activity

Copy the take-home direction sheet (page 41) for each student. Include two copies of the word cards on card stock for each student to read. Place all of the materials in a zippered plastic bag.

Working with Sounds in "-ap" and "-at" Words

LESSON 1
BASIC

Isolating Initial Sounds—Model for your students: *Listen carefully. I am going to say a word. The word is sat. What is the first sound you hear in sat? The first sound is /s/.*
Words to practice: *Say the first sound you hear in . . .* hat, bat, mat, rat.

Blending Sounds—Model for students: *Listen carefully. I am going to say the sounds slowly in my secret word. I would like you to blend those sounds together. The sounds are: /m/ /a/ /p/. What is the secret word? When I blend the sounds /m/ /a/ /p/ together, I hear the word* map.
Words to practice: *cap, nap, tap, sap, rap*

MORE CHALLENGING

- *Listen to the words:* mat, cap, rat. *Which words rhyme?* (mat, rat)
- *What word begins with /l/ and rhymes with* nap? (lap)
- *Listen closely because I want to tell you a secret word. It is /g/ /a/ /p/. Say the sounds with me: /g/ /a/ /p/. What is my secret word?* (gap)

- *Listen to the words:* chat, chap, trap. *Which words rhyme?* (chap, trap)
- *Here is another secret word for you. It is /b/ /a/ /t/. Say the sounds: /b/ /a/ /t/. What is my secret word?* (bat)
- *Listen to the words:* sap, cap, sat. *Which words rhyme?* (sap, cap)
- *Say the word* pat. *How many sounds do you hear in* pat? *Hold up your fingers to show me the number.* (three) *Now, say the word without the /p/ sound. What is the new word?* (at)
- *What word begins with /t/ and rhymes with the word* nap? (tap)

LESSON 2
BASIC

Segmenting Sounds—Model for you students: *Listen carefully. I would like you to tell me each sound you hear in a word. If the word is zap, what are the sounds? I would say /z/ /a/ /p/.*
Words to practice: *Tell each sound you hear in . . .* gap, rap, cap, lap.

Adding Sounds—Model for your students: *Listen carefully. I am going to say a word and then add a sound to make a new word. My secret word rhymes with* at and begins with the /r/ sound. *What is the word? (Repeat the sounds: /r/ /at/.) The word is* rat.
Words to practice: *pat, fat, hat, cat, vat.*

MORE CHALLENGING

- *What word rhymes with* rap *and begins with /y/?* (yap)
- *Say each sound you hear in the word* nap. *What are those sounds?* (/n/ /a/ /p/)
- *Now think about the word* map. *How many sounds do you hear in the word?* (three) *Stretch the sounds in the word.* (/m/ /aaaaaa/ /p/)

- *What word begins with /r/ and ends with the sound /ap/?* (rap)
- *Listen closely because I want to tell you a secret word. It is /f/ /a/ /t/. Say the sounds with me: /f/ /a/ /t/. What is the secret word?* (fat)
- *Say each sound you hear in the word* zap. *What are those sounds?* (/z/ /a/ /p/)
- *Listen to the word* at. *What word rhymes with* at *and begins with /p/?* (pat)
- *Here's another word clue: This secret word begins with /s/ and rhymes with the word* cat. *What is the word?* (sat)

LESSON 3
BASIC

Blending Sounds—Model for your students: *Listen carefully. I am going to say some sounds slowly. I would like you to blend those sounds together and then tell me the word. The sounds are /f/ /l/ /a/ /t/. (Repeat the sounds.) What is the word? The word is* flat.
Words to practice: *spat, brat, chat, that, and CVC words*

Substituting Sounds—Model for your students: *Listen to the word* tap. *Let's change the /t/ sound to /z/. What is the new word? I can blend the sounds /z/ /ap/ together to make the word* zap.
Words to practice: *zap*—change /z/ to /g/ = gap; *gap*—change /g/ to /r/ = rap; *rap*—change /r/ to /ch/ = chap

MORE CHALLENGING

- *Say each sound you hear in the word* flap. *What are those sounds?* (/f/ /l/ /a/ /p/)
- *I want to tell you my secret word. It is /c/ /l/ /a/ /p/. (Repeat the sounds.) Blend the sounds together. What word can you make with the sounds?* (clap)
- *Listen to the word* spat. *Say the word* spat *without the /s/ sound. What is the new word?* (pat)

- *Say the word* nap. *Add the sound /s/ to the beginning of the word. Now, what is the new word?* (snap)
- *Listen to the word* chap. *Change the /ch/ sound to /s/. What new word did you make?* (sap)
- *Now listen to the word* brat. *Say the word* brat *without the /b/ sound. What is the new word?* (rat)
- *Listen to the sounds: /th/ /a/ /t/. (Repeat the sounds.) Blend the sounds together. What word can you make with the sounds?* (that)
- *Say the word* slap. *Now, say it without the /s/ sound. What is the new word?* (lap)

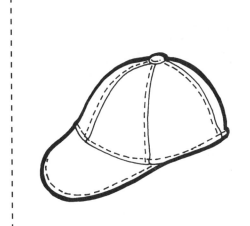

Pictures: cap, map

_ap

_ap

See page 140 for initial letter cards to make words. The pictures and cards for -at words are on page 26.

_ap _ap _ap

Read at Home—the "_ap" and "_at" Word Families

Slap Jack Words

To Parent:
Your child has been learning how to read words that end with "ap" and "at." In the zippered bag you will find two copies of each word card.

Slap Jack Words
How to play the game (two players):
• Cut out the word cards if needed. Mix up the cards and then deal the entire deck, one at a time facedown, to the players so that each has a pile.
• Each player takes the top two cards from his pile and places them faceup. If any of the words match, the player "slaps" that word card, reads it aloud correctly, and collects both cards. The matches can also be made with cards the opponent has.
• Continue the game until all of the matches have been made. The player who collects the most pairs of matching cards wins the game.

Ready, Set, Read! Arrange all of the word cards in several rows on a table. Have your child read the words aloud as a practice run and then a second time at a faster speed!

MEET AND READ THE "-IN" FAMILY

Getting Started! Determine which letter-sound correspondences and letter patterns the student needs to practice.

• **Learning to Read CVC Words**—If the student cannot easily identify the phonemes for the consonants *b, f, k, p, t,* and *w,* use Day 1–5 activities. Otherwise, begin on Day 2. Select CVC words from the list. Start with about six words for the targeted practice on the first day. Add more words when the child is ready for a challenge.

• **Learning to Read CCVC Words**—If the student can read the three-letter words, provide lessons for sounding out and reading CCVC words. Select three days of activities. Introduce the digraphs *th, sh,* and *ch* and consonant clusters with a tactile activity. During the lessons, include CVC words (and words from other word families) to strengthen decoding skills (*tin* with *thin, win* with *twin, kin* with *skin*) and word-recognition fluency.

Word List		
bin*	tin*	skin*
fin*	win*	spin*
in*	chin*	thin*
kin*	grin*	twin*
pin*	shin*	

See page 146 for reproducible word cards.

DAY 1

Materials: Copy the picture of the shark's fin on page 44. Follow the directions for the Molding Words activity on page 15.

• Show the picture for *fin.* Ask the child to tell you the beginning sound of the word (*fin* = /f/) and make the letter in clay. Continue the lesson by calling out other *-in* words. Have the child identify the beginning sounds and make the letters in clay to spell the words.

• To teach CCVC words, form the letters for digraphs, blends, and rimes in clay.

• Have students write the words.

DAY 2

Materials: Copy of letter cards (page 140) and word cards (page 146); racetrack billboard mat (page 131); prepared mini-book

Use letters and selected word cards in the following activities:

• Show and read the words

• Phonemic Awareness (See page 43.)

• Puffy Words—if tactile activity is needed (See page 15.)

• Rev Up for Words (See page 17.)

• Where Is . . . ? (See page 19.)

• Word Family Mini-Book (See page 20.)

DAY 3

Materials: Copy of letter cards (page 140), word cards (page 146), playing catch mat (page 134), and tree house mat (page 136)

Use letters and selected word cards in the following activities:

• Review and use words in sentences. (See Finish the Sentence, page 21.)

• Phonemic Awareness (See page 43.)

• Catch High-Flying Sounds (See page 18.)

• Read 'n' Climb to See the View (See page 19.)

• Write Down—Back to the Ground (See page 21.)

DAY 4

Materials: Copy of letter cards (page 140), word cards (page 146), robot form (page 139), safe mat (page 135), and monster mat (page 137)

Use letters and selected word cards in the following activities:

• Review and use words in sentences. (See Robot Writing!, page 21.)

• Phonemic Awareness (See page 43.)

• Unlock the Code (See page 18.)

• Mr. Word Muncher (See page 19.)

• Feed Mr. Word Muncher (See page 21.)

DAY 5

Materials: Copy of word cards (page 146); children's storybook featuring *-in* words; self-adhesive flags (office supply item)

Select word cards and use them in the following activities:

• Read 'n' Spell Words (Take turns reading aloud a word to a partner who spells it.)

• Flag It!—Take turns reading aloud a passage from a classroom book that has *-in* words in the text. Each time a word-family word is used, mark it with a sticky flag. (Draw attention to the rime *-in.*)

• I Write, You Write! (See page 21.)

More Suggestions!

Spend a few minutes each day introducing or reviewing the *-in* word family by reading aloud passages (pointing to the words) from children's storybooks. Let students be word-family detectives and identify those words used in the text.

Read at Home Activity

Copy the take-home direction sheet (page 44) for each student. Include two copies of the word cards on card stock and a small paper bag for each student. Place all of the materials in a zippered plastic bag.

Working with Sounds in "-in" Words

LESSON 1
BASIC

Isolating Initial Sounds—Model for your students: *Listen carefully. I am going to say a word. The word is pin. What is the first sound you hear in pin? The first sound is /p/.* Words to practice: *Say the first sound you hear in . . .* kin, fin, bin.

Blending Sounds—Model for your students: *Listen carefully. I am going to say the sounds slowly in my secret word. I would like you to blend those sounds together. The sounds are: /w/ /i/ /n/. What is the secret word? When I blend the* sounds /w/ /i/ /n/ *together, I hear the word* win. Words to practice: *fin, pin, bin, tin.*

MORE CHALLENGING

- *Listen to the words:* fin, fun, bin. *Which words rhyme?* (fin, bin)
- *What word begins with /p/ and rhymes with* fin? (pin)
- *Listen closely because I want to tell you a secret word. It is /d/ /i/ /n/. Say the sounds with me: /d/ /i/ /n/. What is my secret word?* (din)
- *Listen to the words:* pan, pin, shin. *Which two words rhyme?* (pin, shin)

- *Here is another secret word for you. It is /k/ /i/ /n/. Say the sounds: /k/ /i/ /n/. What is my secret word?* (kin)
- *Say the word* win. *How many sounds do you hear in the word* win? (three) *Now, say the word without the /w/ sound. What is the new word?* (in)
- *Listen to the words:* tin, win, ton. *Which two words rhyme?* (tin, win)
- *Here is one more secret word for you. It is /b/ /i/ /n/. Say the sounds: /b/ /i/ /n/. What is the secret word?* (bin)

LESSON 2
BASIC

Segmenting Sounds—Model for your students: *Listen carefully. I would like you to tell me each sound you hear in a word. If the word is* bin, *what are the sounds? I would say /b/ /i/ /n/.* Words to practice: *Tell each sound you hear in . . .* win, kin, tin, fin.

Adding Sounds—Model for your students: *Listen carefully. I am going to say a word and then add a sound to make a new word. My secret word ends with /in/ and* begins with the /k/ sound. What is the word? (Repeat the sounds: /k/ /in/.) The word is kin. Words to practice: *bin, fin, pin, tin*

MORE CHALLENGING

- *Say each sound you hear in the word* win. *What are those sounds?* (/w/ /i/ /n/)
- *Listen closely because I want to tell you a secret word. It is /f/ /i/ /n/. Say the sounds with me: /f/ /i/ /n/. What is the secret word?* (fin)
- *What word rhymes with* in *and begins with /sh/?* (shin)
- *Here's another word clue: This* secret word begins with /ch/ and rhymes with the word in. What is the word? (chin)
- *Now think about the word* fin. *How many sounds do you hear in the word?* (three) *Stretch the sounds in the word.* (/fffff/ /iiiiii/ /nnnnnn/)
- *Listen to the word* fin. *What word rhymes with* fin *and begins with /p/?* (pin)
- *What word begins with /th/ and rhymes with* fin? (thin)
- *Say each sound you hear in the word* tin. *What are those sounds?* (/t/ /i/ /n/)

LESSON 3
BASIC

Blending Sounds—Model for your students: *Listen carefully. I am going to say some sounds slowly. I would like you to blend those sounds together and then tell me the word. The sounds are /th/ /i/ /n/. (Repeat the sounds.) What is the word? The word is* thin. Words to practice: *spin, chin, twin, shin, and CVC words*

Substituting Sounds—Model for your students: *Listen to the word* chin. *Let's change the /ch/ sound to /t/. What is the new word? I can blend the sounds /t/ /in/ together to* make the word tin. Words to practice: *tin*—change /t/ to /sh/ = *shin; shin*—change /sh/ to /f/ = *fin; fin*—change /f/ to /th/ = *thin*

MORE CHALLENGING

- *Listen to the word* chin. *Change the /ch/ sound to /d/. What new word did you make?* (din)
- *I want to tell you my secret word. It is /g/ /r/ /i/ /n/. (Repeat the sounds.) Blend the sounds together. What word can you make with the sounds?* (grin)
- *Listen to the sounds: /s/ /p/ /i/ /n/. (Repeat the sounds.) Blend the sounds together. What word* can you make with the sounds? (spin)
- *Say the word* kin. *Add the sound /s/ to the beginning of the word. What is the new word?* (skin)
- *This time say the word* spin. *Now, say it without the /s/ sound. What is the new word?* (pin)
- *Say the sounds /ch/ /i/ /n/. (Repeat the sounds.) Blend the sounds together. What word can you make with the sounds?* (chin)
- *Say the word* win. *Add the sound /t/ to the beginning of the word. What is the new word?* (twin)
- *Listen to the word* shin. *Change the /sh/ sound to /th/. What new word did you make?* (thin)

See page 140 for initial letter cards to make words.

Pictures: fin, twin

_in   _in   _in

Read at Home—the "_in" Word Family

Strike!

To Parent:
Your child has been learning how to read words that end with "in." Provided for you are two copies of each word card and a small paper bag. Please help your child decorate the front of the game bag with markers for this simplified "bowling" activity.

Strike!
How to play the game (two players):
• Cut out the word cards if needed as well as the Wild Cards on this sheet. Place all of the cards in the prepared bag.
• Have your child draw cards from the bag one at a time, read each word out loud, and place the card faceup on the table. When 10 cards have been drawn and read correctly, a "strike" is counted. Cover one of the pins on this sheet with a paper clip and return the word cards to the bag. Play again to earn a second strike and even a third! Watch out for the Wild Cards.

Ready, Set, Read! Arrange all of the word cards in several rows on a table. Have your child read the words aloud as a practice run and then a second time at a faster speed!

Draw 2 cards.

Game over!

Strike! Cover I pin.

Strike! Cover I pin.

MEET AND READ THE "-IT" FAMILY

Getting Started! Determine which letter-sound correspondences and letter patterns the student needs to practice.

- **Learning to Read CVC Words**—If the student cannot easily identify the phonemes for the consonants *b, f, h, k, l, p, s,* and *w,* use Day 1–5 activities. Otherwise, begin on Day 2. Select CVC words from the list. Start with about six words for the targeted practice on the first day. Add more words when the child is ready for a challenge.

- **Learning to Read CCVC Words**—If the student can read the three-letter words, provide lessons for sounding out and reading CCVC words. Select three days of activities. Introduce the consonant clusters with a tactile activity. During the lessons, include CVC words (and words from other word families) to strengthen decoding skills (*lit* with *flit* or *slit, kit* with *skit, pit* with *spit*) and word-recognition fluency.

Word List

bit*	lit*	grit*
fit*	pit*	skit*
hit*	sit*	slit
it*	wit*	spit*
kit*	flit*	

See pages 146 & 147 for reproducible word cards. Add to the set by printing slit on card stock.

DAY 1

Materials: Copy the pictures on page 47. Follow the directions for the Molding Words activity on page 15.

- Show the pictures for *pit* and *hit*. Ask the child to tell you the beginning sound of each word (*pit* = /p/ and *hit* = /h/) and make the letter in clay. Continue the lesson by calling out other *-it* words. Have the child identify the beginning sounds and make the letters in clay to spell the words.
- To teach CCVC words, form the letters for the blends and rimes in clay.
- Have students write the words.

DAY 2

Materials: Copy of letter cards (page 140), word cards (pages 146 and 147), and launch pad mat (page 132); "Sticky" Words materials (page 19); prepared mini-book

Use letters and selected word cards in the following activities:

- Show and read the words.
- Phonemic Awareness (See page 46.)
- Puffy Words—if tactile activity is needed (See page 15.)
- Blast Off! (See page 17.)
- "Sticky" Words (See page 19.)
- Word Family Mini-Book (See page 20.)

DAY 3

Materials: Copy of letter cards (page 140), word cards (pages 146 and 147), safe mat (page 135), and monster mat (page 137)

Use letters and selected word cards in the following activities:

- Review and use words in sentences. (See Finish the Sentence, page 21.)
- Phonemic Awareness (See page 46.)
- Unlock the Code (See page 18.)
- Mr. Word Muncher (See page 19.)
- Feed Mr. Word Muncher (See page 21.)

DAY 4

Materials: Copy of letter cards (page 140), word cards (pages 146 and 147), robot form (page 139), and truck mat (page 133); materials for Yummy Words (page 20) and Clip, Read, 'n' Write (page 20)

Use letters and selected word cards in the following activities:

- Review and use words in sentences. (See Robot Writing!, page 21.)
- Phonemic Awareness (See page 46.)
- Load the Truck (See page 17.)
- Yummy Words (See page 20.)
- Clip, Read, 'n' Write (See page 20.)

DAY 5

Materials: Copy of word cards (pages 146 and 147); children's storybook featuring *-it* words; self-adhesive flags (office supply item)

Select word cards and use them in the following activities:

- Read 'n' Spell Words (Take turns reading aloud a word to a partner who spells it.)
- Flag It!—Take turns reading aloud a passage from a classroom book that has *-it* words in the text. Each time a word-family word is used, mark it with a sticky flag. (Draw attention to the rime *-it*.)
- I Write, You Write! (See page 21.)

More Suggestions!

Spend a few minutes each day introducing or reviewing the *-it* word family by reading aloud passages (pointing to the words) from children's storybooks. Let students be word-family detectives and identify those words used in the text.

Read at Home Activity

Copy the take-home direction sheet (page 47) for each student. Include two copies of the word cards on card stock and a small paper bag for each student. Place all of the materials in a zippered plastic bag.

Working with Sounds in "-it" Words

LESSON 1
BASIC

Isolating Initial Sounds—Model for your students: *Listen carefully. I am going to say a word. The word is sit. What is the first sound you hear in sit? The first sound is /s/.*
Words to practice: *Say the first sound you hear in . . . bit, pit, fit, hit.*

Blending Sounds—Model for your students: *Listen carefully. I am going to say the sounds slowly in my secret word. I would like you to blend those sounds together. The sounds are: /h/ /i/ /t/. What is the secret word? When I blend the sounds /h/ /i/ /t/ together, I say the word hit. Words to practice: lit, kit, wit, fit*

MORE CHALLENGING

- *Listen to the words: bit, bat, pit. Which words rhyme? (bit, pit)*
- *What word begins with /l/ and rhymes with it? (lit)*
- *Listen closely because I want to tell you a secret word. It is /f/ /i/ /t/. Say the sounds with me: /f/ /i/ /t/. What is my secret word? (fit)*
- *Listen to the words: her, hit, fit. Which words rhyme? (hit, fit)*
- *Here is another secret word for you. It is /s/ /i/ /t/. Say the sounds:*

/s/ /i/ /t/. *What is my secret word? (sit)*
- *Listen to the words: spit, spot, sit. Which words rhyme? (spit, sit)*
- *Say the word wit. How many sounds do you hear in wit? Hold up your fingers to show me the number. (three) Now, say the word without the /w/ sound. What is the new word? (it)*
- *What word begins with /k/ and rhymes with the word wit? (kit)*

LESSON 2
BASIC

Segmenting Sounds—Model for your students: *Listen carefully. I would like you to tell me each sound you hear in a word. If the word is pit, what are the sounds? I would say /p/ /i/ /t/.*
Words to practice: *Tell each sound you hear in . . . sit, kit, fit, lit.*

Adding Sounds—Model for your students: *Listen carefully. I am going to say a word and then add a sound to make a new word. My secret word rhymes with it and begins with the /b/ sound. What*

is the word? (Repeat the sounds: /b/ /it/.) The word is bit.
Words to practice: *hit, pit, wit, sit*

MORE CHALLENGING

- *What word rhymes with it and begins with /s/? (sit)*
- *Say each sound you hear in the word pit. What are those sounds? (/p/ /i/ /t/)*
- *Now think about the word lit. How many sounds do you hear in the word? (three) Stretch the sounds in the word. (/llllll/ /iiiiii/ /t/)*
- *What word begins with /w/ and ends with it? (wit)*

- *Listen closely because I want to tell you a secret word. It is /h/ /i/ /t/. Say the sounds with me: /h/ /i/ /t/. What is the secret word? (hit)*
- *Say each sound you hear in the word bit. What are those sounds? (/b/ /i/ /t/)*
- *Listen to the word sit. What word rhymes with sit and begins with /k/? (kit)*
- *Here's another word clue: This secret word begins with /f/ and rhymes with the word sit. What is the word? (fit)*

LESSON 3
BASIC

Blending Sounds—Model for your students: *Listen carefully. I am going to say some sounds slowly. I would like you to blend those sounds together and then tell me the word. The sounds are /s/ /l/ /i/ /t/. (Repeat the sounds.) What is the word? The word is slit.*
Words to practice: *grit, flit, spit, skit, and CVC words*

Substituting Sounds—Model for your students: *Listen to the word bit. Let's change the /b/ sound to /l/. What is the new word? I can blend the sounds /l/ /it/ together to*

make the word lit.
Words to practice: *lit—change /l/ to /h/ = hit; hit—change /h/ to /p/ = pit; slit—change /s/ to /f/ = flit*

MORE CHALLENGING

- *Say each sound you hear in the word skit. What are those sounds? (/s/ /k/ /i/ /t/)*
- *I want to tell you my secret word. It is /s/ /p/ /i/ /t/. (Repeat the sounds.) Blend the sounds together. What word can you make with the sounds? (spit)*
- *Listen to the word slit. Change the /s/ sound to /f/. What new word did you make? (flit)*
- *Say the word kit. Add the sound*

/s/ *to the beginning of the word. Now, what is the new word? (skit)*
- *Listen to the word wit. Change the /w/ sound to /h/. What new word did you make? (hit)*
- *Now listen to the word slit. Say the word slit without the /s/ sound. What is the new word? (lit)*
- *Listen to the sounds: /f/ /l/ /i/ /t/. (Repeat the sounds.) Blend the sounds together. What word can you make with the sounds? (flit)*
- *Say the word spit. Now, say it without the /s/ sound. What is the new word? (pit)*

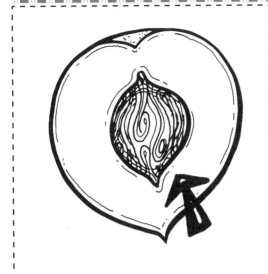

See page 140 for initial letter cards to make words.

Pictures: pit, hit

_it   _it   _it

Read at Home—the "_it" Word Family

Running the Bases

To Parent:
Your child has been learning how to read words that end with "it." Provided for you are two copies of each word card and a small paper bag. Please help your child decorate the front of the paper bag with markers for this simplified "baseball" activity. Make a simple baseball infield diagram (game board) on a sheet of paper. Use coins or other small objects to use as game markers.

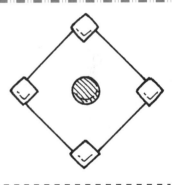

Running the Bases
How to play the game (two players):
• Cut out the word cards if needed as well as the Wild Cards on this sheet. Place the cards in the prepared bag.
• To start the game, have your child draw a card from the bag and read the word out loud. Place a game marker on first base if the word is read correctly. Let your child continue drawing and reading cards to circle the bases and cross home plate. Reading the word incorrectly counts as a strike. When three strikes occur, the player's turn is done and the other player takes a turn. If a player makes it home, record a tally mark on the game board. The other player then takes a turn. Watch out for the Wild Cards!
• The first player to score three runs wins the game.

Ready, Set, Read! Arrange all of the word cards in several rows on a table. Have your child read the words aloud as a practice run and then a second time at a faster speed!

Home run!

Line drive.
Take 2 bases.

Walk to the
next base.

Strike out!
Lose a turn.

MEET AND READ THE "-IP" FAMILY

Getting Started! Determine which letter-sound correspondences and letter patterns the student needs to practice.

• **Learning to Read CVC Words**—If the student cannot easily identify the phonemes for the consonants *d, h, l, r, s, t, y,* and *z,* use Day 1–5 activities. Otherwise, begin on Day 2. Select CVC words from the list. Start with about six words for the targeted practice on the first day. Add more words when the child is ready for a challenge.

• **Learning to Read CCVC Words**—If the student can read the three-letter words, provide activities for sounding out and reading CCVC words. Select three days of lessons. Introduce the digraphs *ch* and *sh* and consonant clusters with a tactile activity. During the lessons, include CVC words to strengthen decoding skills (*lip* with *clip* or *flip, rip* with *drip* or *grip* or *trip, hip* with *chip, sip* with *ship* or *slip*) and word-recognition fluency.

Word List		
dip*	yip	grip
hip*	zip*	ship*
lip*	chip*	skip*
rip*	clip*	slip
sip*	drip*	snip
tip*	flip	trip*

See pages 147 for reproducible word cards. Add to the set by printing other words on card stock.

DAY 1

Materials: Copy the picture for *zip* on page 50. Follow the directions for the Molding Words activity on page 15.

• Show the picture for *zip.* Ask the child to tell you the beginning sound of the word (*zip* = /z/) and make the letter in clay. Continue the lesson by calling out other *-ip* words. Have the child identify the beginning sounds and make the letters in clay to spell the words.
• To teach CCVC words, form the letters for digraphs, blends, and rimes in clay.
• Have students write the words.

DAY 2

Materials: Copy of letter cards (page 140) and word cards (page 147); prepared mini-book

Use letters and selected word cards in the following activities:

• Show and use the words in sentences.
• Phonemic Awareness (See page 49.)
• Puffy Words—if tactile activity is needed (See page 15.)
• What's the Word? (See page 16.)
• Where Is . . . ? (See page 19.)
• Word Family Mini-Book (See page 20.)

DAY 3

Materials: Copy of letter cards (page 140), word cards (page 147), and truck mat (page 133); materials for Yummy Words (page 20) and Clip, Read, 'n' Write (page 20)

Use letters and select word cards in the following activities:

• Review and use words in sentences. (See Finish the Sentence, page 21.)
• Phonemic Awareness (See page 49.)
• Load the Truck (See page 17.)
• Yummy Words (See page 20.)
• Clip, Read, 'n' Write (See page 20.)

DAY 4

Materials: Copy of word cards (page 147) and robot form (139); labeled plastic eggs and egg carton; copy of tree house mat (page 136)

Select word cards and use them in the following activities:

• Review and use words in sentences. (See Robot Writing!, page 21.)
• Phonemic Awareness (See page 49.)
• Pack the Words (See page 18.)
• Read 'n' Climb to See the View (See page 19.)
• Write Down—Back to the Ground (See page 21.)

DAY 5

Materials: Copy of word cards (page 147); children's storybook featuring *-ip* words; self-adhesive flags (office supply item)

Select word cards and use them in the following activities:

• Read 'n' Spell Words (Take turns reading aloud a word to a partner who spells it.)
• Flag It!—Take turns reading aloud a passage from a classroom book that has *-ip* words in the text. Each time a word-family word is used, mark it with a sticky flag. (Draw attention to the rime *-ip.*)
• I Write, You Write! (See page 21.)

More Suggestions!

Spend a few minutes each day introducing or reviewing the *-ip* word family by reading aloud passages (pointing to the words) from children's storybooks. Let students be word-family detectives and identify those words used in the text.

Read at Home Activity

Copy the take-home direction sheet (page 50) for each student. Include a copy of each word card in two different colors of card stock and a small paper bag. Place all of the materials in a zippered plastic bag.

Working with Sounds in "-ip" Words

LESSON 1
BASIC

Isolating Initial Sounds—Model for students: *Listen carefully. I am going to say a word. The word is zip. What is the first sound you hear in zip? The first sound is /z/.*
Words to practice: *Say the first sound you hear in . . .* dip, tip, hip, yip, lip.

Blending Sounds—Model for students: *Listen carefully. I am going to say the sounds slowly in my secret word. I would like you to blend those sounds together. The sounds are: /r/ /i/ /p/. What is the secret word? When I blend the sounds /r/ /i/ /p/ together, I hear the word rip.*
Words to practice: *sip, hip, tip, dip, yip*

MORE CHALLENGING

- *Listen to the words: sip, zap, ship. Which words rhyme? (sip, ship)*
- *What word begins with /z/ and rhymes with hip? (zip)*
- *Listen closely because I want to tell you a secret word. It is /t/ /i/ /p/. Say the sounds with me: /t/ /i/ /p/. What is my secret word? (tip)*
- *Listen to the words: chip, yip, chat. Which two words rhyme? (chip, yip)*
- *Here is another secret word for you. It is /h/ /i/ /p/. Say the sounds: /h/ /i/ /p/. What is my secret word? (hip)*
- *Say the word sip. How many sounds do you hear in the word sip? (three) Now, say the word without the /s/ sound. What is the silly word? (ip)*
- *Listen to the words: dot, dip, tip. Which two words rhyme? (dip, tip)*
- *What word begins with /n/ and rhymes with hip? (nip)*

LESSON 2
BASIC

Segmenting Sounds—Model for students: *Listen carefully. I would like you to tell me each sound you hear in a word. If the word is lip, what are the sounds? I would say /l/ /i/ /p/.*
Words to practice: *Tell each sound you hear in . . .* rip, zip, yip, hip, dip, tip.

Adding Sounds—Model for students: *Listen carefully. I am going to say a word and then add a sound to make a new word. My secret word ends with /ip/ and begins with the /s/ sound. What is the word? (Repeat the sounds: /s/ /ip/.) The word is sip.*
Words to practice: *tip, rip, zip, yip, hip*

MORE CHALLENGING

- *Say each sound you hear in the word ship. What are those sounds? (/sh/ /i/ /p/)*
- *Listen closely because I want to tell you a secret word. It is /l/ /i/ /p/. Say the sounds with me: /l/ /i/ /p/. What is the secret word? (lip)*
- *What word rhymes with hip and begins with /r/? (rip)*
- *Here's another word clue: This secret word begins with /y/ and rhymes with the word hip. What is the word? (yip)*
- *Now think about the word zip. How many sounds do you hear in the word? (three) Stretch the sounds in the word. (/zzzzzz/ /iiiiii/ /p/)*
- *Listen to the word yip. What word rhymes with yip and begins with /s/? (sip)*
- *What word begins with /n/ and ends with /ip/? (nip)*
- *Say each sound you hear in the word chip. What are those sounds? (/ch/ /i/ /p/)*

LESSON 3
BASIC

Blending Sounds—Model for students: *Listen carefully. I am going to say some sounds slowly. I would like you to blend those sounds together and then tell me the word. The sounds are /sh/ /i/ /p/. (Repeat the sounds.) What is the word? The word is ship.*
Words to practice: *chip, trip, snip, drip, and CVC words*

Substituting Sounds—Model for students: *Listen to the word hip. Let's change the /h/ sound to /ch/. What is the new word? I can blend the sounds /ch/ /ip/ together to make the word chip.*
Words to practice: *chip—change /ch/ to /d/ = dip; dip—change /d/ to /y/ = yip; yip—change /y/ to /sh/ = ship*

MORE CHALLENGING

- *Listen to the word lip. Change the /l/ sound to /sh/. What new word did you make? (ship)*
- *I want to tell you my secret word. It is /d/ /r/ /i/ /p/. (Repeat the sounds.) Blend the sounds together. What word can you make with the sounds? (drip)*
- *Listen to the sounds: /c/ /l/ /i/ /p/. (Repeat the sounds.) Blend the sounds together. What word can you make with the sounds? (clip)*
- *Say the word clip. Change the /k/ sound to /f/. What is the new word? (flip)*
- *This time say the word drip. Now, say it without the /d/ sound. What is the new word? (rip) Is this a real word? (yes)*
- *Say the sounds /ch/ /i/ /p/. (Repeat the sounds.) Blend the sounds together. What word can you make with the sounds? (chip)*
- *Say the word rip. Add the sound /g/ to the beginning of the word. What is the new word? (grip)*
- *Listen to the word flip. Now, say it without the /f/ sound. What new word did you make? (lip)*

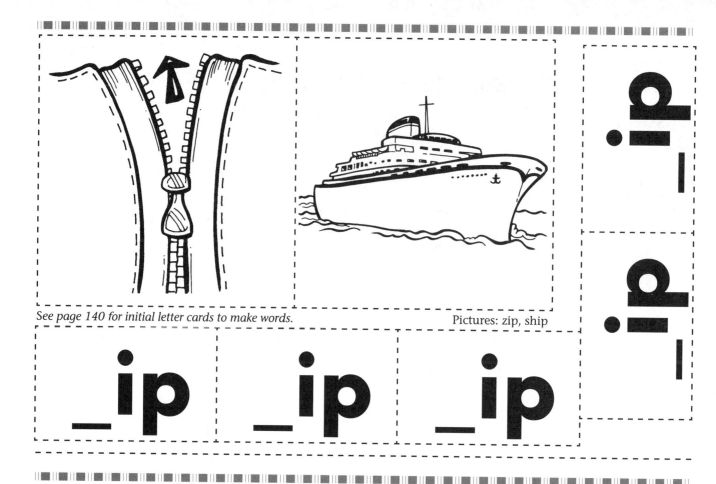

See page 140 for initial letter cards to make words.

Pictures: zip, ship

_ip _ip _ip

_ip _ip

Ship Out with Words

To Parent:
Your child has been learning how to read words that end with "ip." Provided for you are two copies of each word card and a small paper bag.

Ship Out with Words
How to play the game:

- Cut out the word cards if needed and the Game Bag Label on this sheet. Glue the label to the front of the paper bag.
- To play this memory match game, take turns with your child turning over two cards to find matching pairs. When a pair is found, the player picks up those cards. If the cards do not match, turn them facedown.
- The first player to collect six pairs of word cards becomes the captain of the ship! That player places all of the matches in the bag and ships out!

Ready, Set, Read! Arrange all of the word cards in several rows on a table. Have your child read the words aloud as a practice run and then a second time at a faster speed!

Game Bag Label

Ship Out with Words

MEET AND READ "-IG" AND "-IP" FAMILIES

Getting Started! Determine which letter-sound correspondences and letter patterns the student needs to practice.

- **Learning to Read CVC Words**—If the student cannot easily identify the phonemes for the consonants, use Day 1–5 activities. Otherwise, begin on Day 2. Select CVC words from the list. Start with about 10 words for the targeted practice on the first day. Add more words when the child is ready for a challenge.

- **Learning to Read CCVC Words**—If the student can read the three-letter words, provide lessons for sounding out and reading CCVC words. Select three days of activities. Introduce the digraphs *ch* and *sh* and consonant clusters with a tactile activity. During the lessons, include pairings of CVC and CCVC words to strengthen decoding skills (*dig* or *dip* with *drip*, *rig* or *rip* with *brig*, *fig* with *flip*, *wig* with *twig* or *swig*, *sip* with *slip*, *gig* or *rip* with *grip*, *zig* with *zip*) and word-recognition fluency.

Word List

big*	rig*	dip*	yip	grip
dig*	wig*	hip*	zip*	ship*
fig*	zig*	lip*	chip*	skip*
gig*	brig*	rip*	clip*	slip
jig*	swig*	sip*	drip*	snip
pig*	twig*	tip*	flip	trip*

See pages 147 & 148 for reproducible word cards. Add to the set by printing other words on card stock.

DAY 1

Materials: Copy the pictures on pages 50 and 53. Follow the directions for the Molding Words and Pinching Letters activities on page 15.

- Show the pictures for *zip* and the *wig*. Ask the child to tell you the beginning sound of each word (*zip* = /z/ and *wig* = /w/) and make the letters in clay. Continue the lesson by calling out other selected words. Let the child identify the beginning sounds and make the letters in clay to spell the words.
- Have students write the words.
- Pinching Letters (See page 15.)

DAY 2

Materials: Copy of letter cards (page 140), word cards (pages 147 and 148), and stone wall mat (page 130); "Sticky" Words materials (page 19); prepared mini-book

Use letters and selected word cards in the following activities:

- Show and read the words.
- Phonemic Awareness (See page 52.)
- Puffy Words—if tactile activity is needed (See page 15.)
- Letters on Stones (See page 16.)
- "Sticky" Words (See page 19.)
- Word Family Mini-Book (See page 20.)

DAY 3

Materials: Copy of word cards (pages 147 and 148); labeled plastic eggs and egg carton; copy of tree house mat (page 136)

Select word cards and use them in the following activities:

- Review and use words in sentences. (See Finish the Sentence, page 21.)
- Phonemic Awareness (See page 52.)
- Pack the Words (See page 18.)
- Read 'n' Climb to See the View (See page 19.)
- Write Down—Back to the Ground (See page 21.)

DAY 4

Materials: Copy of letter cards (page 140), word cards (pages 147 and 148), robot form (page 139), playing catch mat (page 134), and monster mat (page 137)

Use letters and selected word cards in the following activities:

- Review and use words in sentences. (See Robot Writing!, page 21.)
- Phonemic Awareness (See page 52.)
- Catch High-Flying Sounds (See page 18.)
- Mr. Word Muncher (See page 19.)
- Feed Mr. Word Muncher (See page 21.)

DAY 5

Materials: Copy of word cards (pages 147 and 148); storybook featuring *-ig* and *-ip* words; self-adhesive flags (office supply item)

Select word cards and use them in the following activities:

- Read 'n' Spell Words (Take turns reading aloud a word to a partner who spells it.)
- Flag It!—Take turns reading aloud a passage from a classroom book that has *-ig* and *-ip* words in the text. Each time a word-family word is used, mark it with a sticky flag.
- I Write, You Write! (See page 21.)

More Suggestions!

Spend a few minutes each day introducing or reviewing the *-ig* and *-ip* word families by reading aloud passages (pointing to the words) from children's storybooks. Let students be word-family detectives and identify those words used in the text.

Read at Home Activity

Copy the take-home direction sheet and pig picture (page 53) for each student. Include two copies of the word cards on card stock, the ship picture (page 50), and a paper bag. Place the materials in a zippered plastic bag.

Working with Sounds in "-ig" and "-ip" Words

LESSON 1
BASIC

Isolating Initial Sounds—Model for your students: *Listen carefully. I am going to say a word. The word is rig. What is the first sound you hear in rig? The first sound is /r/.*
Words to practice: *Say the first sound you hear in . . . zig, fig, dig, wig.*

Blending Sounds—Model for your students: *Listen carefully. I am going to say the sounds slowly in my secret word. I would like you to blend those sounds together. The sounds are: /d/ /i/ /p/. What is the secret word? When I blend the sounds /d/ /i/ /p/ together, I hear the word dip.*
Words to practice: *lip, zip, yip, tip, and other CVC words*

MORE CHALLENGING

- *Listen to the words: rip, rig, big. Which words rhyme?* (rig, big)
- *What word begins with /d/ and rhymes with big?* (dig)
- *Listen closely because I want to tell you a secret word. It is /f/ /i/ /g/. Say the sounds with me: /f/ /i/ /g/. What is my secret word?* (fig)
- *Listen to the words: wig, dip, dig. Which words rhyme?* (wig, dig)

- *Here is another secret word for you. It is /l/ /i/ /p/. Say the sounds: /l/ /i/ /p/. What is my secret word?* (lip)
- *Listen to the words: jig, zig, zip. Which words rhyme?* (jig, zig)
- *Say the word big. How many sounds do you hear in big? Hold up your fingers to show me the number.* (three) *Now, say the word without the /b/ sound. What is the silly word?* (ig)
- *What word begins with /h/ and ends with /ip/?* (hip)

LESSON 2
BASIC

Segmenting Sounds—Model for your students: *Listen carefully. I would like you to tell me each sound you hear in a word. If the word is sip, what are the sounds? I would say /s/ /i/ /p/.*
Words to practice: *Tell each sound you hear in . . . hip, tip, lip, zip.*

Adding Sounds—Model for your students: *Listen carefully. I am going to say a word and then add a sound to make a new word. My secret word rhymes with dig and begins with the /b/ sound. What is the word?* (Repeat the sounds: /b/ /ig/.) *The word is big.*
Words to practice: *jig, pig, gig, fig*

MORE CHALLENGING

- *What word rhymes with ship and begins with /z/?* (zip)
- *Say each sound you hear in the word sip. What are those sounds?* (/s/ /i/ /p/)
- *Now think about the word rig. How many sounds do you hear in the word?* (three) *Stretch the sounds in the word.* (/rrrrrr/ /iiiiii/ /g/)

- *What word begins with /n/ and ends with /ip/?* (nip)
- *Listen closely because I want to tell you a secret word. It is /t/ /i/ /p/. Say the sounds with me: /t/ /i/ /p/. What is the secret word?* (tip)
- *Say each sound you hear in the word dig. What are those sounds?* (/d/ /i/ /g/)
- *Listen to the word rig. What word rhymes with rig and begins with /f/?* (fig)
- *Here's another word clue: This secret word begins with /w/ and rhymes with the word rig. What is the word?* (wig)

LESSON 3
BASIC

Blending Sounds—Model for your students: *Listen carefully. I am going to say some sounds slowly. I would like you to blend those sounds together and then tell me the word. The sounds are /t/ /w/ /i/ /g/.* (Repeat the sounds.) *What is the word? The word is twig.*
Words to practice: *dig, brig, swig, jig, and other CVC words*

Substituting Sounds—Model for your students: *Listen to the word lip. Let's change the /l/ sound to /z/. What is the new word? I can blend the sounds /z/ /ip/ together to make the word zip.*
Words to practice: *zip—change /z/ to /h/ = hip; hip—change /h/ to /sh/ = ship; ship—change /sh/ to /ch/ = chip*

MORE CHALLENGING

- *Say each sound you hear in the word brig. What are those sounds?* (/b/ /r/ /i/ /g/)
- *I want to tell you my secret word. It is /g/ /r/ /i/ /p/.* (Repeat the sounds.) *Blend the sounds together. What word can you make with the sounds?* (grip)
- *Listen to the word chip. Change the /ch/ sound to /sh/. What new word did you make?* (ship)

- *Say the word part /ip/. Add the sound /y/ to the beginning of /ip/. Now, what is the new word?* (yip)
- *Listen to the word flip. Change the /f/ sound to /k/. What new word did you make?* (clip)
- *Now listen to the word brig. Say the word brig without the /b/ sound. What is the new word?* (rig)
- *Listen to the sounds: /t/ /w/ /i/ /g/.* (Repeat the sounds.) *Blend the sounds together. What word can you make with the sounds?* (twig)
- *Say the word drip. Now, say it without the /d/ sound. What is the new word?* (rip)

See page 140 for initial letter cards to make words. The pictures and cards for -ip words are on page 50.

Pictures: pig, wig

_ig   _ig   _ig

.ig   .ig

Read at Home—the "_ig" and "_ip" Word Families

Pig or Ship?

To Parent:
Your child has been learning how to read words that end with "ig" or "ip." Two copies of each word card, pictures of a pig and a ship, and a small paper bag have been provided.

On the Pig or Ship?
How to play the game (two players):
• Cut out the Wild Cards and place them with the word cards in the paper bag.
• Ask your child to choose either the pig (for "ig" words) or the ship (for "ip" words). (You will match the remaining object.)
• Take turns with your child drawing a card without looking in the bag and reading the word out loud. If the selected word belongs in the player's chosen word family, set the card near the corresponding object. If not, return the card to the bag. Watch out for the Wild Cards. If the "Game over!" card is drawn, the player with the most cards wins the game.
• The first player to collect five cards wins the game.

Ready, Set, Read! Arrange all of the word cards on a table. Have your child read the words aloud as a practice run and then a second time at a faster speed!

Draw 2 cards.

Pig is not in pen.
Lose a turn.

Ship is not at dock.
Lose a turn.

Ship is loaded!
Game over!

Pig is napping!
Game over!

MEET AND READ "-ID" AND "-IN" FAMILIES

Getting Started! Determine which letter-sound correspondences and letter patterns the student needs to practice.

• **Learning to Read CVC Words**—If the student cannot easily identify the phonemes for the consonants, use Day 1–5 activities. Otherwise, begin on Day 2. Select CVC words from the list. Start with about six words for the targeted practice on the first day. Add more words when the child is ready for a challenge.

• **Learning to Read CCVC Words**—If the student can read the three-letter words, provide lessons for sounding out and reading CCVC words. Select three days of activities. Introduce the digraphs *ch*, *sh*, and *th* and consonant clusters with a tactile activity. During the lessons, include pairings of CVC and CCVC words to strengthen decoding skills (*rid* with *grid*, *tin* with *thin*, *kid* with *skid*, *lid* with *slid*, *kid* or *kin* with *skin*, *hid* with *shin*, *pin* with *spin*, *win* or *tin* with *twin*, *grid* with *grin*) and word-recognition fluency.

Word List

bid*	rid*	in*	grin*
did*	grid*	kin*	shin*
hid*	skid*	pin*	skin*
kid*	slid*	tin*	spin*
lid*	bin*	win*	thin*
mid*	fin*	chin*	twin*

See pages 146 & 148 for reproducible word cards.

DAY 1

Materials: Copy the pictures on pages 44 and 56. Follow the directions for the Molding Words and Pinching Letters activities on page 15.

• Show the pictures for *fin* and *hid*. Ask the child to tell you the beginning sound of each word (*fin* = /f/ and *hid* = /h/) and make the letters in clay. Continue the lesson by calling out other selected words. Let the child identify the beginning sounds and make the letters in clay to spell the words.
• Have students write the words.
• Pinching Letters (See page 15.)

DAY 2

Materials: Copy of letter cards (page 140) and word cards (pages 146 and 148); racetrack billboard mat (page 131); prepared mini-book

Use letters and selected word cards in the following activities:

• Show and read the words.
• Phonemic Awareness (See page 55.)
• Puffy Words—if tactile activity is needed (See page 15.)
• Rev Up for Words (See page 17.)
• Where Is . . . ? (See page 19.)
• Word Family Mini-Book (See page 20.)

DAY 3

Materials: Copy of letter cards (page 140) and word cards (pages 146 and 148); playing catch mat (page 134) and monster mat (page 137)

Use letters and selected word cards in the following activities:

• Review and use words in sentences. (See Finish the Sentence, page 21.)
• Phonemic Awareness (See page 55.)
• Catch High-Flying Sounds (See page 18.)
• Mr. Word Muncher (See page 19.)
• Feed Mr. Word Muncher (See page 21.)

DAY 4

Materials: Copy of letter cards (page 140), word cards (pages 146 and 148), robot form (page 139), and safe mat (page 135); materials for Yummy Words (page 20) and Clip, Read, 'n' Write (page 20)

Use letters and selected word cards in the following activities:

• Review and use words in sentences. (See Robot Writing!, page 21.)
• Phonemic Awareness (See page 55.)
• Unlock the Code (See page 18.)
• Yummy Words (See page 20.)
• Clip, Read, 'n' Write (See page 20.)

DAY 5

Materials: Copy of word cards (pages 146 and 148); storybooks featuring -*id* and -*in* words; self-adhesive flags (office supply item)

Select word cards and use them in the following activities:

• Read 'n' Spell Words (Take turns reading aloud a word to a partner who spells it.)
• Flag It!—Take turns reading aloud a passage from a classroom book that has -*id* and -*in* words in the text. Each time a word-family word is used, mark it with a sticky flag.
• I Write, You Write! (See page 21.)

More Suggestions!

Spend a few minutes each day introducing or reviewing the -*id* and -*in* word families by reading aloud passages (pointing to the words) from children's storybooks. Let students be word-family detectives and identify those words used in the text.

Read at Home Activity

Copy the take-home direction sheet (page 56) for each student. Include a copy of each word card on card stock in two different colors. Place all of the materials in a zippered plastic bag.

Working with Sounds in "-id" and "-in" Words

LESSON 1
BASIC

Isolating Initial Sounds—Model for your students: *Listen carefully. I am going to say a word. The word is mid. What is the first sound you hear in mid? The first sound is /m/.* Words to practice: *Say the first sound you hear in . . .* rid, did, hid, lid, bid.

Blending Sounds—Model for your students: *Listen carefully. I am going to say the sounds slowly in my secret word. I would like you to blend those sounds together. The sounds are: /p/ /i/ /n/. What is the secret word? When I blend the sounds /p/ /i/ /n/ together, I hear the word pin.* Words to practice: *tin, bin, fin, win*

MORE CHALLENGING

- *Listen to the words: bin, bid, rid. Which words rhyme?* (bid, rid)
- *What word begins with /l/ and rhymes with* did? (lid)
- *Listen closely because I want to tell you a secret word. It is /d/ /i/ /d/. Say the sounds with me: /d/ /i/ /d/. What is my secret word?* (did)
- *Listen to the words: kin, kid, win. Which two words rhyme?* (kin, win)

- *Here is another secret word for you. It is /ch/ /i/ /n/. Say the sounds: /ch/ /i/ /n/. What is my secret word?* (chin)
- *Say the word pin. How many sounds do you hear in the word pin?* (three) *Now, say the word without the /p/ sound. What is the new word?* (in)
- *Listen to the words: grid, lid, grin. Which two words rhyme?* (grid, lid)
- *Here is one more secret word for you. It is /f/ /i/ /n/. Say the sounds: /f/ /i/ /n/. What is the secret word?* (fin)

LESSON 2
BASIC

Segmenting Sounds—Model for your students: *Listen carefully. I would like you to tell me each sound you hear in a word. If the word is* chin, *what are the sounds? I would say /ch/ /i/ /n/.* Words to practice: *Tell each sound you hear in . . .* tin, pin, kin, shin.

Adding Sounds—Model for your students: *Listen carefully. I am going to say a word and then add a sound to make a new word. My secret word rhymes with* mid *and begins with the /d/ sound. What is the word? (Repeat the sounds: /d/ /id/.) The word is* did. Words to practice: *bid, rid, lid, hid*

MORE CHALLENGING

- *Say each sound you hear in the word* mid. *What are those sounds?* (/m/ /i/ /d/)
- *Listen closely because I want to tell you a secret word. It is /l/ /i/ /d/. Say the sounds with me: /l/ /i/ /d/. What is the secret word?* (lid)
- *What word rhymes with* thin *and begins with /w/?* (win)
- *Here's another word clue: This secret word begins with /ch/ and rhymes with the word* thin. *What is the word?* (chin)
- *Now think about the word* rid. *How many sounds do you hear in the word?* (three) *Stretch the sounds in the word.* (/rrrrrr/ /iiiiii/ /d/)
- *Listen to the word* kid. *What word rhymes with* kid *and begins with /b/?* (bid)
- *What word begins with /h/ and ends with /id/?* (hid)
- *Say each sound you hear in the word* tin. *What are those sounds?* (/t/ /i/ /n/)

LESSON 3
BASIC

Blending Sounds—Model for your students: *Listen carefully. I am going to say some sounds slowly. I would like you to blend those sounds together and then tell me the word. The sounds are /g/ /r/ /i/ /d/. (Repeat the sounds.) What is the word? The word is* grid. Words to practice: *skid, slid, and CVC words*

Substituting Sounds—Model for your students: *Listen to the word* tin. *Let's change the /t/ sound to /th/. What is the new word? I can blend the sounds /th/ /in/ together* to make the word thin. Words to practice: *thin—change /th/ to /b/ =* bin; *bin—change /b/ to /sh/ =* shin; *shin—change /sh/ to /ch/ =* chin

MORE CHALLENGING

- *Listen to the word* chin. *Change the /ch/ sound to /t/. What new word did you make?* (tin)
- *I want to tell you my secret word. It is /s/ /l/ /i/ /d/. (Repeat the sounds.) Blend the sounds together. What word can you make with the sounds?* (slid)
- *Listen to the sounds: /s/ /k/ /i/ /d/. (Repeat the sounds.) Blend the sounds together. What word can* you make with the sounds? (skid)
- *Say the word* twin. *Now, say it without the /t/ sound. What is the new word?* (win)
- *This time say the word* skin. *Now, say it without the /s/ sound. What is the new word?* (kin)
- *Say the sounds /ch/ /i/ /n/. (Repeat the sounds.) Blend the sounds together. What word can you make with the sounds?* (chin)
- *Say the word* rid. *Add the sound /g/ to the beginning of the word. What is the new word?* (grid)
- *Listen to the word* pin. *Add the sound /s/ to the beginning of the word. What new word did you make?* (spin)

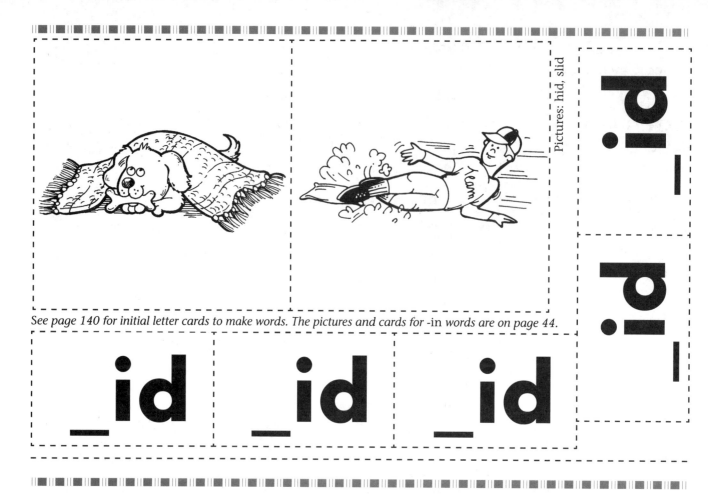

Pictures: hid, slid

_id   _id   _id

_id   _id

See page 140 for initial letter cards to make words. The pictures and cards for -in words are on page 44.

Read at Home—the "_id" and "_in" Word Families

To Parent:

Twin Word Fun

Your child has been learning how to read words that end with "id" and "in." In the zippered bag you will find two sets of word cards, each in a different color.

Twin Word Fun

How to play the game (two players):

• Cut out the word cards if needed. Sort them into two groups by color.

• Scatter the first set of cards faceup in the center of the playing area.

• Choose a word in the second set and draw one or two stars on that card to make a "Wild Word Card." Place the second set of cards facedown in a pile.

• Take turns drawing a card from the pile, reading the word, and finding its twin. If the card is not read correctly, the player returns the card to the bottom of the pile. If the "Wild Word Card" is drawn, the player reads that card and then draws another one. Keep this matching activity game-like for a fun time!

Ready, Set, Read! Arrange all of the word cards in several rows on a table. Have your child read the words aloud as a practice run and then a second time at a faster speed!

MEET AND READ "-IM" AND "-IT" FAMILIES

Getting Started! Determine which letter-sound correspondences and letter patterns the student needs to practice.

• **Learning to Read CVC Words**—If the student cannot easily identify the phonemes for the consonants, use Day 1–5 activities. Otherwise, begin on Day 2. Select CVC words from the list. Start with about 10 words for the targeted practice on the first day. Add more words when the child is ready for a challenge.

• **Learning to Read CCVC Words**—If the student can read the three-letter words, provide lessons for sounding out and reading CCVC words. Select three days of activities. Introduce the consonant clusters with a tactile activity. During the lessons, include pairings of CVC and CCVC words to strengthen decoding skills (*him* with *hit*, *rim* with *brim*, *Tim* with *trim*, *fit* with *flit*, *lit* with *slit*, *pit* with *spit*, *slim* with *slit*) and word-recognition fluency.

Word List

dim*	brim*	hit*	wit*
him*	slim*	it*	flit*
Jim*	swim*	kit*	grit*
Kim*	trim*	lit*	skit*
rim*	bit*	pit*	slit
Tim*	fit*	sit*	spit*

*See pages 146–149 for reproducible word cards. Add to the set by printing slit on card stock.

DAY 1
Materials: Copy the pictures on pages 47 and 59. Follow the directions for the Molding Words and Pinching Letters activities on page 15.

• Show the pictures for *hit* and *rim*. Ask the child to tell you the beginning sound of each word (*hit* = /h/ and *rim* = /r/) and make the letters in clay. Continue the lesson by calling out other selected words. Let the child identify the beginning sounds and make the letters in clay to spell the words.
• Have students write the words.
• Pinching Letters (See page 15.)

DAY 2
Materials: Copy of letter cards (page 140), word cards (pages 146–149), and launch pad mat (page 132); "Sticky" Words materials (page 19); prepared mini-book

Use letters and selected word cards in the following activities:

• Show and read the words.
• Phonemic Awareness (See page 58.)
• Puffy Words—if tactile activity is needed (See page 15.)
• Blast Off! (See page 17.)
• "Sticky" Words (See page 19.)
• Word Family Mini-Book (See page 20.)

DAY 3
Materials: Copy of letter cards (page 140), word cards (pages 146–149), and safe mat (page 135); materials for Yummy Words (page 20) and Clip, Read, 'n' Write (page 20)

Use letters and selected word cards in the following activities:

• Review and use words in sentences. (See Finish the Sentence, page 21.)
• Phonemic Awareness (See page 58.)
• Unlock the Code (See page 18.)
• Yummy Words (See page 20.)
• Clip, Read, 'n' Write (See page 20.)

DAY 4
Materials: Copy of letter cards (page 140), word cards (pages 146–149), robot form (page 139), truck mat (page 133), and tree house mat (page 136)

Use letters and selected word cards in the following activities:

• Review and use words in sentences. (See Robot Writing!, page 21.)
• Phonemic Awareness (See page 58.)
• Load the Truck (See page 17.)
• Read 'n' Climb to See the View (See page 19.)
• Write Down—Back to the Ground (See page 21.)

DAY 5
Materials: Copy of word cards (pages 146–149); storybooks featuring -im and -it words; self-adhesive flags (office supply item)

Select word cards and use them in the following activities:

• Read 'n' Spell Words (Take turns reading aloud a word to a partner who spells it.)
• Flag It!—Take turns reading aloud a passage from a classroom book that has -im and -it words in the text. Each time a word-family word is used, mark it with a sticky flag.
• I Write, You Write! (See page 21.)

More Suggestions!
Spend a few minutes each day introducing or reviewing the -im and -it word families by reading aloud passages (pointing to the words) from children's storybooks. Let students be word-family detectives and identify those words used in the text.

Read at Home Activity
Copy the take-home direction sheet (page 59) for each student. Include two copies of the word cards on card stock. Place all of the materials in a zippered plastic bag.

Working with Sounds in "-im" and "-it" Words

LESSON 1
BASIC

Isolating Initial Sounds—Model for your students: *Listen carefully. I am going to say a word. The word is* him. *What is the first sound you hear in* him? *The first sound is /h/.* Words to practice: *Say the first sound you hear in . . .* Tim, dim, Jim.

Blending Sounds—Model for your students: *Listen carefully. I am going to say the sounds slowly in my secret word. I would like you to blend those sounds together. The sounds are: /b/ /i/ /t/. What is the secret word? When I blend the sounds /b/ /i/ /t/ together, I hear the word* bit. Words to practice: *kit, hit, lit*

MORE CHALLENGING

• *Listen to the words:* him, hit, Jim. *Which words rhyme?* (him, Jim)
• *What word begins with /p/ and rhymes with* it? (pit)
• *Listen closely because I want to tell you a secret word. It is /t/ /i/ /m/. Say the sounds with me: /t/ /i/ /m/. What is my secret word?* (Tim)
• *Listen to the words:* Kim, lit, kit. *Which words rhyme?* (lit, kit)

• *Here is another secret word for you. It is /h/ /i/ /t/. Say the sounds: /h/ /i/ /t/. What is my secret word?* (hit)
• *Listen to the words:* sit, fit, fan. *Which words rhyme?* (sit, fit)
• *Say the word* bit. *How many sounds do you hear in* bit? *Hold up your fingers to show me the number.* (three) *Now, say the word without the /b/ sound. What is the new word?* (it)
• *What word begins with /r/ and ends with /im/?* (rim)

LESSON 2
BASIC

Segmenting Sounds—Model for your students: *Listen carefully. I would like you to tell me each sound you hear in a word. If the word is* wit, *what are the sounds? I would say /w/ /i/ /t/.* Words to practice: *Tell each sound you hear in . . .* fit, sit, pit.

Adding Sounds—Model for your students: *Listen carefully. I am going to say a word and then add a sound to make a new word. My secret word rhymes with* Tim *and begins with the /r/ sound. What is the word? (Repeat the sounds: /r/ /im/.) The word is* rim. Words to practice: *Kim, dim, Jim*

MORE CHALLENGING

• *What word rhymes with* it *and begins with /b/?* (bit)
• *Say each sound you hear in the name* Jim. *What are those sounds?* (/j/ /i/ /m/)
• *Now think about the word* sit. *How many sounds do you hear in the word?* (three) *Stretch the sounds in the word.* (/sssssss/ /iiiiiii/ /t/)

• *What word begins with /d/ and ends with /im/?* (dim)
• *Listen closely because I want to tell you a secret word. It is /w/ /i/ /t/. Say the sounds with me: /w/ /i/ /t/. What is the secret word?* (wit)
• *Say each sound you hear in the word* lit. *What are those sounds?* (/l/ /i/ /t/)
• *Listen to the name* Jim. *What name rhymes with* Jim *and begins with /t/?* (Tim)
• *Here's another word clue: This secret word begins with /h/ and rhymes with the word* it. *What is the word?* (hit)

LESSON 3
BASIC

Blending Sounds—Model for your students: *Listen carefully. I am going to say some sounds slowly. I would like you to blend those sounds together and then tell me the word. The sounds are /t/ /r/ /i/ /m/. (Repeat the sounds.) What is the word? The word is* trim. Words to practice: *brim, slim, swim, and CVC words*

Substituting Sounds—Model for students: *Listen to the word* hit. *Let's change the /h/ sound to /l/. What is the new word? I can blend the sounds /l/ /it/ together to make the word* lit. Words to practice: *lit*—change /l/ to /s/ = *sit*; *pit*—change /p/ to /w/ = *wit*; *slit*—change /s/ to /f/ = *flit*

MORE CHALLENGING

• *Say each sound you hear in the word* brim. *What are those sounds?* (/b/ /r/ /i/ /m/)
• *I want to tell you my secret word. It is /s/ /l/ /i/ /m/. (Repeat the sounds.) Blend the sounds together. What word can you make with the sounds?* (slim)
• *Listen to the word* bit. *Change the /b/ sound to /w/. What new word did you make?* (wit)
• *Say the word* kit. *Add the sound /s/ to the beginning of the word. Now, what is the new word?* (skit)
• *Listen to the word* trim. *Change the /t/ sound to /b/. What new word did you make?* (brim)
• *Now listen to the word* brim. *Say the word* brim *without the /b/ sound. What is the new word?* (rim)
• *Listen to the sounds: /s/ /p/ /i/ /t/. (Repeat the sounds.) Blend the sounds together. What word can you make with the sounds?* (spit)
• *Say the word* flit. *Now, say it without the /f/ sound. What is the new word?* (lit)

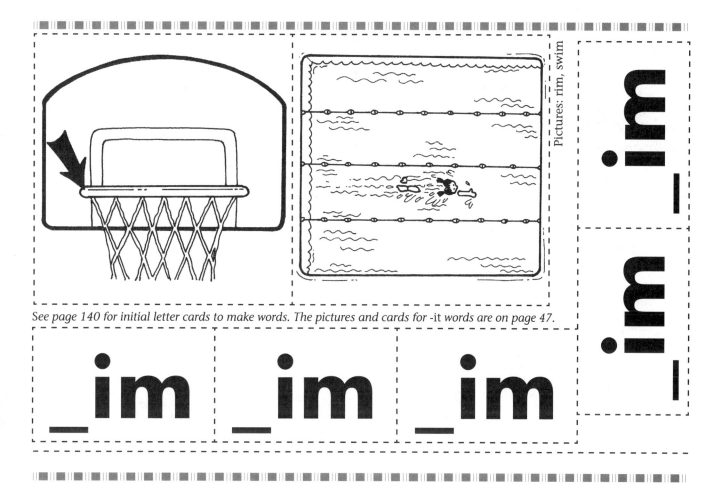

Pictures: rim, swim

See page 140 for initial letter cards to make words. The pictures and cards for -it words are on page 47.

_im _im _im

Swim with Words

To Parent:
Your child has been learning how to read words that end with "im" and "it." In the zippered bag you will find two copies of each word. Please provide two game markers.

Twin Word Fun
How to play the game (two players):
- Cut out the word cards if needed. Choose two cards and draw smiley faces on them to make "Wild Word Cards." Shuffle the cards and arrange them facedown in a pile.
- Take turns drawing a card from the pile, reading the word, and moving a game marker to the next box. If the card is not read correctly, the player returns the card to the bottom of the pile. If a "Wild Word Card" is drawn, the player moves a game marker ahead two boxes after reading the given word correctly.
- The first player who "swims" a lap (moves down the game board to touch the wall and then moves back to the start position) wins the game.

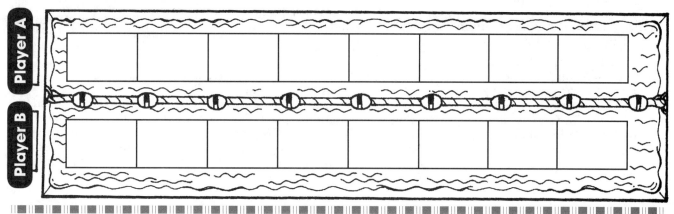

MEET AND READ THE "-OP" FAMILY

Getting Started! Determine which letter-sound correspondences and letter patterns the student needs to practice.

• **Learning to Read CVC Words**—If the student cannot easily identify the phonemes for the consonants *b, c, h, m, p,* and *t,* use Day 1–5 activities. Otherwise, begin on Day 2. Select CVC words from the list. Start with about six words for the targeted practice on the first day. Add words from word families previously studied as a review when the child is ready for a challenge.

• **Learning to Read CCVC Words**—If the student can read the three-letter words, provide lessons for sounding out and reading CCVC words. Select three days of activities. Introduce the digraphs *ch* and *sh* and the consonant clusters with a tactile activity. During the lessons, include CVC words (and words from other word families) to strengthen decoding skills (*hop* with *chop* or *shop, cop* with *crop, pop* with *plop* or *prop*) and word-recognition fluency.

Word List

bop*	**top***	**plop***
cop*	**chop***	**prop***
hop*	**crop***	**shop***
mop*	**drop***	**stop***
pop*	**flop***	

*See page 149 for reproducible word cards.

DAY 1

Materials: Copy the picture for *hop* on page 62. Follow the directions for the Molding Words activity on page 15.

• Show the picture for *hop.* Ask the child to tell you the beginning sound of the word (*hop* = /h/) and make the letter in clay. Continue the lesson by calling out other *-op* words. Have the child identify the beginning sounds and make the letters in clay to spell the words.

• To teach CCVC words, form the letters for digraphs, blends, and rimes in clay.

• Have students write the words.

DAY 2

Materials: Copy of letter cards (page 140) and word cards (page 149); prepared mini-book

Use letters and selected word cards in the following activities:

• Show and use the words in sentences.
• Phonemic Awareness (See page 61.)
• Puffy Words—if tactile activity is needed (See page 15.)
• What's the Word? (See page 16.)
• Where Is . . . ? (See page 19.)
• Word Family Mini-Book (See page 20.)

DAY 3

Materials: Copy of letter cards (page 140), word cards (page 149), truck mat (page 133), and tree house mat (page 136)

Use letters and selected word cards in the following activities:

• Review and use words in sentences. (See Finish the Sentence, page 21.)
• Phonemic Awareness (See page 61.)
• Load the Truck (See page 17.)
• Read 'n' Climb to See the View (See page 19.)
• Write Down—Back to the Ground (See page 21.)

DAY 4

Materials: Copy of word cards (page 149) and robot form (page 139); labeled plastic eggs and egg carton; copy of monster mat (page 137)

Select word cards and use them in the following activities:

• Review and use words in sentences. (See Robot Writing!, page 21.)
• Phonemic Awareness (See page 61.)
• Pack the Words (See page 18.)
• Mr. Word Muncher (See page 19.)
• Feed Mr. Word Muncher (See page 21.)

DAY 5

Materials: Copy of word cards (page 149); children's storybook featuring *-op* words; self-adhesive flags (office supply item)

Select word cards and use them in the following activities:

• Read 'n' Spell Words (Take turns reading aloud a word to a partner who spells it.)
• Flag It!—Take turns reading aloud a passage from a classroom book that has *-op* words in the text. Each time a word-family word is used, mark it with a sticky flag. (Draw attention to the rime *-op.*)
• I Write, You Write! (See page 21.)

More Suggestions!

Spend a few minutes each day introducing or reviewing the *-op* word family by reading aloud passages (pointing to the words) from children's storybooks. Let students be word-family detectives and identify those words used in the text.

Read at Home Activity

Copy the take-home direction sheet (page 62) for each student. Print two copies of the selected word cards on card stock. Place all of the materials in a zippered plastic bag.

Working with Sounds in "-op" Words

LESSON 1
BASIC

Isolating Initial Sounds—Model for your students: *Listen carefully. I am going to say a word. The word is top. What is the first sound you hear in top? The first sound is /t/.* Words to practice: *Say the first sound you hear in . . .* bop, mop, pop, shop.

Blending Sounds—Model for your students: *Listen carefully. I am going to say the sounds slowly in my secret word. I would like you to blend those sounds together. The sounds are: /m/ /o/ /p/. What is*

the secret word? When I blend the sounds /m/ /o/ /p/ together, I hear the word mop.* Words to practice: *hop, cop, top, chop*

MORE CHALLENGING
- *Listen to the words:* hop, top, hit. *Which words rhyme?* (hop, top)
- *What word begins with /k/ and rhymes with* hop? (cop)
- *Listen closely because I want to tell you a secret word. It is /h/ /o/ /p/. Say the sounds with me: /h/ /o/ /p/. What is my secret word?* (hop)
- *Listen to the words:* bib, bop,

stop. *Which two words rhyme?* (bop, stop)
- *Here is another secret word for you. It is /m/ /o/ /p/. Say the sounds: /m/ /o/ /p/. What is my secret word?* (mop)
- *Say the word* bop. *How many sounds do you hear in the word* bop? (three) *Now, say the word without the /b/ sound. What is the silly word?* (op)
- *Listen to the words:* mop, mad, pop. *Which two words rhyme?* (mop, pop)
- *Here is one more secret word for you. It is /t/ /o/ /p/. Say the sounds: /t/ /o/ /p/. What is the secret word?* (top)

LESSON 2
BASIC

Segmenting Sounds—Model for your students: *Listen carefully. I would like you to tell me each sound you hear in a word. If the word is* hop, *what are the sounds? I would say* /h/ /o/ /p/. Words to practice: *Tell each sound you hear in . . .* pop, hop, top, pop.

Adding Sounds—Model for your students: *Listen carefully. I am going to say a word and then add a sound to make a new word. My secret word ends with /op/ and begins with the /k/ sound. What*

is the word? (Repeat the sounds: /k/ /op/.) The word is* cop. Words to practice: *mop, top, chop*

MORE CHALLENGING
- *Say each sound you hear in the word* mop. *What are those sounds?* (/m/ /o/ /p/)
- *Listen closely because I want to tell you a secret word. It is /b/ /o/ /p/. Say the sounds with me: /b/ /o/ /p/. What is the secret word?* (bop)
- *What word rhymes with* hop *and begins with /p/?* (pop)
- *Here's another word clue: This secret word begins with /ch/ and*

rhymes with the word* hop. What is the word?* (chop)
- *Now think about the word* shop. *How many sounds do you hear in the word?* (three) *Stretch the sounds in the word.* (/sh/ /oooooo/ /p/)
- *Listen to the word* hop. *What word rhymes with* hop *and begins with /t/?* (top)
- *What word begins with /m/ and ends with /op/?* (mop)
- *Say each sound you hear in the word* cop. *What are those sounds?* (/k/ /o/ /p/)

LESSON 3
BASIC

Blending Sounds—Model for your students: *Listen carefully. I am going to say some sounds slowly. I would like you to blend those sounds together and then tell me the word. The sounds are /sh/ /o/ /p/. (Repeat the sounds.) What is the word? The word is* shop. Words to practice: *drop, flop, prop, stop, and CVC words*

Substituting Sounds—Model for your students: *Listen to the word* bop. *Let's change the /b/ sound to /p/. What is the new word? I can blend the sounds /p/ /op/ together*

to make the word* pop. Words to practice: *pop*—change /p/ to /ch/ = chop; chop—change /ch/ to /sh/ = shop; prop—change /p/ to /d/ = drop

MORE CHALLENGING
- *Listen to the word* bop. *Change the /b/ sound to /ch/. What new word did you make?* (chop)
- *I want to tell you my secret word. It is /d/ /r/ /o/ /p/. (Repeat the sounds.) Blend the sounds together. What word can you make with the sounds?* (drop)
- *Listen to the sounds: /f/ /l/ /o/ /p/. (Repeat the sounds.) Blend the sounds together. What word can*

you make with the sounds?* (flop)
- *Say each sound you hear in the word* crop. *What are those sounds?* (/k/ /r/ /o/ /p/)
- *This time say the word* stop. *Now, say each sound you hear in the word. What are those sounds?* (/s/ /t/ /o/ /p/)
- *Say the sounds /p/ /r/ /o/ /p/. (Repeat the sounds.) Blend the sounds together. What word can you make with the sounds?* (prop)
- *Say the word* flop. *Change the /f/ sound to /p/. What new word did you make?* (plop)
- *Listen to the word* bop. *Change the /b/ sound to /sh/. What new word did you make?* (shop)

See page 140 for initial letter cards to make words.

Pictures: hop, drop

_op   _op   _op

op
_op
_op

Hop on Words

To Parent:

Your child has been learning how to read words that end with "op." In the zippered bag you will find two copies of each word. Please provide masking tape and a watercolor marker.

Hop on Words

Here's what to do:

- Cut out the word cards if needed.
- On the floor, use masking tape to make a grid with three columns and six rows.
- Choose six different words. Place each word randomly in the grid by writing it on a piece of masking tape. Do this step three times for each word.
- Shuffle all of word cards and place them *facedown* in a pile.
- Have your child draw a word, read it, and then hop across the grid by stepping on the matching words. If the word is not shown on the floor, then it's "rev up for reading" time! Let your child jog around the grid. Continue playing the activity as time and interest allow.

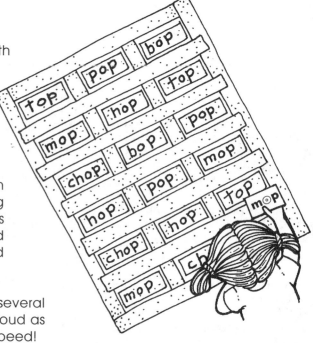

Ready, Set, Read! Arrange all of the word cards in several rows on a table. Have your child read the words aloud as a practice run and then a second time at a faster speed!

MEET AND READ THE "-OT" FAMILY

Getting Started! Determine which letter-sound correspondences and letter patterns the student needs to practice.

• **Learning to Read CVC Words**—If the student cannot easily identify the phonemes for the consonants *c, d, g, h, j, l, n, p, r,* and *t,* use Day 1–5 activities. Otherwise, begin on Day 2. Select CVC words from the list. Start with about six words for the targeted practice on the first day. Add new words as needed for a challenge. Include a few words from word families previously studied as a review.

• **Learning to Read CCVC Words**—If the student can read the three-letter words, provide lessons for sounding out and reading CCVC words. Select three days of activities. Introduce the digraph *sh* and consonant clusters with a tactile activity. During the lessons, include CVC words (and words from other lessons) to strengthen decoding skills (*lot* with *blot* or *plot* or *slot, hot* with *shot, pot* with *spot, rot* with *trot*) and word-recognition fluency.

Word List

cot*	not*	shot*
dot*	pot*	slot*
got*	rot*	spot*
hot*	tot*	trot*
jot*	blot*	
lot*	plot*	

See pages 149 & 150 for reproducible word cards.

DAY 1

Materials: Copy the pictures on page 65. Follow the directions for the Molding Words activity on page 15.

• Show the pictures for *hot* and *cot.* Ask the child to tell you the beginning sound of each word (*hot* = /h/ and *cot* = /k/) and make the letter in clay. Continue the lesson by calling out other *-ot* words. Have the child identify the beginning sounds and make the letters in clay to spell the words.
• To teach CCVC words, form the letters for the digraph, blends, and rimes in clay.
• Have students write the words.

DAY 2

Materials: Copy of letter cards (page 140), word cards (pages 149 and 150), and stone wall mat (page 130); materials for "Sticky" Words (page 19); prepared mini-book

Use letters and selected word cards in the following activities:

• Show and read the words.
• Phonemic Awareness (See page 64.)
• Puffy words—if tactile activity is needed (See page 15.)
• Letters on Stones (See page 16.)
• "Sticky" Words (See page 19.)
• Word Family Mini-Book (See page 20.)

DAY 3

Materials: Copy of word cards (pages 149 and 150); labeled plastic eggs and egg carton; copy of monster mat (page 137)

Select word cards and use them in the following activities:

• Review and use words in sentences. (See Finish the Sentence, page 21.)
• Phonemic Awareness (See page 64.)
• Pack the Words (See page 18.)
• Mr. Word Muncher (See page 19.)
• Feed Mr. Word Muncher (See page 21.)

DAY 4

Materials: Copy of letter cards (page 140), word cards (pages 149 and 150), robot form (page 139), and playing catch mat (page 134); materials for Yummy Words (page 20) and Clip, Read, 'n' Write (page 20)

Use letters and selected word cards in the following activities:

• Review and use words in sentences. (See Robot Writing!, page 21.)
• Phonemic Awareness (See page 64.)
• Catch High-Flying Sounds (See page 18.)
• Yummy Words (See page 20.)
• Clip, Read, 'n' Write (See page 20.)

DAY 5

Materials: Copy of word cards (pages 149 and 150); children's storybook featuring *-ot* words; self-adhesive flags (office supply item)

Select word cards and use them in the following activities:

• Read 'n' Spell Words (Take turns reading aloud a word to a partner who spells it.)
• Flag It!—Take turns reading aloud a passage from a classroom book that has *-ot* words in the text. Each time a word-family word is used, mark it with a sticky flag. (Draw attention to the rime *-ot*.)
• I Write, You Write! (See page 21.)

More Suggestions!

Spend a few minutes each day introducing or reviewing the *-ot* word family by reading aloud passages (pointing to the words) from children's storybooks. Let students be word-family detectives and identify those words used in the text.

Read at Home Activity

Copy the take-home direction sheet (page 65) for each student. Include two copies of the word cards on card stock, plus a sheet of construction paper and a paper bag. Place the materials in a zippered plastic bag.

Working with Sounds in "-ot" Words

LESSON 1
BASIC
Isolating Initial Sounds—Model for your students: *Listen carefully. I am going to say a word. The word is* dot. *What is the first sound you hear in* dot? *The first sound is /d/.* Words to practice: *Say the first sound you hear in . . .* got, not, rot, cot.

Blending Sounds—Model for your students: *Listen carefully. I am going to say the sounds slowly in my secret word. I would like you to blend those sounds together. The sounds are: /t/ /o/ /t/. What is the secret word? When I blend the sounds /t/ /o/ /t/ together, I hear the word* tot. Words to practice: *jot, lot, hot, pot*

MORE CHALLENGING
• *Listen to the words:* cut, cot, dot. *Which words rhyme?* (cot, dot)
• *What word begins with /j/ and rhymes with* dot? (jot)
• *Listen closely because I want to tell you a secret word. It is /p/ /o/ /t/. Say the sounds with me: /p/ /o/ /t/. What is my secret word?* (pot)
• *Listen to the words:* not, nod, lot. *Which words rhyme?* (not, lot)
• *Here is another secret word for you.* It is /k/ /o/ /t/. Say the sounds: /k/ /o/ /t/. What is my secret word? (cot)
• *Listen to the words:* rot, hot, hug. *Which words rhyme?* (rot, hot)
• *Say the word* rot. *How many sounds do you hear in* rot? *Hold up your fingers to show me the number.* (three) *Now, say the word without the /r/ sound. What is the silly word?* (ot)
• *What word begins with /g/ and ends with /ot/?* (got)

LESSON 2
BASIC
Segmenting Sounds—Model for your students: *Listen carefully. I would like you to tell me each sound you hear in a word. If the word is* got, *what are the sounds? I would say /g/ /o/ /t/.* Words to practice: *Tell each sound you hear in . . .* dot, jot, rot, hot.

Adding Sounds—Model for your students: *Listen carefully. I am going to say a word and then add a sound to make a new word. My secret word ends with /ot/ and begins with the /l/ sound. What is the word?* (Repeat the sounds: /l/ /ot/.) *The word is* lot. Words to practice: *cot, not, tot, pot*

MORE CHALLENGING
• *What word rhymes with* dot *and begins with /n/?* (not)
• *Say each sound you hear in the word* dot. *What are those sounds?* (/d/ /o/ /t/)
• *Now think about the word* rot. *How many sounds do you hear in the word?* (three) *Stretch the sounds in the word.* (/rrrrrr/ /oooooo/ /t/)
• *What word begins with /p/ and rhymes with* dot? (pot)
• *Listen closely because I want to tell you a secret word. It is /sh/ /o/ /t/. Say the sounds with me: /sh/ /o/ /t/. What is the secret word?* (shot)
• *Say each sound you hear in the word* got. *What are those sounds?* (/g/ /o/ /t/)
• *Listen to the word* dot. *What word rhymes with* dot *and begins with /n/?* (not)
• *Here's another word clue: This secret word begins with /l/ and rhymes with the word* dot. *What is the word?* (lot)

LESSON 3
BASIC
Blending Sounds—Model for your students: *Listen carefully. I am going to say some sounds slowly. I would like you to blend those sounds together and then tell me the word. The sounds are /s/ /p/ /o/ /t/.* (Repeat the sounds.) *What is the word? The word is* spot. Words to practice: *trot, blot, shot, plot,* and CVC words

Substituting Sounds—Model for students: *Listen to the word* jot. *Let's change the /j/ sound to /sh/. What is the new word? I can blend the sounds /sh/ /ot/ together to make the word* shot. Words to practice: *shot—change /sh/ to /p/ = pot; pot—change /p/ to /r/ = rot; blot—change /b/ to /s/ = slot*

MORE CHALLENGING
• *Say each sound you hear in the word* tot. *What are those sounds?* (/t/ /o/ /t/)
• *I want to tell you my secret word. It is /t/ /r/ /o/ /t/.* (Repeat the sounds.) *Blend the sounds together. What word can you make with the sounds?* (trot)
• *Listen to the word* jot. *Change the /j/ sound to /sh/. What new word did you make?* (shot)
• *Say the word* rot. *Add the sound /t/ to the beginning of the word. Now, what is the new word?* (trot)
• *Listen to the sounds: /b/ /l/ /o/ /t/.* (Repeat the sounds.) *Blend the sounds together. What word can you make with the sounds?* (blot)
• *Now listen to the word* plot. *Say the word* plot *without the /p/ sound. What is the new word?* (lot)
• *Listen to the sounds: /s/ /l/ /o/ /t/. Blend the sounds together. What word can you make with the sounds?* (slot)
• *Say the word* spot. *Now, say it without the /s/ sound. What is the new word?* (pot)

See page 140 for initial letter cards to make words.

Pictures: hot, cot

_ot _ot _ot

ot

ot

Read at Home—the "_ot" Word Families

Got Dots

To Parent:
Your child has been learning how to read words that end with "ot." Provided are two copies of word cards, a sheet of construction paper, and a small paper bag. Please make 10 dots by tracing a milk jug cap on the paper and cutting out the circles. On the back of one circle, draw a smiley face.

Got Dots
How to play the game (two players):
• Cut out the word cards if needed and place them in the paper bag.
• Scatter the 10 dots randomly on the tabletop. Be sure the smiley face on the back of one dot is hidden.
• Take turns drawing a card from the bag without looking in it, reading the word out loud, and picking up a dot if the word is read correctly. If the word card is not read correctly, the player returns the card to the bag. Whoever picks up the smiley face gets to collect the remaining dots!
• The player who collects the most dots wins the game.

Ready, Set, Read! Arrange all of the word cards in several rows on a table. Have your child read the words aloud as a practice run and then a second time at a faster speed!

MEET AND READ THE "-OG" FAMILY

Getting Started! Determine which letter-sound correspondences and letter patterns the student needs to practice.

• **Learning to Read CVC Words**—If the student cannot easily identify the phonemes for the consonants *b, c, d, f, h, j,* and *l,* use Day 1–5 activities. Otherwise, begin on Day 2. Select CVC words from the list. Start with about six words for the targeted practice on the first day. Add words from word families previously studied as a review.

• **Learning to Read CCVC Words**—If the student can read the three-letter words, provide lessons for sounding out and reading CCVC words. Select three days of activities. Introduce the consonant clusters with a tactile activity. During the lessons, include CVC words (and words from other word families) to strengthen decoding skills (*log* or *cog* with *clog, fog* with *frog*) and word-recognition fluency.

Word List	
bog*	jog*
cog*	log*
dog*	clog*
fog*	frog*
hog*	smog*

See page 150 for reproducible word cards.

DAY 1

Materials: Copy the picture for *dog* on page 68. Follow the directions for the Molding Words activity on page 15.

• Show the dog picture. Ask the child to tell you the beginning sound of the word (*dog* = /d/) and make the letter in clay. Continue the lesson by calling out other -og words. Have the child identify the beginning sounds and make the letters in clay to spell the words.
• To teach CCVC words, form the letters for blends and rimes in clay.
• Have students write the words.

DAY 2

Materials: Copy of letter cards (page 140) and word cards (page 150); racetrack billboard mat (page 131); prepared mini-book

Use letters and selected word cards in the following activities:

• Show and read the words.
• Phonemic Awareness (See page 67.)
• Puffy Words—if tactile activity is needed (See page 15.)
• Rev Up for Words (See page 17.)
• Where Is . . . ? (See page 19.)
• Word Family Mini-Book (See page 20.)

DAY 3

Materials: Copy of letter cards (page 140), word cards (page 150), and playing catch mat (page 134); materials for Yummy Words (page 20) and Clip, Read, 'n' Write (page 20)

Use letters and selected word cards in the following activities:

• Review and use words in sentences. (See Finish the Sentence, page 21.)
• Phonemic Awareness (See page 67.)
• Catch High-Flying Sounds (See page 18.)
• Yummy Words (See page 20.)
• Clip, Read, 'n' Write (See page 20.)

DAY 4

Materials: Copy of letter cards (page 140), word cards (page 150), robot form (page 139), safe mat (page 135), and tree house mat (page 136)

Use letters and selected word cards in the following activities:

• Review and use words in sentences. (See Robot Writing!, page 21.)
• Phonemic Awareness (See page 67.)
• Unlock the Code (See page 18.)
• Read 'n' Climb to See the View (See page 19.)
• Write Down—Back to the Ground (See page 21.)

DAY 5

Materials: Copy of word cards (page 150); children's storybook featuring -og words; self-adhesive flags (office supply item)

Select word cards and use them in the following activities:

• Read 'n' Spell Words (Take turns reading aloud a word to a partner who spells it.)
• Flag It!—Take turns reading aloud a passage from a classroom book that has -og words in the text. Each time a word-family word is used, mark it with a sticky flag. (Draw attention to the rime -og.)
• I Write, You Write! (See page 21.)

More Suggestions!

Spend a few minutes each day introducing or reviewing the -og word family by reading aloud passages (pointing to the words) from children's storybooks. Let students be word-family detectives and identify those words used in the text.

Read at Home Activity

Copy the take-home direction sheet and dog and frog pictures (page 68) for each student. Include two copies of the word cards on card stock, plus a sheet of brown construction paper. Place the materials in a zippered plastic bag.

Working with Sounds in "-og" Words

LESSON 1
BASIC

Isolating Initial Sounds—Model for your students: *Listen carefully. I am going to say a word. The word is* dog. *What is the first sound you hear in* dog? *The first sound is* /d/. Words to practice: *Say the first sound you hear in . . .* log, jog, fog (and words from other lessons).

Blending Sounds—Model for your students: *Listen carefully. I am going to say the sounds slowly in my secret word. I would like you to blend those sounds together. The sounds are:* /f/ /o/ /g/. *What is the secret word? When I blend the sounds* /f/ /o/ /g/ *together, I hear the word* fog. Words to practice: *cog, hog, log*

MORE CHALLENGING
- *Listen to the words:* dog, dot, log. *Which words rhyme?* (dog, log)
- *What word begins with* /f/ *and rhymes with* dog? (fog)
- *Listen closely because I want to tell you a secret word. It is* /l/ /o/ /g/. *Say the sounds with me:* /l/ /o/ /g/. *What is my secret word?* (log)
- *Listen to the words:* jet, fog, jog. *Which two words rhyme?* (fog, jog)
- *Here is another secret word for you. It is* /b/ /o/ /g/. *Say the sounds:* /b/ /o/ /g/. *What is my secret word?* (bog)
- *Say the word* jog. *How many sounds do you hear in the word* jog? (three) *Now, say the word without the* /j/ *sound. What is the silly word?* (og)
- *Listen to the words:* frog, bog, bun. *Which two words rhyme?* (frog, bog)
- *Here is one more secret word for you. It is* /k/ /o/ /g/. *Say the sounds:* /k/ /o/ /g/. *What is the secret word?* (cog)

LESSON 2
BASIC

Segmenting Sounds—Model for your students: *Listen carefully. I would like you to tell me each sound you hear in a word. If the word is* jog, *what are the sounds? I would say* /j/ /o/ /g/. Words to practice: *Tell each sound you hear in . . .* cog, dog, bog (and words from other lessons).

Adding Sounds—Model for your students: *Listen carefully. I am going to say a word and then add a sound to make a new word. My secret word ends with* /og/ *and begins with the* /l/ *sound. What is the word? (Repeat the sounds:* /l/ /og/.) *The word is* log. Words to practice: *fog, jog, hog*

MORE CHALLENGING
- *Say each sound you hear in the word* bog. *What are those sounds?* (/b/ /o/ /g/)
- *Listen closely because I want to tell you a secret word. It is* /h/ /o/ /g/. *Say the sounds with me:* /h/ /o/ /g/. *What is the secret word?* (hog)
- *What word rhymes with* dog *and begins with* /j/? (jog)
- *Here's another word clue: This secret word begins with* /k/ *and rhymes with the word* dog. *What is the word?* (cog)
- *Now think about the word* fog. *How many sounds do you hear in the word?* (three) *Stretch the sounds in the word.* (/ffffff/ /oooooo/ /g/)
- *Listen to the word* dog. *What word rhymes with* dog *and begins with* /l/? (log)
- *What word begins with* /f/ *and ends with* /og/? (fog)
- *Say each sound you hear in the word* dog. *What are those sounds?* (/d/ /o/ /g/)

LESSON 3
BASIC

Blending Sounds—Model for your students: *Listen carefully. I am going to say some sounds slowly. I would like you to blend those sounds together and then tell me the word. The sounds are* /f/ /r/ /o/ /g/. *(Repeat the sounds.) What is the word? The word is* frog. Words to practice: *smog, clog, log, cog, and other CVC words*

Substituting Sounds—Model for your students: *Listen to the word* bog. *Let's change the* /b/ *sound to* /d/. *What is the new word? I can blend the sounds* /d/ /og/ *together to make the word* dog. Words to practice: *dog*—change /d/ to /l/ = *log*; *log*—change /l/ to /k/ = *cog*; *cog*—change /k/ to /h/ = *hog*

MORE CHALLENGING
- *Listen to the word* jog. *Change the* /j/ *sound to* /f/. *What new word did you make?* (fog)
- *I want to tell you my secret word. It is* /s/ /m/ /o/ /g/. *(Repeat the sounds.) Blend the sounds together. What word can you make with the sounds?* (smog)
- *Listen to the sounds:* /k/ /l/ /o/ /g/. *(Repeat the sounds.) Blend the sounds together. What word can you make with the sounds?* (clog)
- *Say the word* bog. *Change the* /b/ *sound to* /l/. *What is the new word?* (log)
- *This time say the word* log. *Change the* /l/ *sound to* /d/. *What is the new word?* (dog)
- *Say the sounds* /f/ /r/ /o/ /g/. *(Repeat the sounds.) Blend the sounds together. What word can you make with the sounds?* (frog)
- *Say the word* log. *Add the sound* /k/ *to the beginning of the word. What is the new word?* (clog)
- *Listen to the word* fog. *Change the* /f/ *sound to* /b/. *What new word did you make?* (bog)

See page 140 for initial letter cards to make words.   Pictures: dog, frog

_og _og _og

og _og _og

Read at Home—the "_og" Word Family

Where Is the Dog?

To Parent:
Your child has been learning how to read words that end with "og." In the zippered bag are two copies of the word cards, dog and frog pictures, and a brown sheet of paper. Please provide tape.

Where Is the Dog?
Here's what to do:
- Cut out the phrase cards.
- Roll the brown sheet of paper lengthwise to make a log and tape it to hold that shape. Place the log in the center of the playing area.
- Turn the cards facedown.
- Have your child turn over a phrase card, read it aloud, and show what the phrase means by using the log and the pictures.

Ready, Set, Read! Have your child read the word cards aloud as a practice and then a second time at a faster speed!

dog on the log

dog by the log

frog in the log

frog under the log

dog and frog
not by the log

MEET AND READ "-OP" AND "-AP" FAMILIES

Getting Started! Determine which letter-sound correspondences and letter patterns the student needs to practice.

• **Learning to Read CVC Words**—If the student cannot easily identify the phonemes for the consonants, use Day 1–5 activities. Otherwise, begin on Day 2. Select CVC words from the list. Start with about 10 words for the targeted practice on the first day. Add more words when the child is ready for a challenge.

• **Learning to Read CCVC Words**—If the student can read the three-letter words, provide lessons for sounding out and reading CCVC words. Select three days of activities. Introduce the digraphs *sh* and *ch* and consonant clusters with a tactile activity. During the lessons, include pairings of CVC and CCVC words to strengthen decoding skills (*hop* with *chop* or *shop*, *top* with *stop*, *cap* with *clap*, *cap* with *cop*, *top* with *tap*, *lap* with *flap*, *flap* with *flop*, *mop* with *map*) and word-recognition fluency.

Word List				
bop*	chop*	shop*	nap*	clap*
cop*	crop*	stop*	rap*	chap*
hop*	drop*	cap*	sap*	flap*
mop*	flop*	gap*	tap*	slap*
pop*	plop*	lap*	yap*	snap*
top*	prop*	map*	zap*	trap*

*See pages 145, 146 & 149 for reproducible word cards.

DAY 1

Materials: Copy the pictures on pages 41 and 62. Follow the directions for the Molding Words and Pinching Letters activities on page 15.

• Show the pictures for *cap* and *hop*. Ask the child to tell you the beginning sound of each word (*cap* = /k/ and *hop* = /h/) and make the letters in clay. Continue the lesson by calling out other selected words. Let the child identify the beginning sounds and make the letters in clay to spell the words.
• Have students write the words.
• Pinching Letters (See page 15.)

DAY 2

Materials: Copy of letter cards (page 140), word cards (pages 145, 146, and 149), and launch pad mad (page 132); "Sticky" Words materials (page 19); prepared mini-book

Use letters and selected word cards in the following activities:

• Show and read the words.
• Phonemic Awareness (See page 70.)
• Puffy Words—if tactile activity is needed (See page 15.)
• Blast Off! (See page 17.)
• "Sticky" Words (See page 19.)
• Word Family Mini-Book (See page 20.)

DAY 3

Materials: Copy of letter cards (page 140), word cards (pages 145, 146, and 149), safe mat (page 135), and tree house mat (page 136)

Use letters and selected word cards in the following activities:

• Review and use words in sentences. (See Finish the Sentence, page 21.)
• Phonemic Awareness (See page 70.)
• Unlock the Code (See page 18.)
• Read 'n' Climb to See the View (See page 19.)
• Write Down—Back to the Ground (See page 21.)

DAY 4

Materials: Copy of letter cards (page 140), word cards (pages 145, 146, and 149), robot form (page 139), truck mat (page 133), and monster mat (page 137)

Use letters and selected word cards in the following activities:

• Review and use words in sentences. (See Robot Writing!, page 21.)
• Phonemic Awareness (See page 70.)
• Load the Truck (See page 17.)
• Mr. Word Muncher (See page 19.)
• Feed Mr. Word Muncher (See page 21.)

DAY 5

Materials: Copy of word cards (pages 145, 146, and 149); storybooks featuring -op and -ap words; self-adhesive flags (office supply item)

Select word cards and use them in the following activities:

• Read 'n' Spell Words (Take turns reading aloud a word to a partner who spells it.)
• Flag It!—Take turns reading aloud passages from classroom books that have -op or -ap words in the text. Each time a word-family word is used, mark it with a sticky flag.
• I Write, You Write! (See page 21.)

More Suggestions!

Spend a few minutes each day introducing or reviewing the -op and -ap word families by reading aloud passages (pointing to the words) from children's storybooks. Let students be word-family detectives and identify those words used in the text.

Read at Home Activity

Copy the take-home direction sheet (page 71) and the selected word cards on card stock for each student. (The Wild Cards and the word cards must be the same color.) Place all of the materials in a zippered plastic bag.

Working with Sounds in "-op" and "-ap" Words

LESSON 1
BASIC

Isolating Initial Sounds—Model for your students: *Listen carefully. I am going to say a word. The word is mop. What is the first sound you hear in mop? The first sound is /m/.* Words to practice: *Say the first sound you hear in . . . hop, top, cop, pop.*

Blending Sounds—Model for your students: *Listen carefully. I am going to say the sounds slowly in my secret word. I would like you to blend those sounds together. The sounds are: /n/ /a/ /p/. What is*

the secret word? When I blend the sounds /n/ /a/ /p/ together, I hear the word nap.*
Words to practice: *cap, lap, rap, tap, chap*

MORE CHALLENGING
- *Listen to the words: mop, top, map. Which words rhyme? (mop, top)*
- *What word begins with /r/ and rhymes with cap? (rap)*
- *Listen closely because I want to tell you a secret word. It is /s/ /a/ /p/. Say the sounds with me: /s/ /a/ /p/. What is my secret word? (sap)*
- *Listen to the words: cop, cap, tap.*

Which words rhyme? (cap, tap)*
- *Here is another secret word for you. It is /b/ /o/ /p/. Say the sounds: /b/ /o/ /p/. What is my secret word? (bop)*
- *Listen to the words: flap, flop, nap. Which words rhyme? (flap, nap)*
- *Say the word mop. How many sounds do you hear in mop? Hold up your fingers to show me the number. (three) Now, say the word without the /m/ sound. What is the silly word? (op)*
- *What word begins with /ch/ and ends with /op/? (chop)*

LESSON 2
BASIC

Segmenting Sounds—Model for your students: *Listen carefully. I would like you to tell me each sound you hear in a word. If the word is gap, what are the sounds? I would say /g/ /a/ /p/.*
Words to practice: *Tell each sound you hear in . . . yap, zap, map, tap.*

Adding Sounds—Model for your students: *Listen carefully. I am going to say a word and then add a sound to make a new word. My secret word rhymes with mop and begins with the /ch/ sound. What*

is the word? (Repeat the sounds: /ch/ /op/.) The word is chop.*
Words to practice: *bop, pop, top*

MORE CHALLENGING
- *What word rhymes with cap and begins with /y/? (yap)*
- *Say each sound you hear in the word pop. What are those sounds? (/p/ /o/ /p/)*
- *Now think about the word lap. How many sounds do you hear in the word? (three) Stretch the sounds in the word. (/llllll/ /aaaaaa/ /p/)*
- *What word begins with /t/ and ends with /ap/? (tap)*

- *Listen closely because I want to tell you a secret word. It is /m/ /o/ /p/. Say the sounds with me: /m/ /o/ /p/. What is the secret word? (mop)*
- *Say each sound you hear in the word gap. What are those sounds? (/g/ /a/ /p/)*
- *Listen to the word hop. What word rhymes with hop and begins with /b/? (bop)*
- *Here's another word clue: This secret word begins with /t/ and rhymes with the word bop. What is the word? (top)*

LESSON 3
BASIC

Blending Sounds—Model for student: *Listen carefully. I am going to say some sounds slowly. I would like you to blend those sounds together and then tell me the word. The sounds are /d/ /r/ /o/ /p/. (Repeat the sounds.) What is the word? The word is drop.*
Words to practice: *flop, stop, shop, crop, and CVC words*

Substituting Sounds—Model for students: *Listen to the word sap. Let's change the /s/ sound to /ch/. What is the new word? I can blend the sounds /ch/ /ap/ together to*

make the word chap.*
Words to practice: *chap—change /ch/ to /y/ = yap; slap—change /s/ to /f/ = flap; flap—change /f/ to /k/ = clap*

MORE CHALLENGING
- *Say each sound you hear in the word snap. What are those sounds? (/s/ /n/ /a/ /p/)*
- *I want to tell you my secret word. It is /d/ /r/ /o/ /p/. (Repeat the sounds.) Blend the sounds together. What word can you make with the sounds? (drop)*
- *Listen to the word top. Change the /t/ sound to /sh/. What new word did you make? (shop)*

- *Say the word rap. Add the sound /t/ to the beginning of the word. What is the new word? (trap)*
- *Listen to the word flap. Change the /f/ sound to /k/. What new word did you make? (clap)*
- *Now listen to the word snap. Say the word snap without the /s/ sound. What is the new word? (nap)*
- *Listen to the sounds: /ch/ /a/ /p/. (Repeat the sounds.) Blend the sounds together. What word can you make with the sounds? (chap)*
- *Say the word stop. Now, say it without the /s/ sound. What is the new word? (top)*

Chop and Tap Words

To Parent:
Your child has been learning how to read words that end with "op" and "ap." In the zippered bag are two copies of the word cards.

Chop and Tap Words
How to play the game (two players):
- Cut out the word cards if needed and the Wild Cards on this paper. Mix up the cards and then deal the entire deck facedown to the players so that each has a pile.
- Each player takes the top two cards from his pile and places them faceup. If any of the words are from the same word family, the player "chops" (_op family) or "taps" (_ap family) that word card, reads it aloud correctly, and collects both cards. A match can also be made with one of the opponent's cards. Set aside the matches. Any cards not used should be returned to the bottom of the piles.
- Continue drawing cards from the pile until all of the matches have been made. The player who has the most matches wins the game. Watch out for the "Game over!" card. Then, the player who has collected the most word cards wins.

Read and Sort Words: Place all of the word cards in a small paper bag. Set aside the Game over! card and drop the remaining Wild Cards in the bag, too. Arrange the Word Family Labels in front of each player. Take turns drawing a card, reading the word out loud, and placing it in the corresponding word family. The first player to collect five cards for one of the word families wins the game.

Ready, Set, Read! Arrange all of the word cards in several rows on a table. Have your child read the words aloud for a practice run and then a second time at a faster speed!

Word Family Labels

Labels for Player A

_op Words

_ap Words

Labels for Player B

_op Words

_ap Words

Wild Cards

Draw and read
2 cards.

Draw and read
2 cards.

Lose a turn.

Lose a turn.

Game over!

MEET AND READ "-OT" AND "-IT" FAMILIES

Getting Started! Determine which letter-sound correspondences and letter patterns the student needs to practice.

• **Learning to Read CVC Words**—If the student cannot easily identify the phonemes for the consonants, use Day 1–5 activities. Otherwise, begin on Day 2. Select CVC words from the list. Start with about 10 words for the targeted practice on the first day. Add more words when the child is ready for a challenge.

• **Learning to Read CCVC Words**—If the student can read the three-letter words, provide lessons for sounding out and reading CCVC words. Select three days of activities. Introduce the digraph *sh* and consonant clusters with a tactile activity. During the lessons, include pairings of CVC and CCVC words to strengthen decoding skills (*hot* with *hit* or *shot*, *spot* with *spit*, *slot* with *blot* or *plot* or *slit*, *pot* with *spot* or *pit*, *lit* with *wit* or *slit*) and word-recognition fluency.

Word List				
cot*	not*	shot*	hit*	wit*
dot*	pot*	slot*	it*	flit*
got*	rot*	spot*	kit*	grit*
hot*	tot*	trot*	lit*	skit*
jot*	blot*	bit*	pit*	slit
lot*	plot*	fit*	sit*	spit*

*See pages 146, 147, 149 & 150 for reproducible word cards. Add to the set by printing slit on card stock.

DAY 1

Materials: Copy the pictures on pages 47 and 65. Follow the directions for the Molding Words and Pinching Letters activities on page 15.

• Show the pictures for *pit* and *cot*. Ask the child to tell you the beginning sound of each word (*pit* = /p/ and *cot* = /k/) and make the letters in clay. Continue the lesson by calling out other selected words. Let the child identify the beginning sounds and make the letters in clay to spell the words.
• Have students write the words.
• Pinching Letters (See page 15.)

DAY 2

Materials: Copy of letter cards (page 140) and word cards (pages 146, 147, 149, and 150); prepared mini-book

Use letters and selected word cards in the following activities:

• Show and use the words in sentences.
• Phonemic Awareness (See page 73.)
• Puffy Words—if tactile activity is needed (See page 15.)
• What's the Word? (See page 16.)
• Where Is . . . ? (See page 19.)
• Word Family Mini-Book (See page 20.)

DAY 3

Materials: Copy of letter cards (page 140), word cards (pages 146, 147, 149, and 150), truck mat (page 133) and monster mat (page 137)

Use letters and selected word cards in the following activities:

• Review and use words in sentences. (See Finish the Sentence, page 21.)
• Phonemic Awareness (See page 73.)
• Load the Truck (See page 17.)
• Mr. Word Muncher (See page 19.)
• Feed Mr. Word Muncher (See page 21.)

DAY 4

Materials: Copy of word cards (pages 146, 147, 149, and 150) and robot form (page 139); labeled plastic eggs and egg carton; materials for Yummy Words (page 20) and Clip, Read, 'n' Write (page 20)

Select word cards and use them in the following activities:

• Review and use words in sentences. (See Robot Writing!, page 21.)
• Phonemic Awareness (See page 73.)
• Pack the Words (See page 18.)
• Yummy Words (See page 20.)
• Clip, Read, 'n' Write (See page 20.)

DAY 5

Materials: Copy of word cards (pages 146, 147, 149, and 150); storybooks featuring -ot and -it words; self-adhesive flags (office supply item)

Select word cards and use them in the following activities:

• Read 'n' Spell Words (Take turns reading aloud a word to a partner who spells it.)
• Flag It!—Take turns reading aloud passages from classroom books that have -ot and -it words in the text. Each time a word-family word is used, mark it with a sticky flag.
• I Write, You Write! (See page 21.)

More Suggestions!

Spend a few minutes each day introducing or reviewing the -ot and -it word families by reading aloud passages (pointing to the words) from children's storybooks. Let students be word-family detectives and identify those words used in the text.

Read at Home Activity

Copy the take-home direction sheet (page 74) for each student. Include a copy of the selected word cards on card stock and two small paper bags. Place all of the materials in a zippered plastic bag.

Working with Sounds in "-ot" and "-it" Words

LESSON 1
BASIC

Isolating Initial Sounds—Model for your students: *Listen carefully. I am going to say a word. The word is* wit. *What is the first sound you hear in* wit? *The first sound is* /w/.
Words to practice: *Say the first sound you hear in . . .* lit, hit, bit, sit.

Blending Sounds—Model for your students: *Listen carefully. I am going to say the sounds slowly in my secret word. I would like you to blend those sounds together. The sounds are:* /n/ /o/ /t/. *What is the secret word? When I blend the sounds* /n/ /o/ /t/ *together, I hear the word* not.
Words to practice: *got, lot, cot, jot*

MORE CHALLENGING
- *Listen to the words:* pit, pot, jot. *Which words rhyme?* (pot, jot)
- *What word begins with* /h/ *and rhymes with* sit? (hit)
- *Listen closely because I want to tell you a secret word. It is* /g/ /o/ /t/. *Say the sounds with me:* /g/ /o/ /t/. *What is my secret word?* (got)
- *Listen to the words:* lit, lot, spit. *Which two words rhyme?* (lit, spit)
- *Here is another secret word for you.* It is /b/ /i/ /t/. *Say the sounds:* /b/ /i/ /t/. *What is my secret word?* (bit)
- *Say the word* kit. *How many sounds do you hear in the word* kit? (three) *Now, say the word without the* /k/ *sound. What is the new word?* (it)
- *Listen to the words:* trot, plot, grit. *Which two words rhyme?* (trot, plot)
- *Here is one more secret word for you. It is* /d/ /o/ /t/. *Say the sounds:* /d/ /o/ /t/. *What is the secret word?* (dot)

LESSON 2
BASIC

Segmenting Sounds—Model for your students: *Listen carefully. I would like you to tell me each sound you hear in a word. If the word is* shot, *what are the sounds? I would say* /sh/ /o/ /t/.
Words to practice: *Tell each sound you hear in . . .* tot, hot, dot, rot.

Adding Sounds—Model for your students: *Listen carefully. I am going to say a word and then add a sound to make a new word. My secret word rhymes with* it *and begins with the* /f/ *sound. What is* the word? (Repeat the sounds: /f/ /it/.) *The word is* fit.
Words to practice: *kit, pit, bit, hit*

MORE CHALLENGING
- *Say each sound you hear in the word* lot. *What are those sounds?* (/l/ /o/ /t/)
- *Listen closely because I want to tell you a secret word. It is* /n/ /o/ /t/. *Say the sounds with me:* /n/ /o/ /t/. *What is the secret word?* (not)
- *What word rhymes with* pit *and begins with* /k/? (kit)
- *Here's another word clue: This secret word begins with* /f/ *and ends with* it. *What is the word?* (fit)
- *Now think about the word* sit. *How many sounds do you hear in the word?* (three) *Stretch the sounds in the word.* (/sssss/ /iiiiii/ /t/)
- *Listen to the word* cot. *What word rhymes with* cot *and begins with* /t/? (tot)
- *What word begins with* /r/ *and ends with* /ot/? (rot)
- *Say each sound you hear in the word* wit. *What are those sounds?* (/w/ /i/ /t/)

LESSON 3
BASIC

Blending Sounds—Model for your students: *Listen carefully. I am going to say some sounds slowly. I would like you to blend those sounds together and then tell me the word. The sounds are* /s/ /k/ /i/ /t/. *(Repeat the sounds.) What is the word? The word is* skit.
Words to practice: *spit, grit, flit, slit, and CVC words*

Substituting Sounds—Model for your students: *Listen to the word* got. *Let's change the* /g/ *sound to* /sh/. *What is the new word? I can blend the sounds* /sh/ /ot/ *together to make the word* shot.
Words to practice: shot—change /sh/ to /l/ = lot; blot—change /b/ to /s/ = slot; slot—change /s/ to /p/ = plot

MORE CHALLENGING
- *Listen to the word* pot. *Change the* /p/ *sound to* /t/. *What new word did you make?* (tot)
- *I want to tell you my secret word. It is* /s/ /l/ /i/ /t/. *(Repeat the sounds.) Blend the sounds together. What word can you make with the sounds?* (slit)
- *Listen to the sounds:* /s/ /p/ /o/ /t/. *(Repeat the sounds.) Blend the sounds together. What word can you make with the sounds?* (spot)
- *Say the word* flit. *Now, say it without the* /f/ *sound. What is the new word?* (lit)
- *This time say the word* skit. *Now, say it without the* /s/ *sound. What is the new word?* (kit) *Is this a real word?* (yes)
- *Say the word* pit. *Add the sound* /s/ *to the beginning of the word. What is the new word?* (spit)
- *Say the sounds* /g/ /r/ /i/ /t/. *(Repeat the sounds.) Blend the sounds together. What word can you make with the sounds?* (grit)
- *Listen to the word* lot. *Add the sound* /s/ *to the beginning of the word. What new word did you make?* (slot)

- 73 -

"Hot" Words

To Parent:
Your child has been learning how to read words that end with "ot" and "it." In the zippered bag are two copies of the word cards along with two small paper bags. Please roll down the edges of one of the bags to form a small bowl shape for a "fire pit." Have your child decorate it with red flames. If you have a play firefighter hat, let your child wear it while doing these activities!

Hot Words
How to play the game (two players):

- Cut out the word cards if needed and the Wild Cards on this page. Place all of the cards in a paper bag.
- Take turns with your child drawing a card and reading the word out loud. If the word ends with "ot," it is a "hot" word, and the player should say "ouch" before setting it down. (Those words could be placed in the fire pit!) If the word ends with "it," set it near the fire pit because it is not "hot."
- The first player to read six cards correctly wins the game. Watch out for the "Game over!" card. Then, the player who has collected the most word cards wins.

Read and Sort Words: Place all of the word cards in a small paper bag. Set aside the Game over! card and drop the remaining Wild Cards in the bag, too. Arrange the Word Family Labels in front of each player. Take turns drawing a card, reading the word out loud, and placing it in the corresponding word family. The first player to collect five cards for one of the word families wins the game.

Ready, Set, Read! Arrange all of the word cards in several rows on a table. Have your child read the words aloud as a practice run and then a second time at a faster speed!

Word Family Labels

Labels for Player A

_ot Words

_it Words

Labels for Player B

_ot Words

_it Words

Wild Cards

Draw and read 2 cards.

Cold day! Stand near the fire. Lose a turn.

Cold day! Stand near the fire. Lose a turn.

Draw and read 2 cards.

Game over!

MEET AND READ "-OG" AND "-IG" FAMILIES

Getting Started! Determine which letter-sound correspondences and letter patterns the student needs to practice.

- **Learning to Read CVC Words**—If the student cannot easily identify the phonemes for the consonants, use Day 1–5 activities. Otherwise, begin on Day 2. Select CVC words from the list. Start with about 10 words for the targeted practice on the first day. Add more words when the child is ready for a challenge.

- **Learning to Read CCVC Words**—If the student can read the three-letter words, provide lessons for sounding out and reading CCVC words. Select three days of activities. Introduce the consonant clusters with a tactile activity. During the lessons, include pairings of CVC and CCVC words to strengthen decoding skills (*bog* with *big*, *dog* with *dig*, *fig* with *fog*, *jig* with *jog*, *big* with *brig*, *log* with *clog* or *cog*, *fog* with *frog*, *wig* with *swig* or *twig*, *rig* with *brig*) and word-recognition fluency.

Word List			
bog*	log*	fig*	zig*
cog*	clog*	gig*	brig*
dog*	frog*	jig*	swig*
fog*	smog*	pig*	twig*
hog*	big*	rig*	
jog*	dig*	wig*	

*See pages 148 & 150 for reproducible word cards.

DAY 1

Materials: Copy the pictures on pages 53 and 68. Follow the directions for the Molding Words and Pinching Letters activities on page 15.

- Show the pictures for *dog* and *wig*. Ask the child to tell you the beginning sound of each word (*dog* = /d/ and *wig* = /w/) and make the letters in clay. Continue the lesson by calling out other selected words. Let the child identify the beginning sounds and make the letters in clay to spell the words.
- Have students write the words.
- Pinching Letters (See page 15.)

DAY 2

Materials: Copy of letter cards (page 140), word cards (pages 148 and 150), and stone wall mat (page 130); materials for "Sticky" Words (page 19); prepared mini-book

Use letters and selected word cards in the following activities:

- Show and read the words.
- Phonemic Awareness (See page 76.)
- Puffy Words—if tactile activity is needed (See page 15.)
- Letters on Stones (See page 16.)
- "Sticky" Words (See page 19.)
- Word Family Mini-Book (See page 20.)

DAY 3

Materials: Copy of word cards (pages 148 and 150); labeled plastic eggs and egg carton; materials for Yummy Words (page 20) and Clip, Read, 'n' Write (page 20)

Use letters and selected word cards in the following activities:

- Review and use words in sentences. (See Finish the Sentence, page 21.)
- Phonemic Awareness (See page 76.)
- Pack the Words (See page 18.)
- Yummy Words (See page 20.)
- Clip, Read, 'n' Write (See page 20.)

DAY 4

Materials: Copy of letter cards (page 140), word cards (pages 148 and 150), robot form (page 139), playing catch mat (page 134), and tree house mat (page 136)

Use letters and selected word cards in the following activities:

- Review and use words in sentences. (See Robot Writing!, page 21.)
- Phonemic Awareness (See page 76.)
- Catch High-Flying Sounds (See page 18.)
- Read 'n' Climb to See the View (See page 19.)
- Write Down—Back to the Ground (See page 21.)

DAY 5

Materials: Copy of word cards (pages 148 and 150); storybooks featuring *-og* and *-ig* words; self-adhesive flags (office supply item)

Select word cards and use them in the following activities:

- Read 'n' Spell Words (Take turns reading aloud a word to a partner who spells it.)
- Flag It!—Take turns reading aloud passages from classroom books that have *-og* and *-ig* words in the text. Each time a word-family word is used, mark it with a sticky flag.
- I Write, You Write! (See page 21.)

More Suggestions!

Spend a few minutes each day introducing or reviewing the *-og* and *-ig* word families by reading aloud passages (pointing to the words) from children's storybooks. Let students be word-family detectives and identify those words used in the text.

Read at Home Activity

Copy the take-home direction sheet (page 77) for each student. Include two copies of the word cards on card stock and a paper bag. Place all of the materials in a zippered plastic bag.

Working with Sounds in "-og" and "-ig" Words

LESSON 1
BASIC
Isolating Initial Sounds—Model for your students: *Listen carefully. I am going to say a word. The word is jog. What is the first sound you hear in jog? The first sound is /j/.* Words to practice: *Say the first sound you hear in . . .* bog, log, dog, fog.

Blending Sounds—Model for your students: *Listen carefully. I am going to say the sounds slowly in my secret word. I would like you to blend those sounds together. The sounds are: /f/ /i/ /g/. What is the secret*

word? *When I blend the sounds /f/ /i/ /g/ together, I hear the word* fig. Words to practice: *zig, dig, jig, big, fig*

MORE CHALLENGING
- *Listen to the words:* gig, fog, fig. *Which words rhyme?* (gig, fig)
- *What word begins with /d/ and rhymes with* jig? (dig)
- *Listen closely because I want to tell you a secret word. It is /w/ /i/ /g/. Say the sounds with me: /w/ /i/ /g/. What is my secret word?* (wig)
- *Listen to the words:* rig, twig, cog. *Which words rhyme?* (rig, twig)
- *Here is another secret word for*

you. *It is /b/ /o/ /g/. Say the sounds: /b/ /o/ /g/. What is my secret word?* (bog)
- *Say the word* rig. *How many sounds do you hear in* rig? *Hold up your fingers to show me the number.* (three) *Now, say the word without the /r/ sound. What is the silly word?* (ig)
- *Listen to the words:* brig, bog, smog. *Which words rhyme?* (bog, smog)
- *What word begins with /h/ and rhymes with the word* dog? (hog)

LESSON 2
BASIC
Segmenting Sounds—Model for your students: *Listen carefully. I would like you to tell me each sound you hear in a word. If the word is* wig, *what are the sounds? I would say /w/ /i/ /g/.*
Words to practice: *Tell each sound you hear in . . .* rig, pig, gig, dig.

Adding Sounds—Model for your students: *Listen carefully. I am going to say a word and then add a sound to make a new word. My secret word rhymes with* dog *and begins with the /k/ sound. What*

is the word? *(Repeat the sounds: /k/ /og/.) The word is* cog.
Words to practice: *log, fog, jog, dog*

MORE CHALLENGING
- *What word rhymes with* jig *and begins with /p/?* (pig)
- *Say each sound you hear in the word* jig. *What are those sounds?* (/j/ /i/ /g/)
- *Now think about the word* dog. *How many sounds do you hear in the word?* (three) *Stretch the sounds in the word.* (/d/ /oooooo/ /g/)
- *What word begins with /j/ and ends with /ig/?* (jig)

- *Listen closely because I want to tell you a secret word. It is /f/ /o/ /g/. Say the sounds with me: /f/ /o/ /g/. What is the secret word?* (fog)
- *Say each sound you hear in the word* big. *What are those sounds?* (/b/ /i/ /g/)
- *Listen to the word* dog. *What word rhymes with* dog *and begins with /k/?* (cog)
- *Here's another word clue: This secret word begins with /b/ and rhymes with the word* dog. *What is the word?* (bog)

LESSON 3
BASIC
Blending Sounds—Model for your students: *Listen carefully. I am going to say some sounds slowly. I would like you to blend those sounds together and then tell me the word. The sounds are /s/ /m/ /o/ /g/. (Repeat the sounds.) What is the word? The word is* smog.
Words to practice: *frog, clog,* and CVC words

Substituting Sounds—Model for your students: *Listen to the word* big. *Let's change the /b/ sound to /r/. What is the new word? I can blend the sounds /r/ /ig/ together to*

make the word rig.
Words to practice: *rig*—change /r/ to /w/ = *wig; swig*—change /s/ to /t/ = *twig; pig*—change /p/ to /g/ = *gig*

MORE CHALLENGING
- *Say each sound you hear in the word* frog. *What are those sounds?* (/f/ /r/ /o/ /g/)
- *I want to tell you my secret word. It is /j/ /i/ /g/. (Repeat the sounds.) Blend the sounds together. What word can you make with the sounds?* (jig)
- *Listen to the word* wig. *Change the /w/ sound to /z/. What new word did you make?* (zig)

- *Say the word* rig. *Add the sound /b/ to the beginning of the word. Now, what is the new word?* (brig)
- *Listen to the word* jog. *Change the /j/ sound to /l/. What new word did you make?* (log)
- *Now listen to the word* twig. *Say the word* twig *without the /t/ sound. What is the new word?* (wig)
- *Listen to the sounds: /s/ /m/ /o/ /g/. Blend the sounds together. What word can you make with the sounds?* (smog)
- *Listen to the sounds: /k/ /l/ /o/ /g/. Blend the sounds together. What word can you make with the sounds?* (clog)

Jogging with Words

To Parent:
Your child has been learning how to read words that end with "og" and "ig." In the zippered bag you will find two copies of each word along with a paper bag. Please provide two game markers.

Jogging with Words
How to play the game (two players):
- Cut out the word cards if needed and the Wild Cards on this page. Choose two word cards and draw smiley faces in front of the words to make "Extra Special Word Cards." Cut out the Game Bag Label below and glue it to the paper bag. Put all of the cards in the paper bag.
- Take turns drawing a card from the bag, reading the word, and moving a game marker to the next box. If the card is not read correctly, the player returns the card to the paper bag. If an "Extra Special Word Card" is drawn, the player moves a game marker ahead two boxes after reading the selected word correctly.
- The first player who jogs to the wall and back to the start position wins the game. Watch out for the "Game over!" card because that means the player who is ahead wins the game!

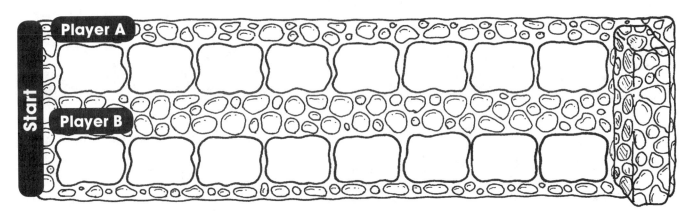

Player A

Start

Player B

Game Bag Label

Jogging with Words

Wild Cards

Draw and read 2 cards.

Hot day! Stop for water. Lose a turn.

Hot day! Stop for water. Lose a turn.

Draw and read 2 cards.

Game over!

MEET AND READ THE "-ET" FAMILY

Getting Started! Determine which letter-sound correspondences and letter patterns the student needs to practice.

- **Learning to Read CVC Words**—If the student cannot easily identify the phonemes for the consonants *b, g, j, l, m, n, p,* and *s,* use Day 1–5 activities. Otherwise, begin on Day 2. Select CVC words from the list. Start with about six words for the targeted practice on the first day. Add more words and the letter-sound relationship for *v, w,* and *y* when the child is ready for a challenge.

- **Learning to Read CCVC Words**—If the student can read the three-letter words, provide lessons for sounding out and reading CCVC words. Select three days of activities. Introduce the digraph *ch* and consonant cluster *fr* with a tactile activity. During the lessons, include pairings of CVC and CCVC words (and words from other word families) to strengthen decoding skills (*jet* or *yet* with *Chet, bet* with *fret*) and word-recognition fluency.

Word List

bet*	net*	yet*
get*	pet*	Chet*
jet*	set*	fret*
let*	vet*	
met*	wet*	

*See page 151 for reproducible word cards.

DAY 1

Materials: Copy the pictures on page 80. Follow the directions for the Molding Words activity on page 15.

- Show the pictures for *jet* and *vet.* Ask the child to tell you the beginning sound of each word (*jet* = /j/ and *vet* = /v/) and make the letter in clay. Continue the lesson by calling out other *-et* words. Have the child identify the beginning sounds and make the letters in clay to spell the words.
- To teach CCVC words, form the letters for the digraph, blend, and rimes in clay.
- Have students write the words.

DAY 2

Materials: Copy of letter cards (page 140), word cards (page 151), and racetrack billboard mat (page 131); prepared mini-book

Use letters and selected word cards in the following activities:

- Show and read the words
- Phonemic Awareness (See page 79.)
- Puffy Words—if tactile activity is needed (See page 15.)
- Rev Up for Words (See page 17.)
- Where Is . . . ? (See page 19.)
- Word Family Mini-Book (See page 20.)

DAY 3

Materials: Copy of letter cards (page 140), word cards (page 151); playing catch scene mat (page 134), and tree house mat (page 136)

Use letters and selected word cards in the following activities:

- Review and use words in sentences. (See Finish the Sentence, page 21.)
- Phonemic Awareness (See page 79.)
- Catch High-Flying Sounds (See page 18.)
- Read 'n' Climb to See the View (See page 19.)
- Write Down—Back to the Ground (See page 21.)

DAY 4

Materials: Copy of letter cards (page 140), word cards (page 151), robot form (page 139), safe mat (page 135), and monster mat (page 137)

Use letters and selected word cards in the following activities:

- Review and use words in sentences. (See Robot Writing!, page 21.)
- Phonemic Awareness (See page 79.)
- Unlock the Code (See page 18.)
- Mr. Word Muncher (See page 19.)
- Feed Mr. Word Muncher (See page 21.)

DAY 5

Materials: Copy of word cards (page 151); children's storybook featuring *-et* words; self-adhesive flags (office supply item)

Select word cards and use them in the following activities:

- Read 'n' Spell Words (Take turns reading aloud a word to a partner who spells it.)
- Flag It!—Take turns reading aloud a passage from a classroom book that has *-et* words in the text. Each time a word-family word is used, mark it with a sticky flag. (Draw attention to the rime *-et.*)
- I Write, You Write! (See page 21.)

More Suggestions!

Spend a few minutes each day introducing or reviewing the *-et* word family by reading aloud passages (pointing to the words) from children's storybooks. Let students be word-family detectives and identify those words used in the text.

Read at Home Activity

Copy the take-home direction sheet (page 80) for each student. Include two copies of the word cards on card stock along with a die. Place the materials in a zippered plastic bag.

- 78 - *Beginning Reader Intervention Activities*

Working with Sounds in "-et" Words

LESSON 1
BASIC

Isolating Initial Sounds—Model for your students: *Listen carefully. I am going to say a word. The word is jet. What is the first sound you hear in jet? The first sound is /j/.*
Words to practice: *Say the first sound you hear in . . .* set, get, met, pet.

Blending Sounds—Model for your students: *Listen carefully. I am going to say the sounds slowly in my secret word. I would like you to blend those sounds together. The sounds are: /w/ /e/ /t/. What is the secret word? When I blend the sounds /w/ /e/ /t/ together, I hear the word* wet.
Words to practice: *bet, yet, let, net*

MORE CHALLENGING
- *Listen to the words:* bet, net, not. *Which words rhyme?* (bet, net)
- *What word begins with /m/ and rhymes with* jet? (met)
- *Listen closely because I want to tell you a secret word. It is /p/ /e/ /t/. Say the sounds with me: /p/ /e/ /t/. What is my secret word?* (pet)
- *Listen to the words:* led, get, let. *Which two words rhyme?* (get, let)
- *Here is another secret word for you. It is /w/ /e/ /t/. Say the sounds: /w/ /e/ /t/. What is my secret word?* (wet)
- *Say the word* bet. *How many sounds do you hear in the word* bet? (three) *Now, say the word without the /b/ sound. What is the silly word?* (et)
- *Listen to the words:* jet, sat, set. *Which two words rhyme?* (jet, set)
- *Here is one more secret word for you. It is /g/ /e/ /t/. Say the sounds: /g/ /e/ /t/. What is the secret word?* (get)

LESSON 2
BASIC

Segmenting Sounds—Model for your students: *Listen carefully. I would like you to tell me each sound you hear in a word. If the word is* set, *what are the sounds? I would say /s/ /e/ /t/.*
Words to practice: *Tell each sound you hear in . . .* jet, yet, pet, get.

Adding Sounds—Model for your students: *Listen carefully. I am going to say a word and then add a sound to make a new word. My secret word rhymes with* set *and begins with the /v/ sound. What is the word? (Repeat the sounds: /v/ /et/.) The word is* vet.
Words to practice: *let, wet, net, bet, met*

MORE CHALLENGING
- *Say each sound you hear in the word* get. *What are those sounds?* (/g/ /e/ /t/)
- *Listen closely because I want to tell you a secret word. It is /s/ /e/ /t/. Say the sounds with me: /s/ /e/ /t/. What is the secret word?* (set)
- *What word rhymes with* jet *and begins with /y/?* (yet)
- *Here's another word clue: This secret word begins with /n/ and rhymes with the word* jet. *What is the word?* (net)
- *Now think about the word* jet. *How many sounds do you hear in the word?* (three) *Stretch the sounds in the word.* (/j/ /eeeeee/ /t/)
- *Listen to the word* net. *What word rhymes with* net *and begins with /l/?* (let)
- *What word begins with /b/ and rhymes with* let? (bet)
- *Say each sound you hear in the word* met. *What are those sounds?* (/m/ /e/ /t/)

LESSON 3
BASIC

Blending Sounds—Model for your students: *Listen carefully. I am going to say some sounds slowly. I would like you to blend those sounds together and then tell me the word. The sounds are /ch/ /e/ /t/. (Repeat the sounds.) What is the word? The word is* Chet.
Words to practice: *fret* and words from other word families

Substituting Sounds—Model for your students: *Listen to the name* Chet. *Let's change the /ch/ sound to /y/. What is the new word? I can blend the sounds /y/ /et/ together to make the word* yet.
Words to practice: *yet*—change /y/ to /j/ = jet; *let*—change /l/ to /w/ = wet; *vet*—change /v/ to /g/ = get

MORE CHALLENGING
- *Listen to the word* wet. *Change the /w/ sound to /ch/. What new word did you make?* (Chet)
- *I want to tell you my secret word. It is /n/ /e/ /t/. (Repeat the sounds.) Blend the sounds together. What word can you make with the sounds?* (net)
- *Listen to the sounds: /b/ /e/ /t/. (Repeat the sounds.) Blend the sounds together. What word can you make with the sounds?* (bet)
- *Say the word* Chet. *Now, say it without the /ch/ sound. What is the silly word?* (et)
- *This time say the word* fret. *Now, say it without the /f/ sound. What is the new word?* (Rhett) *Is this a real word?* (yes)
- *Say the sounds /m/ /e/ /t/. (Repeat the sounds.) Blend the sounds together. What word can you make with the sounds?* (met)
- *Say /et/. Add the sound /l/ to the beginning of /et/. What is the word?* (let)
- *Listen to the word* jet. *Change the /j/ sound to /v/. What new word did you make?* (vet)

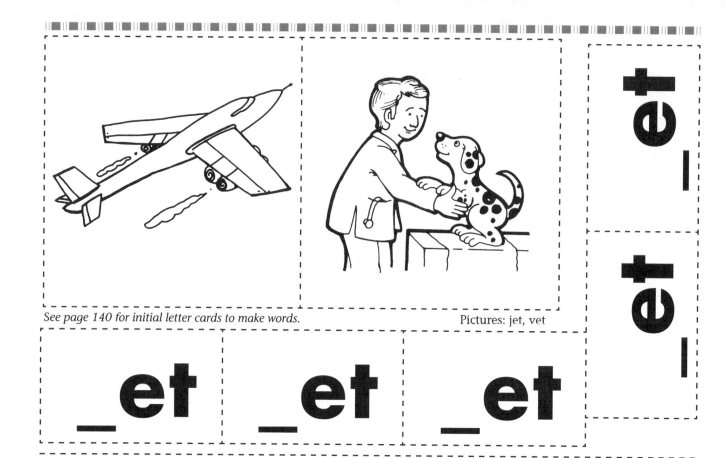

See page 140 for initial letter cards to make words.

Pictures: jet, vet

_et   _et   _et

et et

Read at Home—the "_et" Word Family

Rolling Out a Sentence

To Parent:
Your child has been learning how to read words that end with "et." Please use the word cards and die to play the following game. You will need to provide a sheet of paper and pencil.

Rolling Out a Sentence
How to play the game:
- Cover each face of the die with a small piece of masking tape.
- Choose five "et" words and write them on the die. On the sixth face, write the word *jet*.
- Have your child roll the die and record the word on a sheet of paper. Do this again two more times.
- Then, let your child use the three words in a sentence that can be silly or factual. Record the sentence for your child.
- Continue playing the game as time and interest allow. When you are finished, invite your child to read the sentences that were generated for additional reading practice.

Ready, Set, Read! Have your child read the word cards aloud as a practice run and then a second time at a faster speed!

Reading for Fun: Take turns with your child reading aloud passages from children's storybooks.

MEET AND READ THE "-EN" FAMILY

Getting Started! Determine which letter-sound correspondences and letter patterns the student needs to practice.

• **Learning to Read CVC Words**—If the student cannot easily identify the phonemes for the consonants *b, d, h, k, m, p, t,* and *y,* use Day 1–5 activities. Otherwise, begin on Day 2. Select CVC words from the list. Start with about six words for the targeted practice on the first day. Add more words when the child is ready for a challenge.

• **Learning to Read CCVC Words**—If the student can read the three-letter words, provide lessons for sounding out and reading CCVC words. Select three days of activities. Introduce the digraphs *ch, th,* and *wh,* the silent-letter pair *wr,* and the consonant cluster with a tactile activity. During the lessons, include CVC words (and words from other word families) to strengthen decoding skills (*hen* with *Chen* or *when, when* with *wren, ten* with *then*) and word-recognition fluency.

Word List		
Ben	**pen***	**then***
den*	**ten***	**when***
hen*	**yen***	**wren**
Ken*	**Chen***	
men*	**Glen***	

*See page 151 for reproducible word cards. Add to the set by printing other words on card stock.

DAY 1

Materials: Copy the pictures on page 83. Follow the directions for the Molding Words activity on page 15.

• Show the pictures for *hen* and *pen.* Ask the child to tell you the beginning sound of each word (*hen* = /h/ and *pen* = /p/) and make the letter in clay. Continue the lesson by calling out other *-en* words. Have the child identify the beginning sounds and make the letters in clay to spell the words.
• To teach CCVC words, form the letters for the digraphs, blend, and rimes in clay.
• Have students write the words.

DAY 2

Materials: Copy of letter cards (page 140), word cards (page 151), and launch pad mat (page 132); "Sticky" Words materials (page 19); prepared mini-book

Use letters and selected word cards in the following activities:

• Show and read the words.
• Phonemic Awareness (See page 82.)
• Puffy Words—if tactile activity is needed (See page 15.)
• Blast Off! (See page 17.)
• "Sticky" Words (See page 19.)
• Word Family Mini-Book (See page 20.)

DAY 3

Materials: Copy of letter cards (page 140), word cards (page 151), safe mat (page 135), and monster mat (page 137)

Use letters and selected word cards in the following activities:

• Review and use words in sentences. (See Finish the Sentence, page 21.)
• Phonemic Awareness (See page 82.)
• Unlock the Code (See page 18.)
• Mr. Word Muncher (See page 19.)
• Feed Mr. Word Muncher (See page 21.)

DAY 4

Materials: Copy of letter cards (page 140), word cards (page 151), robot form (page 139), and truck mat (page 133); materials for Yummy Words (page 20) and Clip, Read, 'n' Write (page 20)

Use letters and selected word cards in the following activities:

• Review and use words in sentences. (See Robot Writing!, page 21.)
• Phonemic Awareness (See page 82.)
• Load the Truck (See page 17.)
• Yummy Words (See page 20.)
• Clip, Read, 'n' Write (See page 20.)

DAY 5

Materials: Copy of word cards (page 151); children's storybook featuring *-en* words; self-adhesive flags (office supply item)

Select word cards and use them in the following activities:

• Read 'n' Spell Words (Take turns reading aloud a word to a partner who spells it.)
• Flag It!—Take turns reading aloud a passage from a classroom book that has *-en* words in the text. Each time a word-family word is used, mark it with a sticky flag. (Draw attention to the rime *-en.*)
• I Write, You Write! (See page 21.)

More Suggestions!

Spend a few minutes each day introducing or reviewing the *-en* word family by reading aloud passages (pointing to the words) from children's storybooks. Let students be word-family detectives and identify those words used in the text.

Read at Home Activity

Copy the take-home direction sheet and hen picture (page 83) for each student. Include two copies of the word cards on card stock. Place the materials in a zippered plastic bag.

Working with Sounds in "-en" Words

LESSON 1
BASIC

Isolating Initial Sounds—Model for your students: *Listen carefully. I am going to say a word. The word is men. What is the first sound you hear in men? The first sound is /m/.* Words to practice: *Say the first sound you hear in . . .* den, ten, Ken.

Blending Sounds—Model for your students: *Listen carefully. I am going to say the sounds slowly in my secret word. I would like you to blend those sounds together. The sounds are: /h/ /e/ /n/. What is the secret word? When I blend the* sounds /h/ /e/ /n/ together, I hear the word hen. Words to practice: *Ben, yen, pen*

MORE CHALLENGING
- *Listen to the words:* dip, den, ten. *Which words rhyme?* (den, ten)
- *What word begins with /m/ and rhymes with ten?* (men)
- *Listen closely because I want to tell you a secret word. It is /y/ /e/ /n/. Say the sounds with me: /y/ /e/ /n/. What is my secret word?* (yen)
- *Listen to the words:* then, big, Ben. *Which words rhyme?* (then, Ben)

- *Here is another secret word for you. It is /h/ /e/ /n/. Say the sounds: /h/ /e/ /n/. What is my secret word?* (hen)
- *Listen to the words:* pen, hen, pad. *Which words rhyme?* (pen, hen)
- *Say the word* men. *How many sounds do you hear in men? Hold up your fingers to show me the number.* (three) *Now, say the word without the /m/ sound. What is the silly word?* (en)
- *What word begins with /d/ and rhymes with the word* ten? (den)

LESSON 2
BASIC

Segmenting Sounds—Model for your students: *Listen carefully. I would like you to tell me each sound you hear in a word. If the word is* Chen, *what are the sounds? I would say /ch/ /e/ /n/.* Words to practice: *Tell each sound you hear in . . .* pen, ten, then.

Adding Sounds—Model for your students: *Listen carefully. I am going to say a word and then add a sound to make a new word. My secret word rhymes with* Chen *and begins with the /d/ sound. What* is the word? (Repeat the sounds: /d/ /en/.) *The word is* den. Words to practice: *Ben, hen, yen*

MORE CHALLENGING
- *What word rhymes with* ten *and begins with /h/?* (hen)
- *Say each sound you hear in the word* Ken. *What are those sounds?* (/k/ /e/ /n/)
- *Now think about the word* then. *How many sounds do you hear in the word?* (three) *Stretch the sounds in the word.* (/th/ /eeeeee/ /nnnnnn/)
- *What word begins with /b/ and rhymes with* ten? (Ben)

- *Listen closely because I want to tell you a secret word. It is /t/ /e/ /n/. Say the sounds with me: /t/ /e/ /n/. What is the secret word?* (ten)
- *Say each sound you hear in the word* pen. *What are those sounds?* (/p/ /e/ /n/)
- *Listen to the word* ten. *What word rhymes with* ten *and begins with /d/?* (den)
- *Here's another word clue: This secret word begins with /m/ and rhymes with the word* ten. *What is the word?* (men)

LESSON 3
BASIC

Blending Sounds—Model for your students: *Listen carefully. I am going to say some sounds slowly. I would like you to blend those sounds together and then tell me the word. The sounds are /g/ /l/ /e/ /n/.* (Repeat the sounds.) *What is the word? The name is* Glen. Words to practice: *Chen, then, when,* and CVC words

Substituting Sounds—Model for your students: *Listen to the word* then. *Let's change the /th/ sound to /k/. What is the new word? I can blend the sounds /k/ /en/ together* to make the name Ken. Words to practice: *Ken—change /k/ to /b/ = Ben; Ben—change /b/ to /ch/ = Chen; Chen—change /ch/ to /wh/ = when*

MORE CHALLENGING
- *Say each sound you hear in the word* when. *What are those sounds?* (/wh/ /e/ /n/)
- *I want to tell you my secret word. It is /y/ /e/ /n/.* (Repeat the sounds.) *Blend them together. What word can you make with the sounds?* (yen)
- *Listen to the word* yen. *Change the /y/ sound to /k/. What new word did you make?* (Ken)

- *Say the name* Ken. *Change the /k/ sound to /th/. What new word did you make?* (then)
- *Listen to the word* when. *Change the /wh/ sound to /t/. What new word did you make?* (ten)
- *Say each sound you hear in the word* Glen. *What are those sounds?* (/g/ /l/ /e/ /n/)
- *Listen to the sounds: /h/ /e/ /n/.* (Repeat the sounds.) *Blend them together. What word can you make with the sounds?* (hen)
- *Say the word* Glen. *Now, say it without the /g/ sound. What is the silly word?* (len)

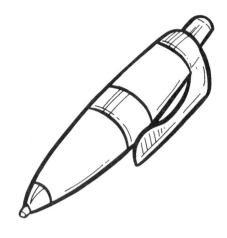

en

See page 140 for initial letter cards to make words.

Pictures: hen, pen

_en **_en** **_en**

_en

Read at Home—the "_en" Word Family

Where Is the Hen?

To Parent:
Your child has been learning how to read words that end with "en." In the zippered bag are two copies of the word cards and a picture of a hen. Please provide a blue pen and a black pen for the activity.

Where Is the Hen?
How to play the game:
- Cut out the phrase cards.
- Set both pens on the playing area.
- Turn the cards facedown.
- Have your child turn over a phrase card and read it aloud.
- Ask your child to show what the phrase means using one of the pens and the picture of the hen.

Ready, Set, Read! Have your child read the word cards aloud as a practice run and then a second time at a faster speed!

hen on a pen

hen near the blue pen

hen by the black pen

hen under a pen

hen not by a pen

MEET AND READ THE "-ED" FAMILY

Getting Started! Determine which letter-sound correspondences and letter patterns the student needs to practice.

- **Learning to Read CVC Words**—If the student cannot easily identify the phonemes for the consonants *b, f, l, n, r, t,* and *w,* use Day 1–5 activities. Otherwise, begin on Day 2. Select CVC words from the list. Start with about six words for the targeted practice on the first day. Add more words when the child is ready for a challenge.

- **Learning to Read CCVC Words**—If the student can read the three-letter words, provide lessons for sounding out and reading CCVC words. Select three days of activities. Introduce the digraph *sh* and consonant clusters with a tactile activity. During the lessons, include pairings of CVC and CCVC words to strengthen decoding skills (*fed* or *red* with *Fred, bed* with *bled, led* with *sled* or *bled, bed* with *sped*) and word-recognition fluency.

Word List		
bed*	red*	Fred*
Ed	Ted*	shed*
fed*	wed*	sled*
led*	bled*	sped*
Ned	fled*	

*See page 152 for reproducible word cards. Add to the set by printing other words on card stock.

DAY 1

Materials: Copy the picture for *bed* on page 86. Follow the directions for the Molding Words activity on page 15.

- Show the picture for *bed.* Ask the child to tell you the beginning sound of the word (*bed* = /b/) and make the letter in clay. Continue the lesson by calling out other *-ed* words. Have the child identify the beginning sounds and make the letters in clay to spell the words.
- To teach CCVC words, form the letters for the digraph, blends, and rimes in clay.
- Have students write the words.

DAY 2

Materials: Copy of letter cards (page 140) and word cards (page 152); prepared mini-book

Use letters and selected word cards in the following activities:

- Show and use the words in sentences.
- Phonemic Awareness (See page 85.)
- Puffy Words—if tactile activity is needed (See page 15.)
- What's the Word? (See page 16.)
- Where Is . . . ? (See page 19.)
- Word Family Mini-Book (See page 20.)

DAY 3

Materials: Copy of letter cards (page 140), word cards (page 152), and truck mat (page 133); materials for Yummy Words (page 20) and Clip, Read, 'n' Write (page 20)

Use letters and selected word cards in the following activities:

- Review and use words in sentences. (See Finish the Sentence, page 21.)
- Phonemic Awareness (See page 85.)
- Load the Truck (See page 17.)
- Yummy Words (See page 20.)
- Clip, Read, 'n' Write (See page 20.)

DAY 4

Materials: Copy of word cards (page 152) and robot form (page 139); labeled plastic eggs and egg carton; copy of tree house mat (page 136)

Select word cards and use them in the following activities:

- Review and use words in sentences. (See Robot Writing!, page 21.)
- Phonemic Awareness (See page 85.)
- Pack the Words (See page 18.)
- Read 'n' Climb to See the View (See page 19.)
- Write Down—Back to the Ground (See page 21.)

DAY 5

Materials: Copy of word cards (page 152); children's storybook featuring *-ed* words; self-adhesive flags (office supply item)

Select word cards and use them in the following activities:

- Read 'n' Spell Words (Take turns reading aloud a word to a partner who spells it.)
- Flag It!—Take turns reading aloud a passage from a classroom book that has *-ed* words in the text. Each time a word-family word is used, mark it with a sticky flag. (Draw attention to the rime *-ed.*)
- I Write, You Write! (See page 21.)

More Suggestions!

Spend a few minutes each day introducing or reviewing the *-ed* word family by reading aloud passages (pointing to the words) from children's storybooks. Let students be word-family detectives and identify those words used in the text.

Read at Home Activity

Copy the take-home direction sheet (page 86) for each student. Include copies of each word card on card stock in two different colors. Place all of the materials in a zippered plastic bag.

Working with Sounds in "-ed" Words

LESSON 1
BASIC
Isolating Initial Sounds—Model for your students: *Listen carefully. I am going to say a word. The word is bed. What is the first sound you hear in bed? The first sound is /b/.* Words to practice: *Say the first sound you hear in . . . Ted, led, wed.*

Blending Sounds—Model for your students: *Listen carefully. I am going to say the sounds slowly in my secret word. I would like you to blend those sounds together. The sounds are: /f/ /e/ /d/. What is the secret word? When I blend the sounds /f/*

LESSON 2
BASIC
Segmenting Sounds—Model for your students: *Listen carefully. I would like you to tell me each sound you hear in a word. If the word is Ted, what are the sounds? I would say /t/ /e/ /d/.*
Words to practice: *Tell each sound you hear in . . . led, Ned, shed.*

Adding Sounds—Model for your students: *Listen carefully. I am going to say a word and then add a sound to make a new word. My secret word rhymes with Ed and begins with the /r/ sound. What*

LESSON 3
BASIC
Blending Sounds—Model for your students: *Listen carefully. I am going to say some sounds slowly. I would like you to blend those sounds together and then tell me the word. The sounds are /s/ /p/ /e/ /d/. (Repeat the sounds.) What is the word? The word is sped.*
Words to practice: *sled, fled, Fred, shed, bled, and CVC words*

Substituting Sounds—Model for your students: *Listen to the word led. Let's change the /l/ sound to /sh/. What is the new word? I can blend the sounds /sh/ /ed/ together*

/e/ /d/ *together, I hear the word* fed. Words to practice: *red, wed, shed*

MORE CHALLENGING
- *Listen to the words:* bed, bad, Ned. *Which words rhyme?* (bed, Ned)
- *What word begins with /f/ and rhymes with* red? (fed)
- *Listen closely because I want to tell you a secret word. It is /b/ /e/ /d/. Say the sounds with me: /b/ /e/ /d/. What is my secret word?* (bed)
- *Listen to the words:* fun, fed, led. *Which two words rhyme?* (fed, led)

is the word? (Repeat the sounds: /r/ /ed/.) *The word is* red.
Words to practice: *fed, wed, bed*

MORE CHALLENGING
- *Say each sound you hear in the word* fed. *What are those sounds?* (/f/ /e/ /d/)
- *Listen closely because I want to tell you a secret word. It is /w/ /e/ /d/. Say the sounds with me: /w/ /e/ /d/. What is the secret word?* (wed)
- *What word rhymes with* red *and begins with /b/?* (bed)
- *Here's another word clue: This secret word begins with /sh/ and*

to make the word shed.
Words to practice: *shed*—change /sh/ to /t/ = *Ted; sled*—change /s/ to /f/ = *fled; fled*—change /f/ to /b/ = *bled*

MORE CHALLENGING
- *Listen to the word* bled. *Change the /b/ sound to /f/. What new word did you make?* (fled)
- *I want to tell you my secret word. It is /sh/ /e/ /d/. (Repeat the sounds.) Blend the sounds together. What word can you make with the sounds?* (shed)
- *Listen to the sounds: /s/ /p/ /e/ /d/. (Repeat the sounds.) Blend the sounds together. What word can you make with the sounds?* (sped)

- *Here is another secret word for you. It is /n/ /e/ /d/. Say the sounds: /n/ /e/ /d/. What is my secret word?* (Ned)
- *Say the word* led. *How many sounds do you hear in the word* led? (three) *Now, say the word without the /l/ sound. What is the new word?* (Ed)
- *Listen to the words:* red, wed, run. *Which two words rhyme?* (red, wed)
- *Here is one more secret word for you. It is /t/ /e/ /d/. Say the sounds: /t/ /e/ /d/. What is the secret word?* (Ted)

rhymes with the word red. *What is the word?* (shed)
- *Now think about the word* red. *How many sounds do you hear in the word?* (three) *Stretch the sounds in the word.* (/rrrrrr/ /eeeeee/ /d/)
- *Listen to the word* shed. *What word rhymes with* shed *and begins with /t/?* (Ted)
- *What name begins with /n/ and ends with* ed? (Ned)
- *Say each sound you hear in the word* led. *What are those sounds?* (/l/ /e/ /d/)

- *Say the word* shred. *Now, say it without the /sh/ sound. What is the new word?* (red)
- *This time say the word* sled. *Now, say it without the /s/ sound. What is the new word?* (led) *Is this a real word?* (yes)
- *Say the word* red. *Add the sound /f/ to the beginning of the word. What is the name?* (Fred)
- *Say the word* led. *Add the sound /b/ to the beginning of the word. What is the new word?* (bled)
- *Listen to the word* bed. *Change the /b/ sound to /t/. What new word did you make?* (Ted)

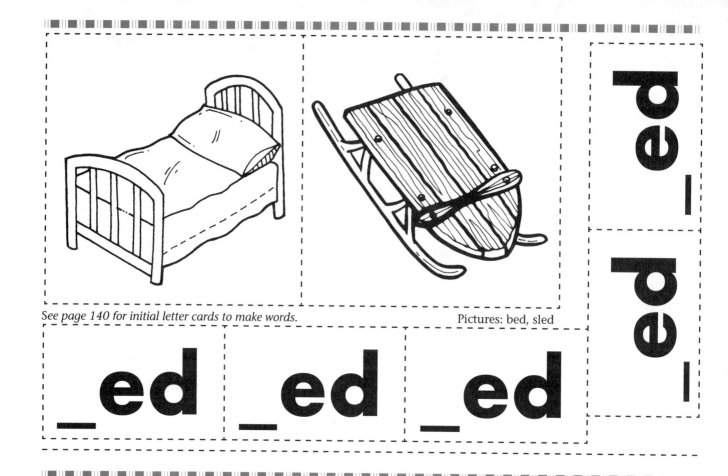

See page 140 for initial letter cards to make words.

Pictures: bed, sled

_ed _ed _ed   _ed _ed

Match and Read

To Parent:
Your child has been learning how to read words that end with "ed." In the zippered bag you will find word cards in two different colors.

Match and Read
How to play the game:
- Cut out the word cards if needed. Sort them into two groups by color.
- Scatter the first set of cards faceup in the center of the playing area.
- Give the second set of cards to your child.
- Have your child find the matching pairs and read each word. You may also take turns finding the matching pairs to keep the activity game-like.

Ready, Set, Read! Arrange all of the word cards in several rows on a table. Have your child read the words aloud as a practice run and then a second time at a faster speed!

READ THE "-EN" AND "-AN" FAMILIES

Getting Started! Determine which letter-sound correspondences and letter patterns the student needs to practice.

• **Learning to Read CVC Words**—If the student cannot easily identify the phonemes for the consonants, use Day 1–5 activities. Otherwise, begin on Day 2. Select CVC words from the list. Start with about 10 words for the targeted practice on the first day. Add more words when the child is ready for a challenge.

• **Learning to Read CCVC Words**—If the student can read the three-letter words, provide lessons for sounding out and reading CCVC words. Select three days of activities. Introduce the digraphs *th*, *wh*, and *ch* and consonant clusters with a tactile activity. During the lessons, include pairings of CVC and CCVC words to strengthen decoding skills (*den* with *Dan*, *men* with *man*, *hen* with *when* or *Chen*, *ban* with *bran*, *can* with *clan* or *scan*, *pen* with *pan*, *pan* with *plan* or *span*, *tan* with *than*, *ten* with *then*) and word-recognition fluency.

Word List				
Ben	ten*	wren	man*	clan*
den*	yen*	an	pan*	plan*
hen*	Chen*	ban	ran*	scan*
Ken*	Glen*	can*	tan*	span*
men*	then*	Dan*	van*	than*
pen*	when*	fan*	bran*	

*See pages 143, 144 & 151 for reproducible word cards. Add to the set by printing other words on card stock.

DAY 1

Materials: Copy the pictures on pages 29 and 83. Follow the directions for the Molding Words and Pinching Letters activities on page 15.

• Show the pictures for *van* and *hen*. Ask the child to tell you the beginning sound of each word (*van* = /v/ and *hen* = /h/) and make the letters in clay. Continue the lesson by calling out other selected words. Let the child identify the beginning sounds and make the letters in clay to spell the words.
• Have students write the words.
• Pinching Letters (See page 15.)

DAY 2

Materials: Copy of letter cards (page 140), word cards (pages 143, 144, and 151), and stone wall mat (page 130); "Sticky" Words materials (page 19); prepared mini-book

Use letters and selected word cards in the following activities:

• Show and read the words.
• Phonemic Awareness (See page 88.)
• Puffy Words—if tactile activity is needed (See page 15.)
• Letters on Stones (See page 16.)
• "Sticky" Words (See page 19.)
• Word Family Mini-Book (See page 20.)

DAY 3

Materials: Copy of word cards (pages 143, 144, and 151); labeled plastic eggs and egg carton; copy of tree house mat (page 136)

Select word cards and use them in the following activities:

• Review and use words in sentences. (See Finish the Sentence, page 21.)
• Phonemic Awareness (See page 88.)
• Pack the Words (See page 18.)
• Read 'n' Climb to See the View (See page 19.)
• Write Down—Back to the Ground (See page 21.)

DAY 4

Materials: Copy of letter cards (page 140), word cards (pages 143, 144, and 151), robot form (page 139), playing catch mat (page 134), and monster mat (page 137)

Use letters and selected word cards in the following activities:

• Review and use words in sentences. (See Robot Writing!, page 21.)
• Phonemic Awareness (See page 88.)
• Catch High-Flying Sounds (See page 18.)
• Mr. Word Muncher (See page 19.)
• Feed Mr. Word Muncher (See page 21.)

DAY 5

Materials: Copy of word cards (pages 143, 144, and 151); storybook featuring *-en* and *-an* words; self-adhesive flags (office supply item)

Select word cards and use them in the following activities:

• Read 'n' Spell Words (Take turns reading aloud a word to a partner who spells it.)
• Flag It!—Take turns reading aloud a passage from a classroom book that has *-en* and *-an* words in the text. Each time a word-family word is used, mark it with a sticky flag.
• I Write, You Write! (See page 21.)

More Suggestions!

Spend a few minutes each day introducing or reviewing the *-en* and *-an* word families by reading aloud passages (pointing to the words) from children's storybooks. Let students be word-family detectives and identify those words used in the text.

Read at Home Activity

Copy the take-home direction sheet (page 89) for each student. Include a copy of the word cards and a small paper bag. Place all of the materials in a zippered plastic bag.

Working with Sounds in "-en" and "-an" Words

LESSON 1
BASIC
Isolating Initial Sounds—Model for your students: *Listen carefully. I am going to say a word. The word is when. What is the first sound you hear in when? The beginning sound is /wh/.*
Words to practice: *Say the first sound you hear in . . . Ken, men, yen, den.*

Blending Sounds—Model for your students: *Listen carefully. I am going to say the sounds slowly in my secret word. I would like you to blend those sounds together. The* sounds are: /p/ /a/ /n/. What is the secret word? When I blend the sounds /p/ /a/ /n/ together, I hear the word pan.
Words to practice: *van, fan, plan, man, ban*

MORE CHALLENGING
- *Listen to the words: man, men, Ken. Which words rhyme? (men, Ken)*
- *What word begins with /th/ and rhymes with an? (than)*
- *Listen closely because I want to tell you a secret word. It is /d/ /e/ /n/. Say the sounds with me: /d/ /e/ /n/. What is my secret word? (den)*

- *Listen to the words: Dan, den, plan. Which words rhyme? (Dan, plan)*
- *Here is another secret word for you. It is /p/ /e/ /n/. Say the sounds: /p/ /e/ /n/. What is my secret word? (pen)*
- *Listen to the words: when, Glen, glad. Which words rhyme? (when, Glen)*
- *Say the word ran. How many sounds do you hear in ran? Hold up your fingers to show me the number. (three) Now, say the word without the /r/ sound. What is the new word? (an)*
- *What name begins with /b/ and rhymes with the word den? (Ben)*

LESSON 2
BASIC
Segmenting Sounds—Model for your students: *Listen carefully. I would like you to tell me each sound you hear in a word. If the word is span, what are the sounds? I would say /s/ /p/ /a/ /n/.*
Words to practice: *Tell each sound you hear in . . . ran, bran, than, pan.*

Adding Sounds—Model for your students: *Listen carefully. I am going to say a word and then add a sound to make a new word. My secret word rhymes with ten and* begins with the /p/ sound. What is the word? (Repeat the sounds: /p/ /en/.) The word is pen.
Words to practice: *Ben, hen, Chen, yen*

MORE CHALLENGING
- *What word rhymes with pen and begins with /t/? (ten)*
- *Say each sound you hear in the word then. What are those sounds? (/th/ /e/ /n/)*
- *Now think about the word plan. How many sounds do you hear in the word? (four) Stretch the sounds in the word. (/p/ /lllll/ /aaaaaa/ /nnnnnn/)*

- *What word begins with /k/ and rhymes with pen? (Ken)*
- *Listen closely because I want to tell you a secret word. It is /f/ /a/ /n/. Say the sounds with me: /f/ /a/ /n/. What is the secret word? (fan)*
- *Say each sound you hear in the word tan. What are those sounds? (/t/ /a/ /n/)*
- *Listen to the word can. What word rhymes with can and begins with /p/? (pan)*
- *Here's another word clue: This secret word begins with /th/ and rhymes with the word ten. What is the word? (then)*

LESSON 3
BASIC
Blending Sounds—Model for your students: *Listen carefully. I am going to say some sounds slowly. I would like you to blend those sounds together and then tell me the word. The sounds are /th/ /e/ /n/. (Repeat the sounds.) What is the word? The word is then.*
Words to practice: *when, Chen, Glen, and CVC words*

Substituting Sounds—Model for your students: *Listen to the word van. Let's change the /v/ sound to /th/. What is the new word? I can blend the sounds /th/ /an/ together* to make the word than.
Words to practice: *than—change /th/ to /t/ = tan; ran—change /r/ to /b/ = ban; clan—change /k/ to /p/ = plan*

MORE CHALLENGING
- *Say each sound you hear in the name Chen. What are those sounds? (/ch/ /e/ /n/)*
- *I want to tell you my secret word. It is /g/ /l/ /e/ /n/. (Repeat the sounds.) Blend the sounds together. What name can you make with the sounds? (Glen)*
- *Listen to the word plan. Change the /p/ sound to /k/. What new word did you make? (clan)*

- *Say the word an. Add the sound /th/ to the beginning of the word. Now, what is the new word? (than)*
- *Listen to the word pan. Add the /s/ sound to the beginning of the word. What new word did you make? (span)*
- *Now listen to the word bran. Say the word bran without the /b/ sound. What is the new word? (ran)*
- *Listen to the sounds: /wh/ /e/ /n/. Blend them together. What word can you make with the sounds? (when)*
- *Say the word scan. Now, say it without the /s/ sound. What is the new word? (can)*

By the Pen or in the Pan?

To Parent:
Your child has been learning how to read words that end with "en" or "an." Along with the word cards and small paper bag that have been provided, please supply a small frying pan and a writing pen for this activity.

By the Pen or in the Pan?
How to play the game (two players):
• Cut out the word cards if needed and the Wild Cards on this paper. Cut out the Game Bag Label below and glue it to the front of the paper bag. Drop all of the cards into the paper bag.
• Ask your child to choose either the pen (for _en words) or the pan (for _an words).
• Take turns with your child drawing a card without looking in the bag and reading the word out loud. If the selected word belongs in the player's chosen word family, set the card near the corresponding object. If not, return the card to the bag. Watch out for the Wild Cards.
• The first player to collect five word cards wins the game.

Ready, Set, Read! Arrange all of the word cards on a table. Have your child read the words aloud as a practice run and then a second time at a faster speed!

Wild Cards

Draw and read 2 cards.

Ouch! Hot pan! Lose a turn.

Pen is broken. Lose a turn.

Draw and read 3 cards.

Draw and read 2 cards.

Put 2 cards back in the bag.

Game Bag Label

Which Word Family? "_en" or "_an"

MEET AND READ THE "-EM," "-ED," AND "-ID" FAMILIES

Getting Started! Determine which letter-sound correspondences and letter patterns the student needs to practice.

• **Learning to Read CVC Words**—If the student cannot easily identify the phonemes for the consonants, use Day 1–5 activities. Otherwise, begin on Day 2. Select CVC words from the list. Start with about 10 words for the targeted practice on the first day. Add more words when the child is ready for a challenge.

• **Learning to Read CCVC Words**—If the student can read the three-letter words, provide lessons for sounding out and reading CCVC words. Select three days of activities. Introduce the digraphs *th* and *sh* and consonant clusters with a tactile activity. During the lessons, include pairings of CVC and CCVC words to strengthen decoding skills (*hem* with *them*, *led* with *fled* or *sled*, *bed* with *bled*, *red* with *Fred*, *rid* with *grid*, *lid* with *slid*, *kid* with *skid*, *fed* with *fled*) and word-recognition fluency.

Word List				
gem*	fed*	bled*	bid*	rid*
hem*	led*	fled*	did*	grid*
stem*	Ned	Fred*	hid*	skid*
them*	red*	shed*	kid*	slid*
bed*	Ted*	sled*	lid*	
Ed	wed*	sped*	mid*	

See pages 148 & 152 for reproducible word cards. Add to the set by printing other words on card stock.

DAY 1

Materials: Copy the pictures on pages 56, 86, and 92. Follow the directions for the Molding Words and Pinching Letters activities on page 15.

• Show the pictures for *hid*, *bed*, and *gem*. Ask the child to tell you the beginning sound of each word (*hid* = /h/, *bed* = /b/, and *gem* = /j/) and make the letters in clay. Continue the lesson by calling out other selected words. Let the child identify the beginning sounds and make the letters in clay to spell the words.
• Have students write the words.
• Pinching Letters (See page 15.)

DAY 2

Materials: Copy of letter cards (page 140) and word cards (pages 148 and 152); racetrack billboard mat (page 131); prepared mini-book

Use letters and selected word cards in the following activities:

• Show and read the words.
• Phonemic Awareness (See page 91.)
• Puffy Words—if tactile activity is needed (See page 15.)
• Rev Up for Words (See page 17.)
• Where Is . . . ? (See page 19.)
• Word Family Mini-Book (See page 20.)

DAY 3

Materials: Copy of letter cards (page 140), word cards (pages 148 and 152), playing catch mat (page 134), and monster mat (page 137)

Use letters and selected word cards in the following activities:

• Review and use words in sentences. (See Finish the Sentence, page 21.)
• Phonemic Awareness (See page 91.)
• Catch High-Flying Sounds (See page 18.)
• Mr. Word Muncher (See page 19.)
• Feed Mr. Word Muncher (See page 21.)

DAY 4

Materials: Copy of letter cards (page 140), word cards (pages 148 and 152), robot form (page 139), and safe mat (page 135); materials for Yummy Words (page 20) and Clip, Read, 'n' Write (page 20)

Use letters and selected word cards in the following activities:

• Review and use words in sentences. (See Robot Writing!, page 21.)
• Phonemic Awareness (See page 91.)
• Unlock the Code (See page 18.)
• Yummy Words (See page 20.)
• Clip, Read, 'n' Write (See page 20.)

DAY 5

Materials: Copy of word cards (pages 148 and 152); storybooks featuring *-em*, *-ed*, and *-id* words; self-adhesive flags (office supply item)

Select word cards and use them in the following activities:

• Read 'n' Spell Words (Take turns reading aloud a word to a partner who spells it.)
• Flag It!—Take turns reading aloud passages from classroom books that have *-em*, *-ed*, and *-id* words in the text. Each time a word-family word is used, mark it with a sticky flag.
• I Write, You Write! (See page 21.)

More Suggestions!

Spend a few minutes each day introducing or reviewing the *-em*, *-ed*, and *-id* word families by reading aloud passages (pointing to the words) from storybooks. Let students be word-family detectives and identify those words used in the text.

Read at Home Activity

Copy the take-home direction sheet (page 92) for each student. Include one or two copies of the selected word cards on card stock. Place all of the materials in a zippered plastic bag.

Working with Sounds in "-em," "-ed," and "-id" Words

LESSON 1
BASIC
Isolating Initial Sounds—Model for your students: *Listen carefully. I am going to say a word. The word is kid. What is the first sound you hear in kid? The first sound is /k/.* Words to practice: *Say the first sound you hear in . . .* them, did, gem, lid, hem.

Blending Sounds—Model for your students: *Listen carefully. I am going to say the sounds slowly in my secret word. I would like you to blend those sounds together. The sounds are: /sh/ /e/ /d/. What is* the secret word? *When I blend the sounds /sh/ /e/ /d/ together, I hear the word* shed. Words to practice: *fed, wed, sped, Ned, Fred*

MORE CHALLENGING
- *Listen to the words:* kid, shed, Ted. *Which words rhyme?* (shed, Ted)
- *What word begins with /n/ and rhymes with* bed? (Ned)
- *Listen closely because I want to tell you a secret word. It is /k/ /i/ /d/. Say the sounds with me: /k/ /i/ /d/. What is my secret word?* (kid)
- *Listen to the words:* lid, let, skid. *Which two words rhyme?* (lid, skid)
- *Here is another secret word for you. It is /th/ /e/ /m/. Say the sounds: /th/ /e/ /m/. What is my secret word?* (them)
- *Say the word* skid. *How many sounds do you hear in the word* skid? (four) *Now, say the word without the /s/ sound. What is the new word?* (kid)
- *Listen to the words:* gem, hid, hem. *Which two words rhyme?* (gem, hem)
- *Here is one more secret word for you. It is /w/ /e/ /d/. Say the sounds: /w/ /e/ /d/. What is the secret word?* (wed)

LESSON 2
BASIC
Segmenting Sounds—Model for your students: *Listen carefully. I would like you to tell me each sound you hear in a word. If the word is* them, *what are the sounds? I would say /th/ /e/ /m/.* Words to practice: *Tell each sound you hear in . . .* Ted, stem, red, sled.

Adding Sounds—Model for your students: *Listen carefully. I am going to say a word and then add a sound to make a new word. My secret word rhymes with* kid *and begins with the /l/ sound. What* is the word? (Repeat the sounds: /l/ /id/.) *The word is* lid. Words to practice: *mid, rid, bid, hid*

MORE CHALLENGING
- *Say each sound you hear in the word* bed. *What are those sounds?* (/b/ /e/ /d/)
- *Listen closely because I want to tell you a secret word. It is /j/ /e/ /m/. Say the sounds with me: /j/ /e/ /m/. What is the secret word?* (gem)
- *What word rhymes with* did *and begins with /h/?* (hid)
- *Here's another word clue: This secret word begins with /r/ and* rhymes with the word bed. *What is the word?* (red)
- *Now think about the word* hem. *How many sounds do you hear in the word?* (three) *Stretch the sounds in the word.* (/hhhhh/ /eeeee/ /mmmmm/)
- *Listen to the word* bed. *What word rhymes with* bed *and begins with /l/?* (led)
- *What word begins with /k/ and ends with /id/?* (kid)
- *Say each sound you hear in the word* did. *What are those sounds?* (/d/ /i/ /d/)

LESSON 3
BASIC
Blending Sounds—Model for your students: *Listen carefully. I am going to say some sounds slowly. I would like you to blend those sounds together and then tell me the word. The sounds are /s/ /t/ /e/ /m/.* (Repeat the sounds.) *What is the word? The word is* stem. Words to practice: *them, grid, skid, slid, and other words*

Substituting Sounds—Model for your students: *Listen to the word* shed. *Let's change the /sh/ sound to /f/. What is the new word? I can blend the sounds /f/ /ed/ together to make the word* fed.

Words to practice: *fed*—change /f/ to /l/ = *led*; *sled*—change /s/ to /b/ = *bled*; *bled*—change /b/ to /f/ = *fled*

MORE CHALLENGING
- *Listen to the word* fled. *Change the /f/ sound to /s/. What new word did you make?* (sled)
- *I want to tell you my secret word. It is /s/ /k/ /i/ /d/.* (Repeat the sounds.) *Blend the sounds together. What word can you make with the sounds?* (skid)
- *Listen to the sounds: /g/ /r/ /i/ /d/.* (Repeat the sounds.) *Blend the sounds together. What word can you make with the sounds?* (grid)
- *Say the word* red. *Add the sound /sh/ to the beginning of the word. What is the new word?* (shred)
- *This time say the word* Fred. *Now, say it without the /f/ sound. What is the new word?* (red)
- *Say the sounds /s/ /t/ /e/ /m/.* (Repeat the sounds.) *Blend them together. What word can you make with the sounds?* (stem)
- *Say the word* lid. *Add the sound /s/ to the beginning of the word. What is the new word?* (slid)
- *Listen to the word* hem. *Change the /h/ sound to /th/. What new word did you make?* (them)

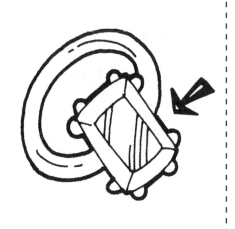

_em _em _em

_em
_em
_em

See page 140 for initial letter cards. Find pictures for -ed words on page 86 and -id words on page 56.

To Parent:
Please supply each player with 10 game markers (paper clips in two colors, coins, etc.).

Read at Home: Three in a Row!

(Game for two players)

- Cut out the word cards and place them facedown in a pile.
- Take turns drawing a card and reading the word. Cover a corresponding space on the grid.
- The first player to cover three spaces in a row ↑, →, ↗, or ↘ wins the game.

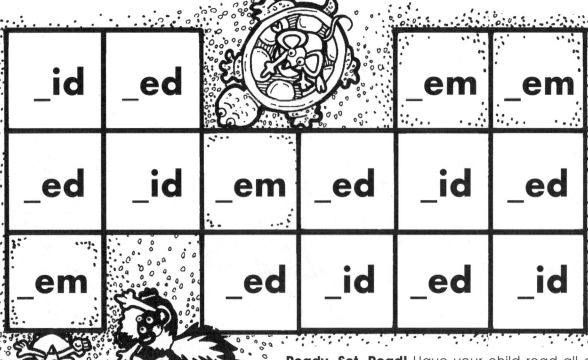

_id	_ed		_em	_em
_ed	_id	_em	_ed	_id	_ed
_em		_ed	_id	_ed	_id

Ready, Set, Read! Have your child read all of the word cards aloud at a fast pace.

KE-804110 © Carson-Dellosa - 92 - *Beginning Reader Intervention Activities*

MEET AND READ THE "-EG," "-ET," AND "-OT" FAMILIES

Getting Started! Determine which letter-sound correspondences and letter patterns the student needs to practice.

• **Learning to Read CVC Words**—If the student cannot easily identify the phonemes for the consonants, use Day 1–5 activities. Otherwise, begin on Day 2. Select CVC words from the list. Start with about 10 words for the targeted practice on the first day. Add more words when the child is ready for a challenge.

• **Learning to Read CCVC Words**—If the student can read the three-letter words, provide lessons for sounding out and reading CCVC words. Select three days of activities. Introduce the digraphs *ch* and *sh* and consonant clusters with a tactile activity. During the lessons, include pairings of CVC and CCVC words to strengthen decoding skills (*beg* with *bet*, *Meg* with *met*, *peg* with *pet*, *get* with *got*, *let* with *lot*, *net* with *not*, *pet* with *pot*, *pot* with *spot*, *rot* with *tot* or *trot*) and word-recognition fluency.

Word List				
beg*	let*	yet*	jot*	plot*
leg*	met*	Chet*	lot*	shot*
Meg*	net*	fret*	not*	slot*
peg*	pet*	cot*	pot*	spot*
bet*	set*	dot*	rot*	trot*
get*	vet*	got*	tot*	
jet*	wet*	hot*	blot*	

*See pages 149–152 for reproducible word cards.

DAY 1

Materials: Copy the pictures on pages 65, 80, and 95. Follow the directions for the Molding Words and Pinching Letters activities on page 15.

• Show the pictures for *hot*, *jet*, and *leg*. Ask the child to tell you the beginning sound of each word (*hot* = /h/, *jet* = /j/, and *leg* = /l/) and make the letters in clay. Continue the lesson by calling out other selected words. Let the child identify the beginning sounds and make the letters in clay to spell the words.
• Have students write the words.
• Pinching Letters (See page 15.)

DAY 2

Materials: Copy of letter cards (page 140), word cards (pages 149–152), and launch pad mat (page 132); "Sticky" Words materials (page 19); prepared mini-book

Use letters and selected word cards in the following activities:

• Show and read the words.
• Phonemic Awareness (See page 94.)
• Puffy Words—if tactile activity is needed (See page 15.)
• Blast Off! (See page 17.)
• "Sticky" Words (See page 19.)
• Word Family Mini-Book (See page 20.)

DAY 3

Materials: Copy of letter cards (page 140), word cards (pages 149–152), and safe mat (page 135); materials for Yummy Words (page 20) and Clip, Read, 'n' Write (page 20)

Use letters and selected word cards in the following activities:

• Review and use words in sentences. (See Finish the Sentence, page 21.)
• Phonemic Awareness (See page 94.)
• Unlock the Code (See page 18.)
• Yummy Words (See page 20.)
• Clip, Read, 'n' Write (See page 20.)

DAY 4

Materials: Copy of letter cards (page 140), word cards (pages 149–152), robot form (page 139); truck mat (page 133), and tree house mat (page 136)

Use letters and selected word cards in the following activities:

• Review and use words in sentences. (See Robot Writing!, page 21.)
• Phonemic Awareness (See page 94.)
• Load the Truck (See page 17.)
• Read 'n' Climb to See the View (See page 19.)
• Write Down—Back to the Ground (See page 21.)

DAY 5

Materials: Copy of word cards (pages 149–152); children storybooks featuring -*eg*, -*et*, and -*ot* words; self-adhesive flags (office supply item)

Select word cards and use them in the following activities:

• Read 'n' Spell Words (Take turns reading aloud a word to a partner who spells it.)
• Flag It!—Take turns reading aloud passages from classroom books that have -*eg*, -*et*, and -*ot* words in the text. Each time a word-family word is used, mark it with a sticky flag.
• I Write, You Write! (See page 21.)

More Suggestions!

Spend a few minutes each day introducing or reviewing the -*eg*, -*et*, and -*ot* word families by reading aloud passages (pointing to the words) from children's storybooks. Let students be word-family detectives and identify those words used in the text.

Read at Home Activity

Copy the take-home direction sheet (page 95) for each student. Include two copies of the word cards on card stock. (*Note:* Need eight -*eg* word cards in the set.) Place all of the materials in a zippered plastic bag.

Working with Sounds in "-eg," "-et," and "-ot" Words

LESSON 1
BASIC

Isolating Initial Sounds—Model for your students: *Listen carefully. I am going to say a word. The word is beg. What is the first sound you hear in beg? The first sound is /b/.* Words to practice: *Say the first sound you hear in . . .* Chet, pet, leg, wet, Meg.

Blending Sounds—Model for your students: *Listen carefully. I am going to say the sounds slowly in my secret word. I would like you to blend those sounds together. The sounds are: /s/ /p/ /o/ /t/. What is*

the secret word? When I blend the sounds /s/ /p/ /o/ /t/. together, I hear the word spot.
Words to practice: *peg, dot, blot, tot, leg, not*

MORE CHALLENGING
- *Listen to the words:* met, Meg, wet. *Which words rhyme?* (met, wet)
- *What word begins with /d/ and rhymes with cot?* (dot)
- *Listen closely because I want to tell you a secret word. It is /j/ /e/ /t/. Say the sounds with me: /j/ /e/ /t/. What is my secret word?* (jet)
- *Listen to the words:* jet, jot, got.

Which words rhyme? (jot, got)
- *Here is another secret word for you. It is /p/ /e/ /g/. Say the sounds: /p/ /e/ /g/. What is my secret word?* (peg)
- *Listen to the words:* Meg, beg, bag. *Which words rhyme?* (Meg, beg)
- *Say the word spot. How many sounds do you hear in spot? Hold up your fingers to show me the number.* (four) *Now, say the word without the /s/ sound. What is the new word?* (pot)
- *What word begins with /r/ and rhymes with the word cot?* (rot)

LESSON 2
BASIC

Segmenting Sounds—Model for your students: *Listen carefully. I would like you to tell me each sound you hear in a word. If the word is* got, *what are the sounds? I would say /g/ /o/ /t/.*
Words to practice: *Tell each sound you hear in . . .* jot, beg, cot, hot, peg.

Adding Sounds—Model for your students: *Listen carefully. I am going to say a word and then add a sound to make a new word. My secret word rhymes with* pet *and*

begins with the /m/ sound. What is the word? (Repeat the sounds: /m/ /et/.) The word is met.
Words to practice: *set, net, jet, yet*

MORE CHALLENGING
- *What word rhymes with* cot *and begins with /n/?* (not)
- *Say each sound you hear in the word* rot. *What are those sounds?* (/r/ /o/ /t/)
- *Now think about the word* leg. *How many sounds do you hear in the word?* (three) *Stretch the sounds in the word.* (/lllllll/ /eeeeee/ /g/)
- *What word begins with /t/ and*

rhymes with cot? (tot)
- *Listen closely because I want to tell you a secret word. It is /ch/ /e/ /t/. Say the sounds with me: /ch/ /e/ /t/. What is the secret word?* (Chet)
- *Say each sound you hear in the word* shot. *What are those sounds?* (/sh/ /o/ /t/)
- *Listen to the word* leg. *What word rhymes with* leg *and begins with /p/?* (peg)
- *Here's another word clue: This secret word begins with /p/ and rhymes with the word* jet. *What is the word?* (pet)

LESSON 3
BASIC

Blending Sounds—Model for your students: *Listen carefully. I am going to say some sounds slowly. I would like you to blend those sounds together and then tell me the word. The sounds are /t/ /r/ /o/ /t/. (Repeat the sounds.) What is the word? The word is* trot.
Words to practice: *fret, Chet, spot, blot, and other words*

Substituting Sounds—Model for your students: *Listen to the word* cot. *Let's change the /k/ sound to /r/. What is the new word? I can blend the sounds /r/ /ot/ together to*

make the word rot.
Words to practice: *rot—change /r/ to /sh/ = shot; Meg—change /m/ to /p/ = peg; plot—change /p/ to /s/ = slot*

MORE CHALLENGING
- *Say each sound you hear in the name* Meg. *What are those sounds?* (/m/ /e/ /g/)
- *I want to tell you my secret word. It is /s/ /p/ /o/ /t/. (Repeat the sounds.) Blend the sounds together. What word can you make with the sounds?* (spot)
- *Listen to the word* met. *Change the /m/ sound to /g/. What new word did you make?* (get)

- *Say the word* pot. *Add the sound /s/ to the beginning of the word. Now, what is the new word?* (spot)
- *Listen to the word* yet. *Change the /y/ sound to /b/. What new word did you make?* (bet)
- *Now listen to the word* rot. *Add the sound /t/ to the beginning of the word. What is the new word?* (trot)
- *Listen to the sounds: /f/ /r/ /e/ /t/. (Repeat the sounds.) Blend the sounds together. What word can you make with the sounds?* (fret)
- *Say the word* blot. *Now, say it without the /b/ sound. What is the new word?* (lot)

See page 140 for initial letter cards. Find pictures for -et words on page 80 and -ot words on page 65.

Pictures: leg, peg

_eg _eg _eg _eg _eg

To Parent: Please provide three game markers (paper clips in three colors, dried pasta pieces, etc.).

Read at Home: Race to the Boat!

• Cut out the word cards and set them facedown in a pile.
• Place a game marker on each animal.
• Take turns drawing a card and reading the word. Each time, move the corresponding game marker ahead one space.
• The first animal to reach the boat wins the game.

Ready, Set, Read! Have your child read all of the word cards aloud at a fast pace.

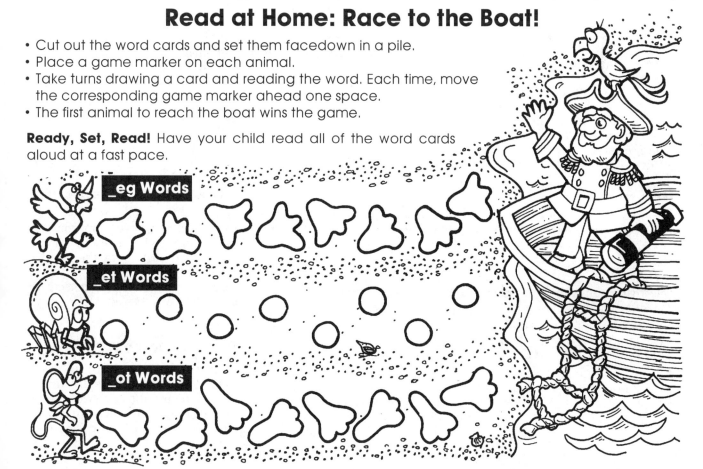

_eg Words

_et Words

_ot Words

MEET AND READ THE "-UG" FAMILY

Getting Started! Determine which letter-sound correspondences and letter patterns the student needs to practice.

• **Learning to Read CVC Words**—If the student cannot easily identify the phonemes for the consonants *b, d, h, j, l, m, p, r,* and *t,* use Day 1–5 activities. Otherwise, begin on Day 2. Select CVC words from the list. Start with about six words for the targeted practice on the first day. Add words from word families previously studied as a review when the child is ready for a challenge.

• **Learning to Read CCVC Words**—If the student can read the three-letter words, provide lessons for sounding out and reading CCVC words. Select three days of activities. Introduce the digraph *ch* and consonant clusters with a tactile activity. During the lessons, include CVC words (and words from other word families) to strengthen decoding skills (*lug* with *plug* or *slug*, *mug* with *smug*, *hug* with *chug*) and word-recognition fluency.

Word List

bug*	mug*	plug*
dug*	pug	slug*
hug*	rug*	smug
jug*	tug*	snug*
lug*	chug*	

See page 153 for reproducible word cards. Add to the set by printing other words on card stock.

DAY 1

Materials: Copy the pictures on page 98. Follow the directions for the Molding Words activity on page 15.

• Show the pictures for *bug* and *mug.* Ask the child to tell you the beginning sound of each word (*bug* = /b/, *mug* = /m/) and make the letter in clay. Continue the lesson by calling out other *-ug* words. Have the child identify the beginning sounds and make the letters in clay to spell the words.
• To teach CCVC words, form the letters for the digraph, blends, and rimes in clay.
• Have students write the words.

DAY 2

Materials: Copy of letter cards (page 140) and word cards (page 153); prepared mini-book

Use letters and selected word cards in the following activities:

• Show and use the words in sentences.
• Phonemic Awareness (See page 97.)
• Puffy Words—if tactile activity is needed (See page 15.)
• What's the Word? (See page 16.)
• Where Is . . . ? (See page 19.)
• Word Family Mini-Book (See page 20.)

DAY 3

Materials: Copy of letter cards (page 140), word cards (page 153), truck mat (page 133), and tree house mat (page 136)

Use letters and selected word cards in the following activities:

• Review and use words in sentences. (See Finish the Sentence, page 21.)
• Phonemic Awareness (See page 97.)
• Load the Truck (See page 17.)
• Read 'n' Climb to See the View (See page 19.)
• Write Down—Back to the Ground (See page 21.)

DAY 4

Materials: Copy of word cards (page 153) and robot form (page 139); labeled plastic eggs and egg carton; copy of monster mat (page 137)

Select word cards and use them in the following activities:

• Review and use words in sentences. (See Robot Writing!, page 21.)
• Phonemic Awareness (See page 97.)
• Pack the Words (See page 18.)
• Mr. Word Muncher (See page 19.)
• Feed Mr. Word Muncher (See page 21.)

DAY 5

Materials: Copy of word cards (page 153); children's storybook featuring *-ug* words; self-adhesive flags (office supply item)

Select word cards and use them in the following activities:

• Read 'n' Spell Words (Take turns reading aloud a word to a partner who spells it.)
• Flag It!—Take turns reading aloud a passage from a classroom book that has *-ug* words in the text. Each time a word-family word is used, mark it with a sticky flag. (Draw attention to the rime *-ug.*)
• I Write, You Write! (See page 21.)

More Suggestions!

Spend a few minutes each day introducing or reviewing the *-ug* word family by reading aloud passages (pointing to the words) from children's storybooks. Let students be word-family detectives and identify those words used in the text.

Read at Home Activity

Copy the take-home direction sheet (page 98) and the bug picture for each student. Include two copies of the word cards on card stock. Place the materials in a zippered plastic bag.

Working with Sounds in "-ug" Words

LESSON 1
BASIC

Isolating Initial Sounds—Model for your students: *Listen carefully. I am going to say a word. The word is* pug. *What is the first sound you hear in* pug? *The first sound is* /p/. Words to practice: *Say the first sound you hear in . . .* hug, tug, rug, lug.

Blending Sounds—Model for your students: *Listen carefully. I am going to say the sounds slowly in my secret word. I would like you to blend those sounds together. The sounds are:* /ch/ /u/ /g/. *What is the secret word? When I blend the sounds* /ch/ /u/ /g/ *together, I hear the word* chug.
Words to practice: *mug, lug, dug, bug* (and words from other lessons)

MORE CHALLENGING
- *Listen to the words:* tug, toe, mug. *Which words rhyme?* (tug, mug)
- *What word begins with* /j/ *and rhymes with* tug? (jug)
- *Listen closely because I want to tell you a secret word. It is* /l/ /u/ /g/. *Say the sounds with me:* /l/ /u/ /g/. *What is my secret word?* (lug)
- *Listen to the words:* dog, dug, bug. *Which two words rhyme?* (dug, bug)
- *Here is another secret word for you. It is* /h/ /u/ /g/. *Say the sounds:* /h/ /u/ /g/. *What is my secret word?* (hug)
- *Say the word* mug. *How many sounds do you hear in the word* mug? (three) *Now, say the word without the* /m/ *sound. What is the silly word?* (ug)
- *Listen to the words:* bug, hug, hut. *Which two words rhyme?* (bug, hug)
- *Here is one more secret word for you. It is* /r/ /u/ /g/. *Say the sounds:* /r/ /u/ /g/. *What is the secret word?* (rug)

LESSON 2
BASIC

Segmenting Sounds—Model for your students: *Listen carefully. I would like you to tell me each sound you hear in a word. If the word is* tug, *what are the sounds? I would say* /t/ /u/ /g/.
Words to practice: *Tell each sound you hear in . . .* pug, bug, dug (and words from other lessons).

Adding Sounds—Model for your students: *Listen carefully. I am going to say a silly word and then add a sound to make a new word. My secret word rhymes with* ug *and begins with the* /h/ *sound. What is the word?* (Repeat the sounds: /h/ /ug/.) *The word is* hug.
Words to practice: *chug, rug, jug* (and words from other lessons)

MORE CHALLENGING
- *Say each sound you hear in the word* tug. *What are those sounds?* (/t/ /u/ /g/)
- *Listen closely because I want to tell you a secret word. It is* /j/ /u/ /g/. *Say the sounds with me:* /j/ /u/ /g/. *What is the secret word?* (jug)
- *What word rhymes with* tug *and begins with* /b/? (bug)
- *Here's another word clue: This secret word begins with* /ch/ *and rhymes with the word* tug. *What is the word?* (chug)
- *Now think about the word* rug. *How many sounds do you hear in the word?* (three) *Stretch the sounds in the word.* (/rrrrrr/ /uuuuuu/ /g/)
- *Listen to the word* tug. *What word rhymes with* tug *and begins with* /h/? (hug)
- *What word begins with* /l/ *and rhymes with* tug? (lug)
- *Say each sound you hear in the word* mug. *What are those sounds?* (/m/ /u/ /g/)

LESSON 3
BASIC

Blending Sounds—Model for your students: *Listen carefully. I am going to say some sounds slowly. I would like you to blend those sounds together and then tell me the word. The sounds are* /s/ /n/ /u/ /g/. (Repeat the sounds.) *What is the word? The word is* snug.
Words to practice: *smug, plug, slug, chug,* and CVC words

Substituting Sounds—Model for your students: *Listen to the word* chug. *Let's change the* /ch/ *sound to* /m/. *What is the new word? I can blend the sounds* /m /ug/ *together to make the word* mug.
Words to practice: *mug*—change /m/ to /l/ = *lug; lug*—change /l/ to /d/ = *dug; plug*—change /p/ to /s/ = *slug*

MORE CHALLENGING
- *Listen to the word* lug. *Change the* /l/ *sound to* /d/. *What new word did you make?* (dug)
- *I want to tell you my secret word. It is* /ch/ /u/ /g/. (Repeat the sounds.) *Blend the sounds together. What word can you make with the sounds?* (chug)
- *Listen to the sounds:* /s/ /l/ /u/ /g/. (Repeat the sounds.) *Blend the sounds together. What word can you make with the sounds?* (slug)
- *Say the word* smug. *Now, say it without the* /s/ *sound. What is the new word?* (mug)
- *This time say the word* plug. *Now, say it without the* /p/ *sound. What is the new word?* (lug)
- *Say the sounds* /s/ /m/ /u/ /g/. (Repeat the sounds.) *Blend the sounds together. What word can you make with the sounds?* (smug)
- *Say the word* lug. *Add the sound* /s/ *to the beginning of the word. What is the new word?* (slug)
- *Listen to the word* mug. *Change the* /m/ *sound to* /ch/. *What new word did you make?* (chug)

See page 140 for initial letter cards to make words.

Pictures: bug, mug

_ug   _ug   _ug

_ug   _ug

Read at Home—the "_ug" Word Family

Where Is the Bug?

To Parent:
Your child has been learning how to read words that end with "ug." In the zippered bag are two copies of the word cards and a picture of a bug. Please provide a mug for the activity.

Where Is the Bug?
How to play the game:
- Cut out the phrase cards.
- Set the mug in the center of the playing area.
- Turn the cards facedown.
- Have your child turn over a phrase card and read it aloud.
- Ask your child to show what the phrase means by using the mug and the picture of the bug.

Ready, Set, Read! Have your child read the word cards aloud as a practice run and then a second time at a faster speed!

bug on the mug

bug behind the mug

bug in the mug

bug under the mug

bug not by the mug

MEET AND READ THE "-UB" FAMILY

Getting Started! Determine which letter-sound correspondences and letter patterns the student needs to practice.

• **Learning to Read CVC Words**—If the student cannot easily identify the phonemes for the consonants *c, d, h, n, r, s,* and *t,* use Day 1–5 activities. Otherwise, begin on Day 2. Select CVC words from the list. Start with about six words for the targeted practice on the first day. Add words from word families previously studied as a review.

• **Learning to Read CCVC Words**—If the student can read the three-letter words, provide lessons for sounding out and reading CCVC words. Select three days of activities. Introduce the the consonant clusters with a tactile activity. During the lessons, include CVC words (and words from other word families) to strengthen decoding skills (*rub* with *grub, tub* with *stub, nub* with *snub*) and word-recognition fluency.

Word List

cub*	rub*	flub*
dub*	sub*	grub
hub*	tub*	snub
nub*	club*	stub*

*See page 153 for reproducible word cards. Add to the set by printing other words on card stock.

DAY 1

Materials: Copy the pictures on page 101. Follow the directions for the Molding Words activity on page 15.

• Show the pictures for *tub* and *sub*. Ask the child to tell you the beginning sound of each word (*tub* = /t/, *sub* = /s/) and make the letter in clay. Continue the lesson by calling out other *-ub* words. Have the child identify the beginning sounds and make the letters in clay to spell the words.
• To teach CCVC words, form the letters for the blends and rimes in clay.
• Have students write the words.

DAY 2

Materials: Copy of letter cards (page 140), word cards (page 153), and stone wall mat (page 130); materials for "Sticky" Words (page 19); prepared mini-book

Use letters and selected word cards in the following activities:

• Show and read the words.
• Phonemic Awareness (See page 100.)
• Puffy Words—if tactile activity is needed (See page 15.)
• Letters on Stones (See page 16.)
• "Sticky" Words (See page 19.)
• Word Family Mini-Book (See page 20.)

DAY 3

Materials: Copy of word cards (page 153); labeled plastic eggs and egg carton; copy of monster mat (page 137)

Select word cards and use them in the following activities:

• Review and use words in sentences. (See Finish the Sentence, page 21.)
• Phonemic Awareness (See page 100.)
• Pack the Words (See page 18.)
• Mr. Word Muncher (See page 19.)
• Feed Mr. Word Muncher (See page 21.)

DAY 4

Materials: Copy of letter cards (page 140), word cards (page 153), robot form (page 139), and playing catch mat (page 134); materials for Yummy Words (page 20) and Clip, Read, 'n' Write (page 20)

Use letters and selected word cards in the following activities:

• Review and use words in sentences. (See Robot Writing!, page 21.)
• Phonemic Awareness (See page 100.)
• Catch High-Flying Sounds (See page 18.)
• Yummy Words (See page 20.)
• Clip, Read, 'n' Write (See page 20.)

DAY 5

Materials: Copy of word cards (page 153); children's storybook featuring *-ub* words; self-adhesive flags (office supply item)

Select word cards and use them in the following activities:

• Read 'n' Spell Words (Take turns reading aloud a word to a partner who spells it.)
• Flag It!—Take turns reading aloud a passage from a classroom book that has *-ub* words in the text. Each time a word-family word is used, mark it with a sticky flag. (Draw attention to the rime *-ub*.)
• I Write, You Write! (See page 21.)

More Suggestions!

Spend a few minutes each day introducing or reviewing the *-ub* word family by reading aloud passages (pointing to the words) from children's storybooks. Let students be word-family detectives and identify those words used in the text.

Read at Home Activity

Copy the take-home direction sheet (page 101) for each student. Include two copies of the word cards on card stock, plus a die. Place the materials in a zippered plastic bag.

Working with Sounds in "-ub" Words

LESSON 1
BASIC

Isolating Initial Sounds—Model for your students: *Listen carefully. I am going to say a word. The word is tub. What is the first sound you hear in tub? The first sound is /t/.*
Words to practice: *Say the first sound you hear in . . .* dub, sub, hub, rub.

Blending Sounds—Model for your students: *Listen carefully. I am going to say the sounds slowly in my secret word. I would like you to blend those sounds together. The sounds are: /n/ /u/ /b/. What is*
the secret word? When I blend the sounds /n/ /u/ /b/ together, I hear the word* nub.
Words to practice: *rub, dub, cub, (and other words)*

MORE CHALLENGING
• *Listen to the words:* hot, sub, hub. *Which words rhyme?* (sub, hub)
• *What word begins with /k/ and rhymes with hub?* (cub)
• *Listen closely because I want to tell you a secret word. It is /s/ /u/ /b/. Say the sounds with me: /s/ /u/ /b/. What is my secret word?* (sub)
• *Listen to the words:* tub, dad, dub. *Which words rhyme?* (tub, dub)

• *Here is another secret word for you. It is /r/ /u/ /b/. Say the sounds: /r/ /u/ /b/. What is my secret word?* (rub)
• *Listen to the words:* rub, hub, rap. *Which words rhyme?* (rub, hub)
• *Say the word* tub. *How many sounds do you hear in* tub? *Hold up your fingers to show me the number.* (three) *Now, say the word without the /t/ sound. What is the silly word?* (ub)
• *What word begins with /n/ and rhymes with the word* rub? (nub)

LESSON 2
BASIC

Segmenting Sounds—Model for your students: *Listen carefully. I would like you to tell me each sound you hear in a word. If the word is* sub, *what are the sounds? I would say /s/ /u/ /b/.*
Words to practice: *Tell each sound you hear in . . .* hub, cub, nub.

Adding Sounds—Model for your students: *Listen carefully. I am going to say a silly word and then add a sound to make a new word. My secret word rhymes with* ub *and begins with the /h/ sound. What is*
the word? (Repeat the sounds: /h/ /ub/.) The word is* hub.
Words to practice: *dub, rub, tub, cub, and other words*

MORE CHALLENGING
• *What word rhymes with* sub *and begins with /r/?* (rub)
• *Say each sound you hear in the word* cub. *What are those sounds?* (/k/ /u/ /b/)
• *Now think about the word* sub. *How many sounds do you hear in the word?* (three) *Stretch the sounds in the word.* (/sssssss/ /uuuuuu/ /b/)
• *What word begins with /d/ and*

rhymes with* sub? (dub)
• *Listen closely because I want to tell you a secret word. It is /h/ /u/ /b/. Say the sounds with me: /h/ /u/ /b/. What is the secret word?* (hub)
• *Say each sound you hear in the word* dub. *What are those sounds?* (/d/ /u/ /b/)
• *Listen to the word* sub. *What word rhymes with* sub *and begins with /n/?* (nub)
• *Here's another word clue: This secret word begins with /t/ and rhymes with the word* sub. *What is the word?* (tub)

LESSON 3
BASIC

Blending Sounds—Model for your students: *Listen carefully. I am going to say some sounds slowly. I would like you to blend those sounds together and then tell me the word. The sounds are /s/ /t/ /u/ /b/. (Repeat the sounds.) What is the word? The word is* stub.
Words to practice: *flub, club, grub, snub, and CVC words*

Substituting Sounds—Model for your students: *Listen to the word* tub. *Let's change the /t/ sound to /r/. What is the new word? I can blend the sounds /r/ /ub/ together*
to make the word* rub.
Words to practice: *rub*—change /r/ to /d/ = *dub*; *dub*—change /d/ to /s/ = *sub*; *club*—change /k/ to /f/ = *flub*

MORE CHALLENGING
• *Say each sound you hear in the word* stub. *What are those sounds?* (/s/ /t/ /u/ /b/)
• *I want to tell you my secret word. It is /c/ /l/ /u/ /b/. (Repeat the sounds.) Blend the sounds together. What word can you make with the sounds?* (club)
• *Listen to the word* rub. *Change the /r/ sound to /s/. What new word did you make?* (sub)

• *Say the word* club. *Change the /k/ sound to /f/. What is the new word?* (flub)
• *Listen to the word* hub. *Change the /h/ sound to /d/. What new word did you make?* (dub)
• *Now listen to the word* stub. *Say the word* stub *without the /s/ sound. What is the new word?* (tub)
• *Listen to the sounds: /f/ /l/ /u/ /b/. (Repeat the sounds.) Blend the sounds together. What word can you make with the sounds?* (flub)
• *Say the word* nub. *Change the /n/ sound to /r/. What is the new word?* (rub)

See page 140 for initial letter cards to make words.

Pictures: tub, sub

_ub _ub _ub

ub _

ub _

Rolling Out a Sentence

To Parent:
Your child has been learning how to read words that end with "ub." Please use the word cards and die to play the following game. You will need to provide a sheet of paper and pencil.

Rolling Out a Sentence

How to play the game:
- Cover each face of the die with a small piece of masking tape.
- Choose five "ub" words and write them on the die. On the sixth face, write the word *cub*.
- Have your child roll the die and record the word on a sheet of paper. Do this again two more times.
- Then, let your child use the three words in a sentence that can be silly or factual. Record the sentence for your child.
- Continue playing the game as time and interest allow. When you are finished, invite your child to read the sentences that were generated for additional reading practice.

Ready, Set, Read! Have your child read the word cards aloud as a practice run and then a second time at a faster speed!

Reading for Fun: Take turns with your child reading aloud passages from children's storybooks.

MEET AND READ "-UT" AND "-UN" FAMILIES

Getting Started! Determine which letter-sound correspondences and letter patterns the student needs to practice.

• **Learning to Read CVC Words**—If the student cannot easily identify the phonemes for certain initial consonants, use Day 1–5 activities. Otherwise, begin on Day 2. Select CVC words from the list. Start with about 10 words for the targeted practice on the first day. Add words when the child is ready for a challenge. Include words from word families previously studied as a review.

• **Learning to Read CCVC Words**—If the student can read the three-letter words, provide lessons for sounding out and reading CCVC words. Select three days of activities. Introduce the digraph *sh* and consonant clusters with a tactile activity. During the lessons, include pairings of CVC and CCVC words to strengthen decoding skills (*hut* with *shut, but* with *bun, sun* with *shun* or *spun* or *stun, rut* with *run*) and word-recognition fluency.

Word List		
but*	rut*	shun*
cut*	shut*	spun*
gut*	bun*	stun*
hut*	fun*	
jut	run*	
nut*	sun*	

*See pages 153 & 154 for reproducible word cards. Add to the set by printing *jut* on card stock.

DAY 1

Materials: Copy the pictures on page 104. Follow the directions for the Molding Words activity on page 15.

• Show the pictures for *cut* and *run*. Ask the child to tell you the beginning sound of each word (*cut* = /k/, *run* = /r/) and make the letter in clay. Continue the lesson by calling out other words. Have the child identify the beginning sounds and make the letters in clay to spell the words.
• To teach CCVC words, form the letters for the digraph, blends, and rimes in clay.
• Have students write the words.

DAY 2

Copy of letter cards (page 140) and word cards (pages 153 and 154); racetrack billboard mat (page 131); prepared mini-book

Use letters and selected word cards in the following activities:

• Show and read the words
• Phonemic Awareness (See page 103.)
• Puffy Words—if tactile activity is needed (See page 15.)
• Rev Up for Words (See page 17.)
• Where Is . . . ? (See page 19.)
• Word Family Mini-Book (See page 20.)

DAY 3

Materials: Copy of letter cards (page 140), word cards (pages 153 and 154), and playing catch mat (page 134); materials for Yummy Words (page 20) and Clip, Read, 'n' Write (page 20)

Use letters and selected word cards in the following activities:

• Review and use words in sentences. (See Finish the Sentence, page 21.)
• Phonemic Awareness (See page 103.)
• Catch High-Flying Sounds (See page 18.)
• Yummy Words (See page 20.)
• Clip, Read, 'n' Write (See page 20.)

DAY 4

Materials: Copy of letter cards (page 140), word cards (pages 153 and 154), robot form (page 139), safe mat (page 135), and tree house mat (page 136)

Use letters and selected word cards in the following activities:

• Review and use words in sentences. (See Robot Writing!, page 21.)
• Phonemic Awareness (See page 103.)
• Unlock the Code (See page 18.)
• Read 'n' Climb to See the View (See page 19.)
• Write Down—Back to the Ground (See page 21.)

DAY 5

Materials: Copy of word cards (pages 153 and 154); storybooks featuring *-ut* and *-un* words; self-adhesive flags (office supply item)

Select word cards and use them in the following activities:

• Read 'n' Spell Words (Take turns reading aloud a word to a partner who spells it.)
• Flag It!—Take turns reading aloud a passage from a classroom book that has *-ut* or *-un* words in the text. Each time a word-family word is used, mark it with a sticky flag. (Draw attention to the rime.)
• I Write, You Write! (See page 21.)

More Suggestions

Spend a few minutes each day introducing or reviewing the *-ut* and *-un* word families by reading aloud passages (pointing to the words) from children's storybooks. Let students be word-family detectives and identify those words used in the text.

Read at Home Activity

Copy the take-home direction sheet (page 104) for each student. Include a copy of each word card in two different colors on card stock. Place all of the materials in a zippered plastic bag.

Working with Sounds in "-ut" and "-un" Words

LESSON 1
BASIC

Isolating Initial Sounds—Model for your students: *Listen carefully. I am going to say a word. The word is rut. What is the first sound you hear in rut? The first sound is /r/.*
Words to practice: *Say the first sound you hear in . . .* but, jut, nut (and words from other lessons).

Blending Sounds—Model for your students: *Listen carefully. I am going to say the sounds slowly in my secret word. I would like you to blend those sounds together. The sounds are: /s/ /u/ /n/. What is the secret word? When I blend the sounds /s/ /u/ /n/ together, I hear the word sun.*
Words to practice: *fun, run, bun, shun* (and words from other lessons)

MORE CHALLENGING
- *Listen to the words:* run, sad, sun. *Which words rhyme?* (run, sun)
- *What word begins with /b/ and rhymes with sun?* (bun)
- *Listen closely because I want to tell you a secret word. It is /n/ /u/ /t/. Say the sounds with me: /n/ /u/ /t/. What is my secret word?* (nut)

- *Listen to the words:* had, hut, but. *Which two words rhyme?* (hut, but)
- *Here is another secret word for you. It is /f/ /u/ /n/. Say the sounds: /f/ /u/ /n/. What is my secret word?* (fun)
- *Say the word* shut. *How many sounds do you hear in the word* shut? (three) *Now, say the word without the /sh/ sound. What is the silly word?* (ut)
- *Listen to the words:* cut, rut, cat. *Which two words rhyme?* (cut, rut)
- *Here is one more secret word for you. It is /g/ /u/ /t/. Say the sounds: /g/ /u/ /t/. What is the secret word?* (gut)

LESSON 2
BASIC

Segmenting Sounds—Model for your students: *Listen carefully. I would like you to tell me each sound you hear in a word. If the word is* bun, *what are the sounds? I would say /b/ /u/ /n/.*
Words to practice: *Tell each sound you hear in . . .* fun, sun, shun, (and words from other lessons).

Adding Sounds—Model for your students: *Listen carefully. I am going to say a silly word and then add a sound to make a new word. My secret word rhymes with ut and begins with the /sh/ sound. What is the word?* (Repeat the sounds: /sh/ /ut/.) *The word is shut.*
Words to practice: *rut, hut, cut,* (and words from other lessons)

MORE CHALLENGING
- *Say each sound you hear in the word* rut. *What are those sounds?* (/r/ /u/ /t/)
- *Listen closely because I want to tell you a secret word. It is /s/ /u/ /n/. Say the sounds with me: /s/ /u/ /n/. What is the secret word?* (sun)
- *What word rhymes with* run *and begins with /b/?* (bun)

- *Here's another word clue: This secret word begins with /k/ and rhymes with the word* hut. *What is the word?* (cut)
- *Now think about the word* hut. *How many sounds do you hear in the word?* (three) *Stretch the sounds in the word.* (/hhhhhh/ /uuuuuu/ /t/)
- *Listen to the word* hut. *What word rhymes with* hut *and begins with /g/?* (gut)
- *What word begins with /sh/ and rhymes with run?* (shun)
- *Say each sound you hear in the word* run. *What are those sounds?* (/r/ /u/ /n/)

LESSON 3
BASIC

Blending Sounds—Model for your students: *Listen carefully. I am going to say some sounds slowly. I would like you to blend those sounds together and then tell me the word. The sounds are /sh/ /u/ /t/.* (Repeat the sounds.) *What is the word? The word is shut.*
Words to practice: CVC words and words from other lessons.

Substituting Sounds—Model for your students: *Listen to the word* fun. *Let's change the /f/ sound to /r/. What is the new word? I can blend the sounds /r/ /un/ together to make the word* run.
Words to practice: *run*—change /r/ to /sh/ = *shun*; *shun*—change /sh/ to /s/ = *sun*; *sun*—change /s/ to /b/ = *bun*

MORE CHALLENGING
- *Listen to the word* cut. *Change the /k/ sound to /j/. What new word did you make?* (jut)
- *I want to tell you my secret word. It is /s/ /p/ /u/ /n/.* (Repeat the sounds.) *Blend the sounds together. What word can you make with the sounds?* (spun)
- *Listen to the sounds: /sh/ /u/ /t/.* (Repeat the sounds.) *Blend the sounds together. What word can you make with the sounds?* (shut)
- *Say the word* spun. *Now, say it without the /s/ sound. What is the new word?* (pun)
- *This time say the word* but. *Change the /t/ sound to /n/. What is the new word?* (bun)
- *Say the sounds /s/ /t/ /u/ /n/.* (Repeat the sounds.) *Blend them together. What word can you make with the sounds?* (stun)
- *Say the word* run. *Change the /n/ sound to /t/. What is the new word?* (rut)
- *Listen to the word* but. *Change the /b/ sound to /sh/. What new word did you make?* (shut)

See page 140 for initial letter cards to make words.

Pictures: cut, run

_ut **_ut**

Memory Match Fun

To Parent:
Your child has been learning how to read words that end with "ut" and "un." In the zippered bag you will find word cards in two different colors.

Memory Match Fun
How to play the game:
- Cut out the word cards if needed. Sort them into two groups by color.
- Arrange the first set of cards facedown in rows in the playing area. Place the second set of cards facedown in rows nearby.
- Take turns playing the memory match game by turning over two cards to see if the words match. If a match is made, collect those pairs of cards. When no match is made, turn those cards facedown again.
- Continue playing until all of the matches have been found.

Ready, Set, Read! Arrange all of the word cards in several rows on a table. Have your child read the words aloud as a practice run and then a second time at a faster speed!

MEET AND READ "-UM" AND "-OG" FAMILIES

Getting Started! Determine which letter-sound correspondences and letter patterns the student needs to practice.

• **Learning to Read CVC Words**—If the student cannot easily identify the phonemes for certain initial consonants, use Day 1–5 activities. Otherwise, begin on Day 2. Select CVC words from the list. Start with about 10 words for the targeted practice on the first day. Add more words when the child is ready for a challenge.

• **Learning to Read CCVC Words**—If the student can read the three-letter words fluently, provide activities for sounding out and reading the CCVC words. Introduce the digraph *ch* and consonant clusters with a tactile activity. During the lessons, include pairings of CVC and CCVC words to strengthen decoding skills (*hum* with *chum*, *fog* with *frog*, *sum* with *scum* or *swum*, *gum* with *glum*, *log* with *clog*) and word-recognition fluency.

Word List

gum*	glum	dog*	frog*
hum*	plum*	fog*	smog*
mum*	scum	hog*	
sum*	swum*	jog*	
chum*	bog*	log*	
drum*	cog*	clog*	

*See pages 150 & 154 for reproducible word cards
Add to the set by printing other words on card stock.*

DAY 1

Materials: Copy the pictures on pages 68 and 107. Follow the directions for the Molding Words and Pinching Letters activities on page 15.

• Show the pictures for *dog* and *gum*. Ask the child to tell you the beginning sound of each word (*dog* = /d/ and *gum* = /g/) and make the letters in clay. Continue the lesson by calling out other selected words. Let the child identify the beginning sounds and make the letters in clay to spell the words.
• Have students write the words.
• Pinching Letters (See page 15.)

DAY 2

Materials: Copy of letter cards (page 140), word cards (pages 150 and 154), and launch pad mat (page 132); "Sticky" Words materials (page 19); prepared mini-book

Use letters and selected word cards in the following activities:

• Show and read the words.
• Phonemic Awareness (See page 106.)
• Puffy Words—if tactile activity is needed (See page 15.)
• Blast Off! (See page 17.)
• "Sticky" Words (See page 19.)
• Word Family Mini-Book (See page 20.)

DAY 3

Materials: Copy of letter cards (page 140), word cards (pages 150 and 154), safe mat (page 135), and tree house mat (page 136)

Use letters and selected word cards in the following activities:

• Review and use words in sentences. (See Finish the Sentence, page 21.)
• Phonemic Awareness (See page 106.)
• Unlock the Code (See page 18.)
• Read 'n' Climb to See the View (See page 19.)
• Write Down—Back to the Ground (See page 21.)

DAY 4

Materials: Copy of letter cards (page 140), word cards (pages 150 and 154), robot form (page 139), truck mat (page 133), and monster mat (page 137)

Use letters and selected word cards in the following activities:

• Review and use words in sentences. (See Robot Writing!, page 21.)
• Phonemic Awareness (See page 106.)
• Load the Truck (See page 17.)
• Mr. Word Muncher (See page 19.)
• Feed Mr. Word Muncher (See page 21.)

DAY 5

Materials: Copy of word cards (pages 150 and 154); storybooks featuring *-um* and *-og* words; self-adhesive flags (office supply item)

Select word cards and use them in the following activities:

• Read 'n' Spell Words (Take turns reading aloud a word to a partner who spells it.)
• Flag It!—Take turns reading aloud passages from classroom books that have *-um* or *-og* words in the text. Each time a word-family word is used, mark it with a sticky flag.
• I Write, You Write! (See page 21.)

More Suggestions!

Spend a few minutes each day introducing or reviewing the *-um* and *-og* word families by reading aloud passages (pointing to the words) from children's storybooks. Let students be word-family detectives and identify those words used in the text.

Read at Home Activity

Copy the take-home direction sheet (page 107) for each student. Include two copies of the word cards on card stock, plus a piece of brown construction paper. Place all of the materials in a zippered plastic bag.

Working with Sounds in "-um" and "-og" Words

LESSON 1
BASIC
Isolating Initial Sounds—Model for your students: *Listen carefully. I am going to say a word. The word is* log. *What is the first sound you hear in* log? *The first sound is* /l/. Words to practice: *Say the first sound you hear in . . .* jog, cog, fog.

Blending Sounds—Model for your students: *Listen carefully. I am going to say the sounds slowly in my secret word. I would like you to blend those sounds together. The sounds are:* /g/ /u/ /m/. *What is the secret word? When I blend the*

sounds /g/ /u/ /m/ *together, I hear the word* gum.
Words to practice: *mum, sum, chum*

MORE CHALLENGING
- *Listen to the words:* chat, chum, gum. *Which words rhyme?* (chum, gum)
- *What word begins with* /j/ *and rhymes with* dog? (jog)
- *Listen closely because I want to tell you a secret word. It is* /s/ /u/ /m/. *Say the sounds with me:* /s/ /u/ /m/. *What is my secret word?* (sum)
- *Listen to the words:* dog, dot, log.

Which words rhyme? (dog, log)
- *Here is another secret word for you. It is* /f/ /o/ /g/. *Say the sounds:* /f/ /o/ /g/. *What is my secret word?* (fog)
- *Listen to the words:* plum, drum, plan. *Which words rhyme?* (plum, drum)
- *Say the word* chum. *How many sounds do you hear in* chum? *Hold up your fingers to show me the number.* (three) *Now, say the word without the* /ch/ *sound. What is the new silly word?* (um)
- *What word begins with* /h/ *and rhymes with the word* gum? (hum)

LESSON 2
BASIC
Segmenting Sounds—Model for your students: *Listen carefully. I would like you to tell me each sound you hear in a word. If the word is* hum, *what are the sounds? I would say* /h/ /u/ /m/.
Words to practice: *Tell each sound you hear in . . .* gum, sum, mum and other CVC words.

Adding Sounds—Model for your students: *Listen carefully. I am going to say a silly word and then add a sound to make a new word. My secret word rhymes with* og and

begins with the /b/ sound. *What is the word?* (Repeat the sounds: /b/ /og/.) *The word is* bog.
Words to practice: *hog, dog, fog*

MORE CHALLENGING
- *What word rhymes with* gum *and begins with* /s/? (sum)
- *Say each sound you hear in the word* bog. *What are those sounds?* (/b/ /o/ /g/)
- *Now think about the word* chum. *How many sounds do you hear in the word?* (three) *Stretch the sounds in the word.* (/ch/ /uuuuuu/ /mmmmmm/)
- *What word begins with* /s/ *and*

rhymes with gum? (sum)
- *Listen closely because I want to tell you a secret word. It is* /l/ /o/ /g/. *Say the sounds with me:* /l/ /o/ /g/. *What is the secret word?* (log)
- *Say each sound you hear in the word* mum. *What are those sounds?* (/m/ /u/ /m/)
- *Listen to the word* dog. *What word rhymes with* dog *and begins with* /k/? (cog)
- *Here's another word clue: This secret word begins with* /f/ *and rhymes with the word* dog. *What is the word?* (fog)

LESSON 3
BASIC
Blending Sounds—Model for your students: *Listen carefully. I am going to say some sounds slowly. I would like you to blend those sounds together and then tell me the word. The sounds are* /f/ /r/ /o/ /g/. (Repeat the sounds.) *What is the word? The word is* frog.
Words to practice: *clog, smog, and CCVC words from other lessons*

Substituting Sounds—Model for your students: *Listen to the word* mum. *Let's change the* /m/ *sound to* /s/. *What is the new word? I can blend the sounds* /s/ /um/ *together*

to make the word sum.
Words to practice: *sum—change* /s/ to /h/ = hum; hum—change /h/ to /ch/ = chum; plum—change /p/ to /g/ = glum

MORE CHALLENGING
- *Say each sound you hear in the word* drum. *What are those sounds?* (/d/ /r/ /u/ /m/)
- *I want to tell you my secret word. It is* /s/ /m/ /o/ /g/. (Repeat the sounds.) *Blend the sounds together. What word can you make with the sounds?* (smog)
- *Listen to the word* glum. *Change the* /g/ *sound to* /p/. *What new word did you make?* (plum)

- *Say each sound you hear in the word* scum. *What are those sounds?* (/s/ /k/ /u/ /m/)
- *Listen to the word* dog. *Change the* /d/ *sound to* /k/. *What new word did you make?* (cog)
- *Now listen to the word* glum. *Say the word* glum *without the* /g/ *sound. What is the silly word?* (lum)
- *Listen to the sounds:* /f/ /r/ /o/ /g/. (Repeat the sounds.) *Blend the sounds together. What word can you make with the sounds?* (frog)
- *Say the word* clog. *Now, say it without the* /k/ *sound. What is the new word?* (log)

See page 140 for initial letter cards to make words. The pictures and cards for -og words are on page 68.

Pictures: gum, drum

_um **_um** **_um**

_um **_um**

Read at Home—the "_um" and "_og" Word Families

Drumming Up Words

To Parent:
Your child has been learning how to read words that end with "um" and "og." In the zippered bag are two copies of the word cards along with sheet of construction paper. Roll the paper into a log shape and tape the overlapping edges together. Please provide a small kettle to be the "drum" and two unsharpened pencils or writing pens.

Drumming Up Words
How to do the activity (two players):
- Cut out the word cards if needed. Shuffle them and place them facedown in a pile.
- Take turns with your child drawing a card and reading the word out loud. If the word ends with "um," place it near the drum. If the word ends with "og," set the card near the log. Whenever the word *drum* is drawn, that player taps a rhythm on the drum.
- Continue the activity until all of the cards have been sorted or one player has tapped on the drum twice.

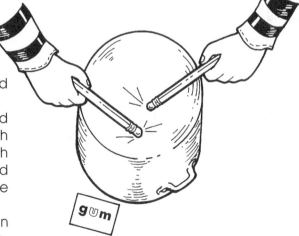

Ready, Set, Read! Arrange all of the word cards in several rows on a table. Have your child read the words aloud as a practice run and then a second time at a faster speed.

MEET AND READ THE "-UD," "-UN," AND "-AT" FAMILIES

Getting Started! Determine which letter-sound correspondences and letter patterns the student needs to practice.

• **Learning to Read CVC Words**—If the student cannot easily identify the phonemes for certain initial consonants, use Day 1–5 activities. Otherwise, begin on Day 2. Select CVC words from the list. Start with about 10 words for the targeted practice on the first day. Add more words when the child is ready for a challenge.

• **Learning to Read CCVC Words**—If the student can read the three-letter words, provide lessons for sounding out and reading CCVC words. Select three days of activities. Introduce the digraphs *th*, *sh*, and *ch* and consonant clusters with a tactile activity. During the lessons, include pairings of CVC and CCVC words to strengthen decoding skills (*rat* with *brat*, *cat* with *scat*, *spud* with *spun*, *bun* with *bud*, *pat* with *spat*, *hat* with *that*, *thud* with *that*) and word-recognition fluency.

Word List

bud*	sun*	fat*	brat*
mud*	shun*	hat*	chat*
spud*	spun*	mat*	flat*
thud*	stun*	pat*	scat
bun*	at	rat*	slat
fun*	bat*	sat*	spat
run*	cat*	vat	that*

*See pages 143 & 154 for reproducible word cards. Add to the set by printing other words on card stock.

DAY 1

Materials: Copy the pictures on pages 26, 104, and 110. Follow the directions for the Molding Words and Pinching Letters activities on page 15.

• Show the pictures for *cat*, *run*, and *mud*. Ask the child to tell you the beginning sound of each word (*cat* = /k/, *run* = /r/, and *mud* = /m/) and make the letters in clay. Continue the lesson by calling out other selected words. Let the child identify the beginning sounds and make the letters in clay to spell the words.
• Have students write the words.
• Pinching Letters (See page 15.)

DAY 2

Materials: Copy of letter cards (page 140) and word cards (pages 143 and 154); prepared mini-book

Use letters and selected word cards in the following activities:

• Show and use the words in sentences.
• Phonemic Awareness (See page 109.)
• Puffy Words—if tactile activity is needed (See page 15.)
• What's the Word? (See page 16.)
• Where Is . . . ? (See page 19.)
• Word Family Mini-Book (See page 20.)

DAY 3

Materials: Copy of letter cards (page 140), word cards (pages 143 and 154), truck mat (page 133) and monster mat (page 137)

Use letters and selected word cards in the following activities:

• Review and use words in sentences. (See Finish the Sentence, page 21.)
• Phonemic Awareness (See page 109.)
• Load the Truck (See page 17.)
• Mr. Word Muncher (See page 19.)
• Feed Mr. Word Muncher (See page 21.)

DAY 4

Materials: Copy of word cards (pages 143 and 154) and robot form (page 139); labeled plastic eggs and egg carton; materials for Yummy Words (page 20) and Clip, Read, 'n' Write (page 20)

Select word cards and use them in the following activities:

• Review and use words in sentences. (See Robot Writing!, page 21.)
• Phonemic Awareness (See page 109.)
• Pack the Words (See page 18.)
• Yummy Words (See page 20.)
• Clip, Read, 'n' Write (See page 20.)

DAY 5

Materials: Copy of word cards (pages 143 and 154); children's storybooks featuring -ud, -un, and -at words; self-adhesive flags (office supply item)

Select word cards and use them in the following activities:

• Read 'n' Spell Words (Take turns reading aloud a word to a partner who spells it.)
• Flag It!—Take turns reading aloud passages from books that have -ud, -un, and -at words in the texts. Each time a word-family word is used, mark it with a sticky flag.
• I Write, You Write! (See page 21.)

More Suggestions!

Spend a few minutes each day introducing or reviewing the -ud, -un, and -at word families by reading aloud passages (pointing to the words) from children's storybooks. Let students be word-family detectives and identify those words used in the text.

Read at Home Activity

Copy the take-home direction sheet (page 110) for each student. Include one or two copies of the word cards on card stock, plus a die and small paper bag. Place all of the materials in a zippered plastic bag.

Working with Sounds in "-ud," "-un," and "-at" Words

LESSON 1
BASIC

Isolating Initial Sounds—Model for your students: *Listen carefully. I am going to say a word. The word is run. What is the first sound you hear in run? The first sound is /r/.* Words to practice: *Say the first sound you hear in . . . sun, fun, shun.*

Blending Sounds—Model for your students: *Listen carefully. I am going to say the sounds slowly in my secret word. I would like you to blend those sounds together. The sounds are: /h/ /a/ /t/. What is the secret word? When I blend the sounds /h/ /a/ /t/ together, I hear the word hat.* Words to practice: *chat, sat, cat, bud, mud, thud*

MORE CHALLENGING

- *Listen to the words: mud, mad, thud. Which words rhyme?* (mud, thud)
- *What word begins with /th/ and rhymes with bat?* (that)
- *Listen closely because I want to tell you a secret word. It is /b/ /u/ /d/. Say the sounds with me: /b/ /u/ /d/. What is my secret word?* (bud)
- *Listen to the words: bat, fun, bun. Which two words rhyme?* (fun, bun)
- *Here is another secret word for you. It is /s/ /a/ /t/. Say the sounds: /s/ /a/ /t/. What is my secret word?* (sat)
- *Say the word pat. How many sounds do you hear in the word pat?* (three) *Now, say the word without the /p/ sound. What is the new word?* (at)
- *Listen to the words: scat, chat, chin. Which two words rhyme?* (scat, chat)
- *Here is one more secret word for you. It is /r/ /u/ /n/. Say the sounds: /r/ /u/ /n/. What is the secret word?* (run)

LESSON 2
BASIC

Segmenting Sounds—Model for your students: *Listen carefully. I would like you to tell me each sound you hear in a word. If the word is rat, what are the sounds? I would say /r/ /a/ /t/.* Words to practice: *Tell each sound you hear in . . . mat, sat, hat, chat.*

Adding Sounds—Model for your students: *Listen carefully. I am going to say a silly word and then add a sound to make a new word. My secret word rhymes with ud and begins with the /m/ sound. What is the word? (Repeat the sounds: /m/ /ud/.) The word is mud.* Words to practice: *bud, shun, bun, thud, fun*

MORE CHALLENGING

- *Say each sound you hear in the word rat. What are those sounds?* (/r/ /a/ /t/)
- *Listen closely because I want to tell you a secret word. It is /m/ /u/ /d/. Say the sounds with me: /m/ /u/ /d/. What is the secret word?* (mud)
- *What word rhymes with mud and begins with /b/?* (bud)
- *Here's another word clue: This secret word begins with /r/ and rhymes with the word fun. What is the word?* (run)
- *Now think about the word shun. How many sounds do you hear in the word?* (three) *Stretch the sounds in the word.* (/sh/ /uuuuu/ /nnnnn/)
- *Listen to the word cat. What word rhymes with cat and begins with /ch/?* (chat)
- *What word begins with /f/ and rhymes with hat?* (fat)
- *Say each sound you hear in the word sun. What are those sounds?* (/s/ /u/ /n/)

LESSON 3
BASIC

Blending Sounds—Model for your students: *Listen carefully. I am going to say some sounds slowly. I would like you to blend those sounds together and then tell me the word. The sounds are /s/ /p/ /u/ /d/. (Repeat the sounds.) What is the word? The word is spud.* Words to practice: *stun, thud, spun, shun, and CVC words*

Substituting Sounds—Model for your students: *Listen to the word bat. Let's change the /b/ sound to /th/. What is the new word? I can blend the sounds /th/ /at/ together to make the word that.* Words to practice: *that—change /th/ to /v/ = vat; vat—change /v/ to /ch/ = chat; flat—change /f/ to /s/ = slat*

MORE CHALLENGING

- *Listen to the word slat. Change the /s/ sound to /f/. What new word did you make?* (flat)
- *I want to tell you my secret word. It is /b/ /r/ /a/ /t/. (Repeat the sounds.) Blend the sounds together. What word can you make with the sounds?* (brat)
- *Listen to the sounds: /s/ /t/ /u/ /n/. (Repeat the sounds.) Blend the sounds together. What word can you make with the sounds?* (stun)
- *Say the word spun. Now, say it without the /s/ sound. What is the new word?* (pun)
- *This time say the word thud. Now, say it without the /th/ sound. What is the new word? (ud) Is this a real word?* (no)
- *Say the sounds /s/ /k/ /a/ /t/. (Repeat the sounds.) Blend the sounds together. What word can you make with the sounds?* (scat)
- *Say the word pat. Add the sound /s/ to the beginning of the word. What is the new word?* (spat)
- *Listen to the word bud. Change the /b/ sound to /m/. What new word did you make?* (mud)

See page 140 for initial letter cards. Find pictures for -un words on page 104 and -at words on page 26.

_ud _ud _ud

Rolling Out Silly Sentences

To Parent:
Your child has been learning how to read words that end with "ud," "un, and "at." Please use the word cards and die to play the following game. You will need to provide a sheet of paper and pencil.

Rolling Out a Sentence
How to play the game:
- Cut out the word cards if needed.
- Cover each face of the die with a small piece of masking tape.
- Choose three "ud," "un," or "at" words and write them on the die. Place the word cards in the paper bag. On each of the other faces, write one word: *cat*, *rat*, or *mud*.
- Have your child roll the die and record the word on a sheet of paper. Do this again two more times.
- Let your child draw three word cards from the bag and write them on the paper. Have your child use the six selected words in one or two sentences that can be silly. Record the sentences for your child.
- Continue playing the game as time and interest allow. When you are finished, invite your child to read the sentences that were generated for additional reading practice.

Ready, Set, Read! Have your child read the word cards aloud as a practice run and then a second time at a faster speed!

 Beginning Reader Intervention Activities

MEET AND READ THE "-UG," "-UT," AND "-IG" FAMILIES

Getting Started! Determine which letter-sound correspondences and letter patterns the student needs to practice.

- **Learning to Read CVC Words**—If the student cannot easily identify the phonemes for the initial consonants, use Day 1–5 activities. Otherwise, begin on Day 2. Select CVC words from the list. Start with about 10 words for the targeted practice on the first day. Add more words when the child is ready for a challenge.

- **Learning to Read CCVC Words**—If the student can read the three-letter words, provide lessons for sounding out and reading CCVC words. Select three days of activities. Introduce the digraphs *ch* and *sh* and consonant clusters with a tactile activity. During the lessons, include pairings of CVC and CCVC words to strengthen decoding skills (*hug* with *hut*, *jug* with *jig*, *mug* with *smug*, *rig* with *rug* or *brig*, *wig* with *twig* or *swig*, *dug* with *dig*, *pig* with *pug*, *lug* with *slug*) and word-recognition fluency.

Word List				
bug*	rug*	but*	shut*	rig*
dug*	tug*	cut*	big*	wig*
hug*	chug*	gut*	dig*	zig*
jug*	plug*	hut*	fig*	brig*
lug*	slug*	jut	gig*	swig*
mug*	smug	nut*	jig*	twig*
pug	snug*	rut*	pig*	

See page 148, 153 & 154 for reproducible word cards. Add to the set by printing other words on card stock.

DAY 1
Materials: Copy the pictures on pages 53, 98, and 104. Follow the directions for the Molding Words and Pinching Letters activities on page 15.

- Show the pictures for *wig*, *bug*, and *cut*. Ask the child to tell you the beginning sound of each word (*wig* = /w/, *bug* = /b/, and *cut* = /k/) and make the letters in clay. Continue the lesson by calling out other selected words. Let the child identify the beginning sounds and make the letters in clay to spell the words.
- Have students write the words.
- Pinching Letters (See page 15.)

DAY 2
Materials: Copy of letter cards (page 140), word cards (pages 148, 153, and 154), and stone wall mat (page 130); materials for "Sticky" Words (page 19); prepared mini-book

Use letters and selected word cards in the following activities:

- Show and read the words.
- Phonemic Awareness (See page 112.)
- Puffy Words—if tactile activity is needed (See page 15.)
- Letters on Stones (See page 16.)
- "Sticky" Words (See page 19.)
- Word Family Mini-Book (See page 20.)

DAY 3
Materials: Copy of word cards (pages 148, 153, and 154); labeled plastic eggs and egg carton; materials for Yummy Words (page 20) and Clip, Read, 'n' Write (page 20)

Use letters and selected word cards in the following activities:

- Review and use words in sentences. (See Finish the Sentence, page 21.)
- Phonemic Awareness (See page 112.)
- Pack the Words (See page 18.)
- Yummy Words (See page 20.)
- Clip, Read, 'n' Write (See page 20.)

DAY 4
Materials: Copy of letter cards (page 140), word cards (pages 148, 153, and 154), robot form (page 139), playing catch mat (page 134), and tree house mat (page 136)

Use letters and selected word cards in the following activities:

- Review and use words in sentences. (See Robot Writing!, page 21.)
- Phonemic Awareness (See p. 112.)
- Catch High-Flying Sounds (See page 18.)
- Read 'n' Climb to See the View (See page 19.)
- Write Down—Back to the Ground (See page 21.)

DAY 5
Materials: Copy of word cards (pages 148, 153, and 154); children's storybooks featuring -ug, -ut, and -ig word families; self-adhesive flags (office supply item)

Select word cards and use them in the following activities:

- Read 'n' Spell Words (Take turns reading aloud a word to a partner who spells it.)
- Flag It!—Take turns reading aloud passages from books that have -ug, -ut, and -ig in the text. Each time a word-family word is used, mark it with a sticky flag.
- I Write, You Write! (See page 21.)

More Suggestions!
Spend a few minutes each day introducing or reviewing the -ug, -ut, and -ig word families by reading aloud passages (pointing to the words) from children's storybooks. Let students be word-family detectives and identify those words used in the text.

Read at Home Activity
Copy the take-home direction sheet (page 113) for each student. Include two copies of the selected word cards on card stock and a small paper bag. (*Note:* Need at least three words for each word family.) Place all of the materials in a zippered plastic bag.

Working with Sounds in "-ug," "-ut," and "-ig" Words

LESSON 1
BASIC
Isolating Initial Sounds—Model for your students: *Listen carefully. I am going to say a word. The word is shut. What is the first sound you hear in* shut? *The first sound is* /sh/. Words to practice: *Say the first sound you hear in . . .* but, jut, cut, gut, hut.

Blending Sounds—Model for your students: *Listen carefully. I am going to say the sounds slowly in my secret word. I would like you to blend those sounds together. The sounds are:* /d/ /u/ /g/. *What is the secret word? When I blend the sounds* /d/ /u/ /g/ *together, I hear the word* dug. Words to practice: *lug, bug, jug, wig, gig, big*

MORE CHALLENGING
- *Listen to the words:* dig, dug, chug. *Which words rhyme?* (dug, chug)
- *What word begins with* /w/ *and rhymes with* dig? (wig)
- *Listen closely because I want to tell you a secret word. It is* /h/ /u/ /g/. *Say the sounds with me:* /h/ /u/ /g/. *What is my secret word?* (hug)
- *Listen to the words:* shut, got, gut. *Which words rhyme?* (shut, gut)
- *Here is another secret word for you. It is* /z/ /i/ /g/. *Say the sounds:* /z/ /i/ /g/. *What is my secret word?* (zig)
- *Listen to the words:* brig, rig, rug. *Which words rhyme?* (brig, rig)
- *Say the word* rut. *How many sounds do you hear in* rut? *Hold up your fingers to show me the number.* (three) *Now, say the word without the* /r/ *sound. What is the silly word?* (ut)
- *What word begins with* /k/ *and ends with* /ut/? (cut)

LESSON 2
BASIC
Segmenting Sounds—Model for your students: *Listen carefully. I would like you to tell me each sound you hear in a word. If the word is* rug, *what are the sounds? I would say* /r/ /u/ /g/. Words to practice: *Tell each sound you hear in . . .* mug, lug, hug, pug.

Adding Sounds—Model for your students: *Listen carefully. I am going to say a silly word and then add a sound to make a new word. My secret word rhymes with* ut *and begins with the* /h/ *sound. What is the word?* (Repeat the sounds: /h/ /ut/.) *The word is* hut. Words to practice: *nut, rut, zig, jig, shut*

MORE CHALLENGING
- *What word rhymes with* dig *and begins with* /f/? (fig)
- *Say each sound you hear in the word* shut. *What are those sounds?* (/sh/ /u/ /t/)
- *Now think about the word* rut. *How many sounds do you hear in the word?* (three) *Stretch the sounds in the word.* (/rrrrrr/ /uuuuuu/ /t/)
- *What word begins with* /j/ *and rhymes with* dug? (jug)
- *Listen closely because I want to tell you a secret word. It is* /g/ /i/ /g/. *Say the sounds with me:* /g/ /i/ /g/. *What is the secret word?* (gig)
- *Say each sound you hear in the word* chug. *What are those sounds?* (/ch/ /u/ /g/)
- *Listen to the word* cut. *What word rhymes with* cut *and begins with* /j/? (jut)
- *Here's another word clue: This secret word begins with* /b/ *and rhymes with the word* dug. *What is the word?* (bug)

LESSON 3
BASIC
Blending Sounds—Model for your students: *Listen carefully. I am going to say some sounds slowly. I would like you to blend those sounds together and then tell me the word. The sounds are* /b/ /r/ /i/ /g/. (Repeat the sounds.) *What is the word? The word is* brig. Words to practice: *swig, twig, shut, and other CCVC words*

Substituting Sounds—Model for your students: *Listen to the word* pug. *Let's change the* /p/ *sound to* /ch/. *What is the new word? I can blend the sounds* /ch/ /ug/ *together to make the word* chug. Words to practice: *chug*—change /ch/ to /l/ = *lug*; *lug*—change /l/ to /t/ = *tug*; *slug*—change /s/ to /p/ = *plug*

MORE CHALLENGING
- *Say each sound you hear in the word* plug. *What are those sounds?* (/p/ /l/ /u/ /g/)
- *I want to tell you my secret word. It is* /s/ /w/ /i/ /g/. (Repeat the sounds.) *Blend the sounds together. What word can you make with the sounds?* (swig)
- *Listen to the word* plug. *Change the* /p/ *sound to* /s/. *What new word did you make?* (slug)
- *Say the word* rig. *Add the sound* /b/ *to the beginning of the word. Now, what is the new word?* (brig)
- *Listen to the word* nut. *Change the* /n/ *sound to* /sh/. *What new word did you make?* (shut)
- *Now listen to the word* smug. *Say the word* smug *without the* /s/ *sound. What is the new word?* (mug)
- *Listen to the sounds:* /s/ /n/ /u/ /g/. (Repeat the sounds.) *Blend the sounds together. What word can you make with the sounds?* (snug)
- *Say the word* twig. *Now, say it without the* /t/ *sound. What is the new word?* (wig)

Smart Bug Clues

To Parent:
Your child has been learning how to read words that end with "ug," "ut," and "ig." In the zippered bag are two copies of the word cards and a small paper bag.

Smart Bug Clues
How to do the activity (two players):

- Cut out the word cards if needed and the pictures of magnifying glasses. Each player should have a set of three different magnifying glasses. Put the word cards in the paper bag.

- Take turns with your child drawing a card and reading the word out loud. The word card should be placed under the corresponding word-family magnifying glass. If the word has already been collected, the player returns the card to the bag.

- The game continues until one of the players has collected two word cards for each magnifying glass to win the game. If the word *bug* is drawn, the game ends abruptly. Then, the player who has collected the most cards wins the game. If time allows, play the game again.

Ready, Set, Read! Arrange all of the word cards in several rows on a table. Have your child read the words aloud for a practice run and then a second time at a faster pace.

Pictures for Player A

_ug   _ut   _ig

Pictures for Player B

_ug   _ut   _ig

MEET AND READ THE "-ACK," "-OCK," AND "-ISH" FAMILIES

Getting Started! Determine which letter-sound correspondences and letter patterns the student needs to practice.

• **Learning to Read CVCC Words**—Use Day 1–5 activities to strengthen letter-sound relationships. Select CVCC words from the list. Start with about 10 words for the targeted practice on the first day. Introduce the silent letter pair *ck*. Add more words when the child is ready for a challenge.

• **Learning to Read CCVCC Words**—Provide activities for sounding out and reading CCVCC words. Select three days of lessons. Review the digraphs and consonant clusters with a tactile activity. During the lessons, include pairings of CVCC and CCVCC words to strengthen decoding skills (*back* with *black*, *lock* with *lack*, *rock* with *rack*, *tack* with *stack*, *stock* with *stack*, *rack* with *track*, *smack* with *snack*, *lock* with *clock* or *block* or *flock*, *lack* with *black*, *wish* with *swish*) and word-recognition fluency.

Word List			
back*	clack*	whack*	smock*
Jack*	crack*	dock*	stock*
lack*	quack*	lock*	dish*
Mack*	shack*	rock*	fish*
pack*	slack*	sock*	wish*
rack*	smack*	block*	swish*
sack*	snack*	clock*	
tack*	stack*	flock*	
black*	track*	shock*	

See pages 155 & 156 for reproducible word cards.

DAY 1

Materials: Copy the pictures on page 115 and provide play clay.

• Show the pictures for *backpack* and *dish*. Ask the child to tell you the ending sound of each word (*backpack* = /k/ and *dish* = /sh/) and make those letters in clay. Talk about how the /k/ sound is represented by the letters *ck* and so on. Continue the lesson by calling out other words. Let the child identify the phonemes and make the corresponding letters in clay to spell the words. Save the clay words for review on Day 3.
• Have students write the words.
• Pinching Letters (See page 15.)

DAY 2

Materials: Copy of letter cards (page 140), word cards (pages 155 and 156), and racetrack billboard mat (page 131); prepared mini-book

Use letters and selected word cards in the following activities:

• Show and read the words.
• Puffy Words—if tactile activity is needed (See page 15.)
• Rev Up for Words (See page 17.)
• Where Is . . . ? (See page 19.)
• Word Family Mini-Book (See page 20.)

DAY 3

Materials: Copy of letter cards (page 140), word cards (pages 155 and 156); playing catch mat (page 134), and tree house mat (page 136)

Use letters and selected word cards in the following activities:

• Review and use words in sentences. (Use clay words or see Finish the Sentence, page 21.)
• Catch High-Flying Sounds (See page 18.)
• Read 'n' Climb to See the View (See page 19.)
• Write Down—Back to the Ground (See page 21.)

DAY 4

Materials: Copy of letter cards (page 140), word cards (pages 155 and 156), robot form (page 139), safe mat (page 135), and monster mat (page 137)

Use letters and selected word cards in the following activities:

• Review and use words in sentences. (See Robot Writing!, page 21.)
• Unlock the Code (See page 18.)
• Mr. Word Muncher (See page 19.)
• Feed Mr. Word Muncher (See page 21.)

DAY 5

Materials: Copy of word cards (pages 155 and 156); children's storybooks featuring -*ack*, -*ock*, and -*ish* word families; self-adhesive flags (office supply item)

Select word cards and use them in the following activities:

• Read 'n' Spell Words (Take turns reading aloud a word to a partner who spells it.)
• Flag It!—Take turns reading aloud passages from classroom books that have -*ack*, -*ock*, and -*ish* in the text. Each time a word-family word is used, mark it with a sticky flag.
• I Write, You Write! (See page 21.)

More Suggestions!

Spend a few minutes each day introducing or reviewing the -*ack*, -*ock*, and -*ish* word families by reading aloud passages (pointing to the words) from children's storybooks. Let students be word-family detectives and identify those words used in the text.

Read at Home Activity

Copy the take-home direction and game sheet (page 116) for each student. Include a copy of the selected word cards on card stock. Place all of the materials in a zippered plastic bag.

The "-ack," "-ock," and "-ish" Word Families

_ish

_ock

_ack

See page 140 for initial letter cards to make words.

Pictures: backpack, jack, clock, block, fish, dish

Player A

| _ack |
| _ock |
| _ish |
| _ack |
| _ack |
| _ock |
| _ish |
| _ack |
| _ack |
| _ish |
| _ock |
| _ack |

Player B

| _ack |
| _ack |
| _ock |
| _ish |
| _ock |
| _ack |
| _ish |
| _ock |
| _ack |
| _ack |
| _ish |
| _ack |

Read and Discover!

To Parent: In the zippered bag are word cards to cut out. Please supply 10 game pieces (pennies, paper clips, etc.) for each player to use. Have your child read the words as a practice run before starting the game.

Place the word cards facedown in a pile near the game board. To play the game, take turns drawing a card and covering one of the corresponding word endings. If all of the boxes with that word ending are already covered, the player's turn is over. The first player to cover FOUR adjacent spaces wins.

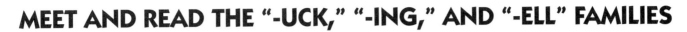

MEET AND READ THE "-UCK," "-ING," AND "-ELL" FAMILIES

Getting Started! Determine which letter-sound correspondences and letter patterns the student needs to practice.

• **Learning to Read CVCC Words**—Use Day 1–5 activities to strengthen letter-sound relationships. Select CVCC words from the list. Start with about 10 words for the targeted practice on the first day. Introduce the digraph *ng* and silent-letter pairs *ck* and *ll*. Add more words when the child is ready for a challenge.

• **Learning to Read CCVCC Words**—Provide activities for sounding out and reading CCVCC words. Select three days of lessons. Review the digraphs and consonant clusters with a tactile activity. During the lessons, include pairings of CVCC and CCVCC words to strengthen decoding skills (*stuck* with *sting*, *luck* with *pluck*, *Chuck* with *cluck*, *wing* with *swing*, *sell* with *smell* or *shell* or *spell*, *sing* with *sting* or *swing* or *sling*, *well* with *swell*) and word-recognition fluency.

Word List				
buck*	pluck*	wing*	thing*	tell*
duck*	stuck*	zing*	bell*	well*
luck*	truck*	bring*	cell*	yell*
puck*	ding*	cling*	dell*	shell*
suck*	king*	fling*	fell*	smell*
tuck*	ping*	sling*	jell*	spell*
Chuck*	ring*	sting*	Nell*	swell*
cluck*	sing*	swing*	sell*	

*See pages 156 & 157 for reproducible word cards.

DAY 1

Materials: Copy the pictures on page 118 and provide play clay.

• Show the pictures for *ring* and *bell*. Ask the child to tell you the ending sound of each word (*ring* = /ng/ and *bell* = /l/) and make those letters in clay. Talk about how the /ng/ sound is represented by the letters *ng* and so on. Continue the lesson by calling out other words. Let the child identify the phonemes and make the corresponding letters in clay to spell the words. Save the clay words for review on Day 3.
• Have students write the words.
• Pinching Letters (See page 15.)

DAY 2

Materials: Copy of letter cards (page 140), word cards (pages 156 and 157), and launch pad mat (page 132); "Sticky" Words materials (page 19); prepared mini-book

Use letters and selected word cards in the following activities:

• Show and read the words.
• Puffy Words—if tactile activity is needed (See page 15.)
• Blast Off! (See page 17.)
• "Sticky" Words (See page 19.)
• Word Family Mini-Book (See page 20.)

DAY 3

Materials: Copy of letter cards (page 140), word cards (pages 156 and 157), safe mat (page 135), and monster mat (page 137)

Use letters and selected word cards in the following activities:

• Review and use words in sentences. (Use clay words or see Finish the Sentence, page 21.)
• Unlock the Code (See page 18.)
• Mr. Word Muncher (See page 19.)
• Feed Mr. Word Muncher (See page 21.)

DAY 4

Materials: Copy of letter cards (page 140), word cards (pages 156 and 157), robot form (page 139), and truck mat (page 133); materials for Yummy Words (page 20) and Clip, Read, 'n' Write (page 20)

Use letters and selected word cards in the following activities:

• Review and use words in sentences. (See Robot Writing, page 21.)
• Load the Truck (See page 17.)
• Yummy Words (See page 20.)
• Clip, Read, 'n' Write (See page 20.)

DAY 5

Materials: Copy of word cards (pages 156 and 157); children's storybooks featuring -*uck*, -*ing*, and -*ell* word families; self-adhesive flags (office supply item)

Select word cards and use them in the following activities:

• Read 'n' Spell Words (Take turns reading aloud a word to a partner who spells it.)
• Flag It!—Take turns reading aloud passages from books that have -*uck*, -*ing*, and -*ell* in the text. Each time a word-family word is used, mark it with a sticky flag.
• I Write, You Write! (See page 21.)

More Suggestions!

Spend a few minutes each day introducing or reviewing the -*uck*, -*ing*, and -*ell* word families by reading aloud passages (pointing to the words) from children's storybooks. Let students be word-family detectives and identify those words used in the text.

Read at Home Activity

Copy the take-home direction and game sheet (page 119) for each student. Include a copy of the selected word cards on card stock. Place all of the materials in a zippered plastic bag.

The "-uck," "-ing," and "-ell" Word Families

See page 140 for initial letter cards to make words.

Pictures: puck, truck, sing, ring, well, bell

To Parent: In the zippered bag are word cards to cut out. Please supply a game piece (penny, dime, paper clip, etc.) for each player to use. Have your child read the words as a practice run before starting the game. Then, place the word cards facedown in a pile near the game board. Using the Key, take turns drawing a card and moving the game piece accordingly.

Summer Word Fun!

The first player to "ring" the bell wins the game!

Key for Moving Spaces
_ing word = Move **1** space.
_ell word = Move **2** spaces.
_uck word = Move **3** spaces.

Start

Ring to win!

MEET AND READ THE "-ICK," "-ULL," AND "-UFF" FAMILIES

Getting Started! Determine which letter-sound correspondences and letter patterns the student needs to practice.

• **Learning to Read CVCC Words**—Use Day 1–5 activities to strengthen letter-sound relationships. Select CVCC words from the list. Start with about 10 words for the targeted practice on the first day. Introduce the silent letter pairs *ck*, *ll*, and *ff*. Add more words when the child is ready for a challenge.

• **Learning to Read CCVCC Words**—Provide activities for sounding out and reading CCVCC words. Select three days of lessons. Review the digraphs and consonant clusters with a tactile activity. During the lessons, include pairings of CVCC and CCVCC words to strengthen decoding skills (*lick* with *click* or *flick* or *slick*, *tick* with *trick* or *thick*, *gull* with *gruff*, *cuff* with *scuff*, *hull* with *huff*, *sick* with *stick* or *slick*, *kick* with *chick*, *muff* with *mull*) and word-recognition fluency.

Word List				
Nick*	tick*	stick*	mull	bluff*
kick*	wick*	thick*	skull*	gruff*
lick*	brick*	trick*	buff*	scuff*
pick*	chick*	dull*	cuff*	stuff*
quick*	click*	gull*	huff*	
Rick*	flick*	hull*	muff*	
sick*	slick*	lull*	puff*	

*See pages 158 & 159 for reproducible word cards. Add to the set by printing mull on card stock.

DAY 1
Materials: Copy the pictures on page 121 and provide play clay.

• Show the pictures for *kick* and *cuff*. Ask the child to tell you the ending sound of each word (*kick* = /k/ and *cuff* = /f/) and make those letters in clay. Talk about how the /f/ sound is represented by the letters *ff* and so on. Continue the lesson by calling out other words. Let the child identify the phonemes and make the corresponding letters in clay to spell the words. Save the clay words for review on Day 3.
• Have students write the words.
• Pinching Letters (See page 15.)

DAY 2
Materials: Copy of letter cards (page 140) and word cards (pages 158 and 159); prepared mini-book

Use letters and selected word cards in the following activities:

• Show and use the words in sentences.
• Puffy Words—if tactile activity is needed (See page 15.)
• What's the Word? (See page 16.)
• Where Is . . . ? (See page 19.)
• Word Family Mini-Book (See page 20.)

DAY 3
Materials: Copy of letter cards (page 140), word cards (pages 158 and 159), and truck mat (page 133); materials for Yummy Words (page 20) and Clip, Read, 'n' Write (page 20)

Use letters and selected word cards in the following activities:

• Review and use words in sentences. (Use clay words or see Finish the Sentence, page 21.)
• Load the Truck (See page 17.)
• Yummy Words (See page 20.)
• Clip, Read, 'n' Write (See page 20.)

DAY 4
Materials: Copy of word cards (pages 158 and 159) and robot form (page 139); labeled plastic eggs and egg carton; copy of tree house mat (page 136)

Select word cards and use them in the following activities:

• Review and use words in sentences. (See Robot Writing!, page 21.)
• Pack the Words (See page 18.)
• Read 'n' Climb to See the View (See page 19.)
• Write Down—Back to the Ground (See page 21.)

DAY 5
Materials: Copy of word cards (pages 158 and 159); storybooks featuring -ick, -ull, and -uff words; self-adhesive flags (office supply item)

Select word cards and use them in the following activities:

• Read 'n' Spell Words (Take turns reading aloud a word to a partner who spells it.)
• Flag It!—Take turns reading aloud a passage from a classroom book that has -ick, -ull, and -uff words in the text. Each time a word-family word is used, mark it with a sticky flag.
• I Write, You Write! (See page 21.)

More Suggestions!
Spend a few minutes each day introducing or reviewing the -ick, -ull, and -uff word families by reading aloud passages (pointing to the words) from children's storybooks. Let students be word-family detectives and identify those words used in the text.

Read at Home Activity
Copy the take-home direction and game sheet (page 122) for each student. Include a copy of the word cards on card stock. Place all of the materials in a zippered plastic bag.

The "-ick," "-ull," and "-uff" Word Families

uff _

ull _

ick _

See page 140 for initial letter cards to make words.

Pictures: kick, brick, hull, gull, cuff, huff or puff

Launch It!

Player A column:
_ick
_ull
_uff
_ick
_uff
_ull
_ick
_uff
_ick
_uff
_ull
_ick

Player B column:
_ull
_ick
_ull
_ick
_uff
_ick
_uff
_ick
_ull
_ick
_uff
_uff

To Parent: In the zippered bag are two copies of the word cards to cut out. Please supply 10 game pieces (pennies, dimes, paper clips, etc.) for each player to use. Have your child read the words as a practice run before starting the game.

Place the word cards facedown in a pile near the game board. To play the game, take turns drawing a card and covering one of the corresponding word endings. If all of the boxes with that word ending are already covered, the player's turn is over. The first player to cover FOUR adjacent spaces "launches" the balloon and wins the game.

Player A

Player B

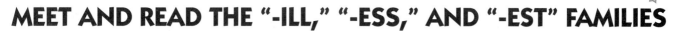

MEET AND READ THE "-ILL," "-ESS," AND "-EST" FAMILIES

Getting Started! Determine which letter-sound correspondences and letter patterns the student needs to practice.

• **Learning to Read CVCC Words**—Use Day 1–5 activities to strengthen letter-sound relationships. Select CVCC words from the list. Start with about 10 words for the targeted practice on the first day. Introduce the final blend *st* and silent letter pairs *ll* and *ss*. Add more words when the child is ready for a challenge.

• **Learning to Read CCVCC Words**—Provide activities for sounding out and reading CCVCC words. Select three days of lessons. Review the digraph *ch* and consonant clusters with a tactile activity. During the lessons, include pairings of CVCC and CCVCC words to strengthen decoding skills (*hill* with *chill*, *sill* with *still* or *skill*, *chest* with *chess*, *pill* with *spill*, *dill* with *drill*, *rest* with *crest*, *fill* with *frill*, *less* with *bless*) and word-recognition fluency.

Word List

bill*	mill*	grill*	chess*	rest*
dill*	pill*	skill*	dress*	test*
fill*	sill*	spill*	press	vest*
gill*	will*	still*	best*	west*
hill*	chill*	less*	jest*	zest*
ill*	drill*	mess*	nest*	chest*
Jill*	frill*	bless	pest*	crest*

*See page 152, 159 & 160 for reproducible word cards. Add to the set by printing other words on card stock.

DAY 1
Materials: Copy the pictures on page 124 and provide play clay.

• Show the pictures for *chess* and *nest*. Ask the child to tell you the ending sound of each word (*chess* = /s/ and *nest* = /t/) and make those letters in clay. Talk about how the /s/ sound in *chess* is represented by the letters *ss* and so on. Continue the lesson by calling out other words. Let the child identify the phonemes and make the corresponding letters in clay to spell the words. Save the clay words for review on Day 3.
• Have students write the words.
• Pinching Letters (See page 15.)

DAY 2
Materials: Copy of letter cards (page 140), word cards (pages 152, 159, and 160), and stone wall mat (page 130); "Sticky" Words materials (page 19); prepared mini-book

Use letters and selected word cards in the following activities:

• Show and read the words.
• Puffy Words—if tactile activity is needed (See page 15.)
• Letters on Stones (See page 16.)
• "Sticky" Words (See page 19.)
• Word Family Mini-Book (See page 20.)

DAY 3
Materials: Copy of word cards (pages 152, 159, and 160); labeled plastic eggs and egg carton; copy of tree house mat (page 136)

Select word cards and use them in the following activities:

• Review and use words in sentences. (Use clay words or see Finish the Sentence, page 21.)
• Pack the Words (See page 18.)
• Read 'n' Climb to See the View (See page 19.)
• Write Down—Back to the Ground (See page 21.)

DAY 4
Materials: Copy of letter cards (page 140), word cards (pages 152, 159, and 160), robot form (page 139), playing catch mat (page 134), and monster mat (page 137)

Use letters and selected word cards in the following activities:

• Review and use words in sentences. (See Robot Writing!, page 21.)
• Catch High-Flying Sounds (See page 18.)
• Mr. Word Muncher (See page 19.)
• Feed Mr. Word Muncher (See page 21.)

DAY 5
Materials: Copy of word cards (pages 152, 159, and 160); storybooks featuring *-ill*, *-ess*, and *-est* words; self-adhesive flags (office supply item)

Select word cards and use them in the following activities:

• Read 'n' Spell Words (Take turns reading aloud a word to a partner who spells it.)
• Flag It!—Take turns reading aloud a passage from a classroom book that has *-ill*, *-ess*, and *-est* words in the text. Each time a word-family word is used, mark it with a sticky flag.
• I Write, You Write! (See page 21.)

More Suggestions!
Spend a few minutes each day introducing or reviewing the *-ill*, *-ess*, and *-est* word families by reading aloud passages (pointing to the words) from children's storybooks. Let students be word-family detectives and identify those words used in the text.

Read at Home Activity
Copy the take-home direction and game sheet (page 125) for each student. Include a copy of the selected word cards on card stock. Place all of the materials in a zippered plastic bag.

The "-ill," "-ess," and "-est" Word Families

See page 140 for initial letter cards to make words.

Pictures: bill, spill, dress, chess, vest, nest

To Parent: In the zippered bag are word cards to cut out. Please supply 10–12 identical game pieces (pennies and dimes, paper clips in two different colors, etc.) for you and your child to use. Have your child read the words as a practice run before starting the game.

Place the word cards facedown in a pile on the game board. To play the game, take turns drawing a card and covering one of the corresponding word endings. If all of the boxes for that word ending are already covered, the player's turn is over. The first player to cover three spaces in a horizontal, vertical, or diagonal row wins the game.

Word Quest

Read at Home—the "_ill," "_ess," and "_est" Word Families

(Game for two players)

Cover three adjacent spaces in a ↑, →, ↗, or ↘ row to win.

_ill	_est	_ill
_ess	_est	_ill
_ill	_est	_ess
_est	_ess	_ill
_ill	_est	_ill
_ill	_ill	_ess
_est	_ill	_ess

Draw pile for game cards

Plan Your Own Five-Day Unit

If your students would benefit from lessons that focus heavily on auditory processing, visual discrimination, phonemic awareness, or spelling-sound relationships, the materials in this book can be easily modified for those special needs. Use the word lists, word cards, phonemic awareness activities, and multisensory activities to create intervention lessons that will help your students make progress in learning to read. Fill in a copy of the planner on page 127 with your refined objectives and activity ideas.

For example, perhaps, your students would benefit from additional word-decoding practice. If they have completed some of the provided lessons that target CVC words from one or two word families during a session, but they still struggle with reading certain words, use the planner to design additional lessons that feature those words along with others for review.

Kinds of Activities to Incorporate During a Session

- **Tactile & Kinesthetic Activities:** See page 15 for ideas.

- **Phonemic Awareness:** Assess how easily the child can blend, segment, and manipulate phonemes in spoken words before determining which activities that child needs to do. To scaffold these phonological skills, follow this sequence: Begin with exercises where the child blends sounds to make words and then move on to segmenting spoken words into individual sounds. The most difficult phonological skill is manipulating phonemes by replacing or deleting certain sounds to make new words. Use various parts of the phonemic awareness lessons in this book to craft your own activities. It is important to help students reach a point of fluency in working with phonemes. Their skills will develop along a continuum, starting with the basic knowledge of the structure of spoken words.

- **Sorting Words by Phonograms Activity:** Gather word cards and picture cards (use as labels for sorting criteria) and have students sort the words into categories by word endings.

- **Matching Sounds to Letters Activities:** See pages 16–18 for ideas.

- **Sounding Out & Reading Words Activities:** See pages 19 and 20 for ideas.

- **Spelling & Writing Activities:** When students spell and write the words in sentences, this helps them retain visual memory of those words. See pages 20 and 21 for ideas.

- **Oral Reading Word Fluency Practice:** Make two copies of page 129. Personalize the fluency boards by filling in the boxes with words from two or three targeted word families. You may have to repeat the selected words several times to reach a total of 96 words for the student to read out loud. Copy the prepared boards on a pale color (like blue) of card stock. Slide the original boards (for the teacher) and the blue boards into sheet protectors to keep them clean.

Have students practice reading the words aloud to find out how many (out of a total of 96) they can read in one minute. For RAN words exercises, let the child read 48 words (two boards) and record the amount of time used by the student.

- **Reading Words in Context:** Supply decodable books for students to read so that they can apply what they have practiced during the lesson.

Five-Day Lesson Planner

Students in Group

Word Families Studied

Objectives (Check those that apply.)

☐ To distinguish short vowel _____

☐ To link sounds to letters

☐ To translate letters into sounds correctly

☐ To blend sounds into words

☐ To sort words into word families

☐ To read targeted words correctly

See page 126 for additional tips. Add phonemic awareness exercises to your lessons as needed.

DAY 1	DAY 2	DAY 3
Tactile Activity:	Matching Sounds to Letters:	Matching Sounds to Letters:
Word Sort: (Word Family Pictures on pages _____)	Sounding Out & Reading:	Sounding Out & Reading:
	Spelling & Writing:	Spelling & Writing:

DAY 4	DAY 5	More Notes
Matching Sounds to Letters:	Oral Reading Word Fluency:	See pages _____ for word cards.
Sounding Out & Reading:	Reading Words in Context (Book Title):	See page(s) _____ for full list of words for each targeted word family.
Spelling & Writing:	I Write, You Write!	

How to Use the Form

- Make photocopies of the form.
- At the end of a five-day unit, evaluate the student's progress and note your assessment on this form.
- Record comments on the back of the form that will be helpful in planning future intervention sessions.

Student Progress Record

Student's Name: _____

Word Family/Families: _____

Level of Mastery

M - mastered

P - needs more practice

Objectives/Skills	Date/Assessment	Date/Assessment
Distinguishes the short vowel ___ or between two sounds: ___ & ___		
Links sounds to letters correctly (Indicate letters not mastered)		
Translates letters into sounds correctly (Indicate letters not mastered)		
Blends sounds into words		
Reads the targeted words correctly (Include word count per minute)		

Assessing Reading Fluency

- Make a copy of this form and indicate which word family or families have been targeted.
- Prepare two copies of page 129 and then print the selected words in the boxes. Repeat the words as needed to fill in four boards (total of 96).
- Make a copy of the prepared boards for the evaluator, inserting them into a plastic sheet protector to mark on with dry erase marker.
- After a practice session, time the students to find out how many words they can read out loud correctly in one minute.

Oral Reading Fluency

Word Families: _____ **Date:** _____ **Date:** _____

Student's Name	# Correct Words	# Correct Words

RAN Letters Boards (page 5): Make copies of this page as needed. Select six letters for a board and fill in the boxes, repeating each letter four times. Copy the master on card stock.
Word Fluency Boards (page 127): Make two copies of the page for one set. Fill in the boxes with selected words. Copy the masters on card stock.

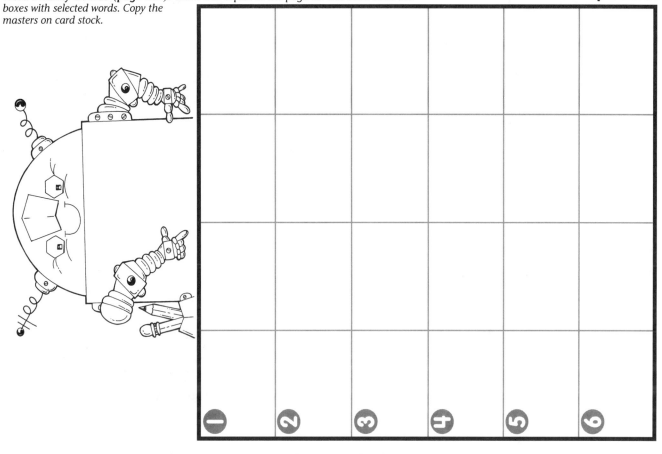

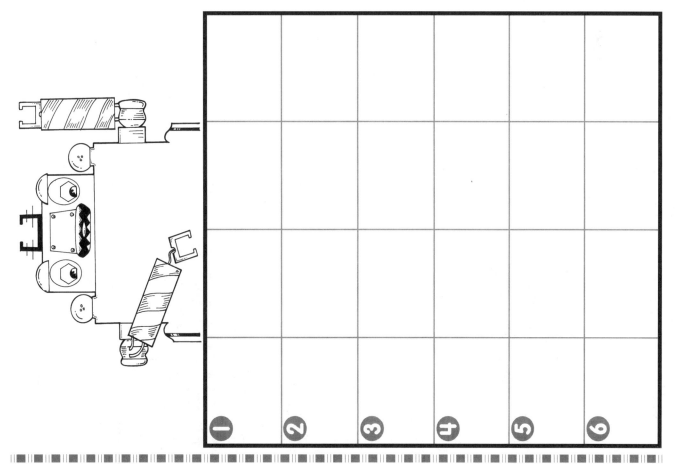

Letters on Stones Mat

See page 16 for directions.

Beginning Reader Intervention Activities

See page 17 for directions.

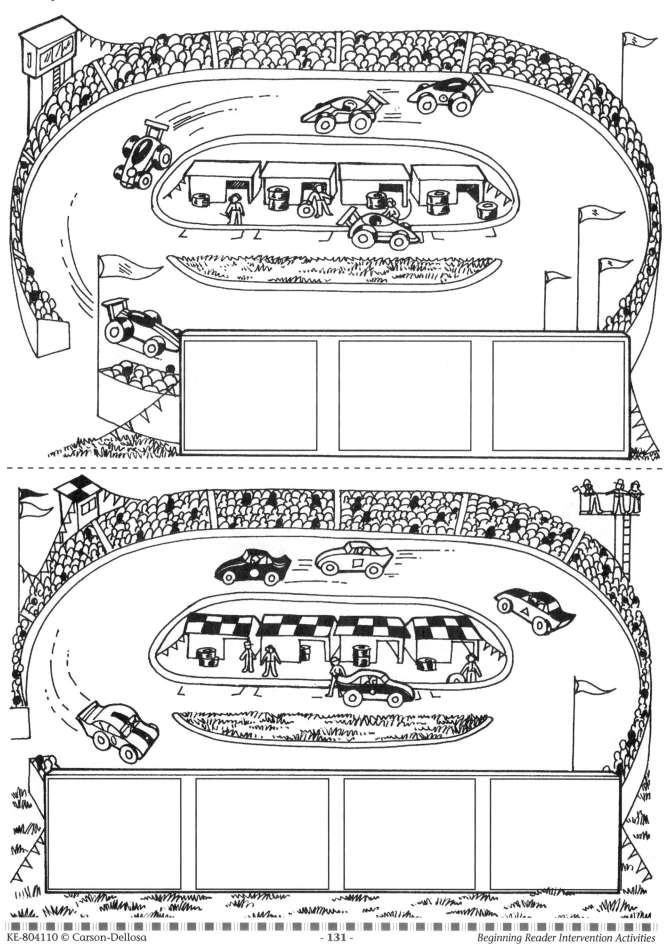

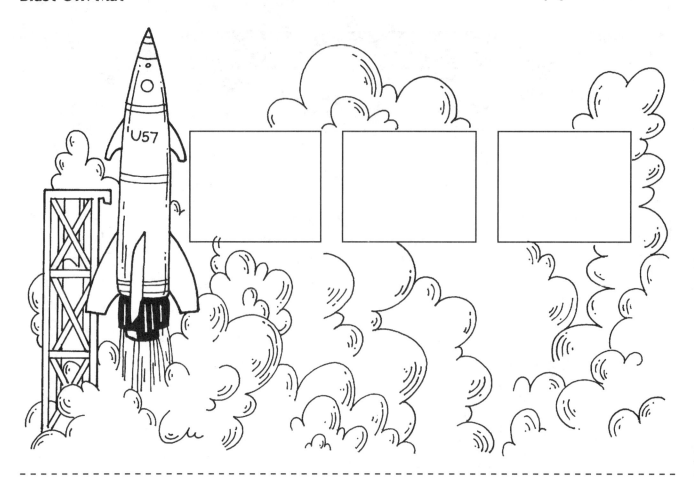

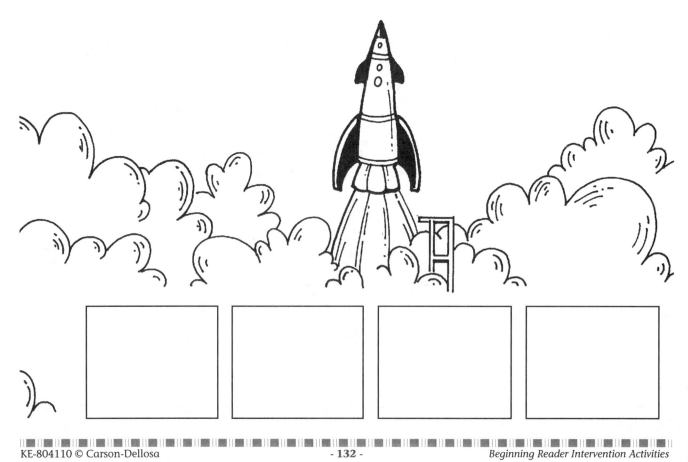

Load the Truck Mat

See page 17 for directions.

See page 18 for directions.

Unlock the Code Mat

See page 18 for directions.

Yummy Words Patterns

See page 20 for directions.

Name: _____

To the teacher: See page 21 for the activity Robot Writing!

Asking Sentence :

Telling Sentence :

Robot Writing!

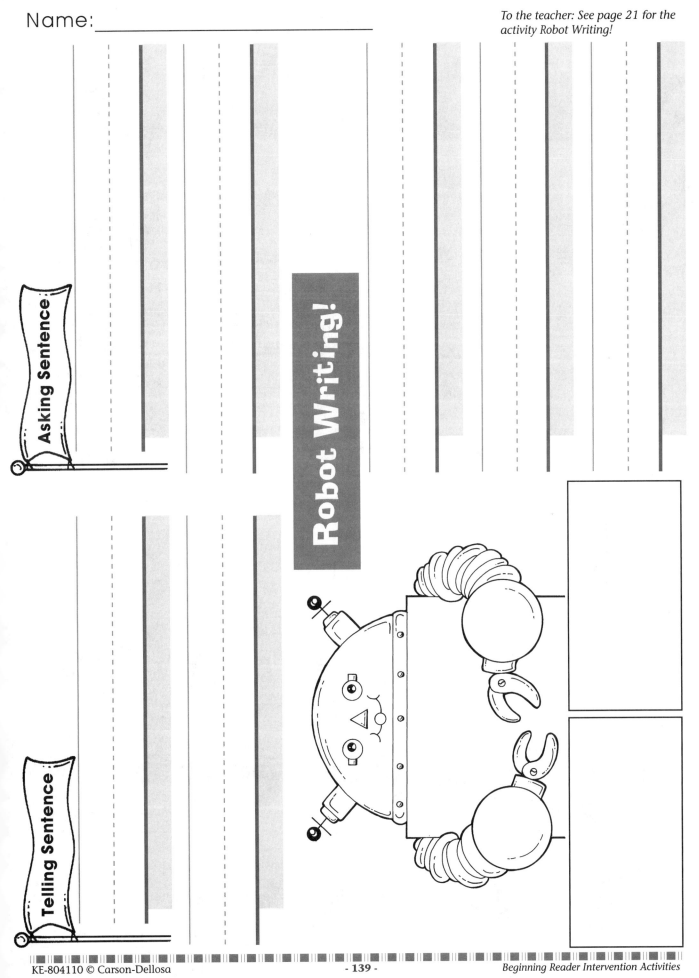

b	b	c	d	d
f	g	g	h	j
k	l	m	n	p
r	s	t	v	w
y	z	a	e	i
o	u	sh	ch	th
ng	wh	ck	qu	
ff	ll	ss	wr	

Rhyme and Write

Name: _____

To the teacher: Print the word family in the boxes below.

Read the word chunk. Write words that end the same way.

Rhyme and Write

Name: _____

To the teacher: Print the word family in the boxes below.

Read the word chunk. Write words that end the same way.

Sentence Writing Template

To the teacher: See page 21 for the activity I Write, You Write Sentences.

Name:

hat	fat	cat	bat
sat	rat	pat	mat
that	flat	chat	brat
man	fan	Dan	can
van	tan	ran	pan
scan	plan	clan	bran

span	than	cab	dab
gab	jab	lab	nab
tab	blab	crab	drab
grab	scab	slab	flab
bad	dad	fad	had
lad	mad	pad	sad

am	Sam	cram	tram	map	tap
glad	ram	clam	swam	lap	sap
clad	Pam	yam	slam	gap	rap
tad	jam	Tam	gram	cap	nap

chap	trap	kin	chin	spin	fit
clap	snap	in	win	skin	bit
zap	slap	fin	tin	shin	twin
yap	flap	bin	pin	grin	thin

lit	flit	dip
sip	clip	trip
kit	wit	spit
rip	chip	skip
it	sit	skit
lip	zip	ship
hit	pit	grit
hip	tip	drip

gig	wig	twig	kid	grid	him
fig	rig	swig	hid	rid	dim
dig	pig	brig	did	mid	slid
big	jig	zig	bid	lid	skid

Tim	rim	Kim	Jim
trim	swim	slim	brim
mop	hop	cop	bop
crop	chop	top	pop
prop	plop	flop	drop
dot	cot	stop	shop

lot	tot	slot	cog	jog	smog
jot	rot	shot	bog	hog	frog
hot	pot	plot	trot	fog	clog
got	not	blot	spot	dog	log

let	jet	get	bet
set	pet	net	met
Chet	yet	wet	vet
Ken	hen	den	fret
yen	ten	pen	men
when	then	Glen	Chen

red	led	fed	bed
fled	bled	wed	Ted
sped	sled	shed	Fred
them	stem	hem	gem
peg	Meg	leg	beg
dress	chess	mess	less

jug	hug	dug	bug
tug	rug	mug	lug
snug	slug	plug	chug
nub	hub	dub	cub
club	tub	sub	rub
cut	but	stub	flub

rut	run	stun	sum	swum	thud
nut	fun	spun	mum	plum	spud
hut	bun	shun	hum	drum	mud
gut	shut	sun	gum	chum	bud

Mack	tack	quack	snack	dock	block
lack	sack	crack	smack	whack	sock
Jack	rack	clack	slack	track	rock
back	pack	black	shack	stack	lock

smock shock flock clock

wish fish dish stock

luck duck buck swish

Chuck tuck suck puck

truck stuck pluck cluck

ring ping king ding

bring	sting	cell	Nell	yell	swell
zing	sling	bell	jell	well	spell
wing	fling	thing	fell	tell	smell
sing	cling	swing	dell	sell	shell

pick	lick	kick	Nick
tick	sick	Rick	quick
click	chick	brick	wick
thick	stick	slick	flick
hull	gull	dull	trick
cuff	buff	skull	lull

bluff	bill	hill	pill	drill
				spill
puff	stuff	gill	mill	chill
				skill
muff	scuff	fill	Jill	will
				grill
huff	gruff	dill	ill	sill
				frill

nest	vest	crest			
jest	test	chest			
best	rest	zest			
still	pest	west			